Political Philosophy

An Historical Introduction

RELATED TITLES

Descartes, Harry M. Bracken, ISBN 1–85168–294–5
God: A Guide for the Perplexed, Keith Ward, ISBN 1–85168–323–2
Kierkegaard, Michael Watts, ISBN 1–85168–317–8
Modern French Philosophy: From Existentialism to Postmodernism,
    Robert Wicks, ISBN 1–85168–318–6
Moral Relativism: A Short Introduction, ISBN 1–85168–305–4
Nietzsche, Robert Wicks, ISBN 1–85168–291–0
Philosophy and Religion: From Plato to Postmodernism, Max Charlesworth,
    ISBN 1–85168–307–0
Sartre, Neil Levy, ISBN 1–85168–290–2
Wittgenstein, Avrum Stroll, ISBN 1–85168–293–7

Political Philosophy

An Historical Introduction

Michael J. White

ONEWORLD

OXFORD

POLITICAL PHILOSOPHY: AN HISTORICAL INTRODUCTION

Oneworld Publications
(Sales and Editorial)
185 Banbury Road
Oxford OX2 7AR
England
www.oneworld-publications.com

ISBN 1–85168–328–3

Cover illustration by Andrzej Klimowski;
cover design by Perks-Willis Graphic Design
Typeset by Jayvee, India
Printed and bound by WS Bookwell, Finland

Contents

Acknowledgments

I should like to thank especially my colleague Jeffrie G. Murphy for his careful reading and perceptive, constructive comments on all of the text of this book. His friendship, encouragement, and wise advice have been immensely important in enabling me to complete the project of writing this book. Thanks are also due to another colleague, Thomas Blackson, whose comments on parts of the text saved me from several egregious blunders, and to an anonymous reader chosen by Oneworld Publications to vet the manuscript for his/her very thoughtful, useful, and kind comments and suggestions. I also very much appreciate the aid, intellectual and practical, supplied by Mel Thompson, Victoria Roddam, and Rebecca Clare at Oneworld.

1

A Short Introduction

It may seem quite obvious that political organization – that whole governmental complex of legislative, administrative, and judicial machinery associated with the residents of a particular geographical area during some temporal period – has some function, purpose or point. On the other hand, it may seem not at all obvious, at least to us inhabitants of Western constitutional states at the beginning of the third millennium, that *human beings* themselves have any such function or point. We humans just seem to be here – with all our individual desires and aversions, our strengths, weaknesses, virtues, and vices, our abilities and accomplishments. Political machinery should do something for us individually – and perhaps collectively. Otherwise, why bother with it?

But, according to a common contemporary view of such matters, we humans ourselves do not have a function or purpose. We may perhaps *choose* to see a purpose or 'larger plan' manifest in our lives or in human affairs more generally; and we may *make commitments* that invest our lives with meaning – for us. But that is a quite individual matter and, at least in the opinion of most of us, not something that is thrust upon human beings in general. We may occasionally invoke the notion of 'human nature', but when we do it is usually simply to connote some ingrained – and often unfortunate – human tendency. And we typically invoke it without the assumption that there should be any rhyme or reason to human nature. In particular, we seldom

1

entertain the thought that human nature should have any normative moral significance – that it should impose certain obligations on us pertaining to how we should live our lives, both individually and socially.

Within the context of the preceding assumptions – which, I think, have become so common as to be pedestrian in the contemporary West – political philosophy faces a large and forbidding task: a further common assumption is that the task of political philosophy is to establish some principled justification of political organization, a justification that will properly discriminate between better and worse forms of polity and that can be used to establish basic norms of political justice. But, according to the point of view I have just sketched, it evidently must accomplish this task without essential reference to a particular conception of a human function or purpose – an idea about which many of us moderns have become skeptical or agnostic. So political philosophy is charged with giving a rich account of the proper rôle of political organization without appeal to any conception (which would almost certainly be controversial) of what human beings are for – that is, without any rich conception of human nature, function, or purpose.

The idea of human nature or the human good as 'function': normative anthropology

I perhaps should say something here about my equation of the ideas of a human nature, function, or purpose: an equation that may strike the contemporary reader as peculiar. Although the very idea of human nature has become controversial, it is an idea that has not completely disappeared. It is often cashed out in terms of claims about 'inbred' human propensities (for example, that humans either are or are not by nature selfish, or religious, or monogamous, etc.) or in terms of claims about human 'needs' (for example, the 'hierarchy of needs' developed by the psychologist Abraham Maslow). As I use the term human 'function' or 'purpose', it may well include such claims about human propensities and needs, but it relates them to some coherent conception of human *functioning* – that is, to some ideal of what human life *should* be all about, some conception of what sort of ultimate concerns should serve as the organizing principle of a human life. The 'should' is significant. According to a classical conception, while human nature (or the human function, in this sense) is a natural and objective feature of the species, it is quite possible for individual humans – or whole communities of humans – to fail to achieve that function or to fail to live up to that nature, for various reasons. The human function, or 'human nature' in this broad sense of the phrase, is a sort of ideal that has normative moral and political consequences for human beings; consequences, in other words, concerning how we should behave both individually and collectively. 'Human nature' in a *narrower* sense of purported empirical facts about human beings (nowadays usually drawn from biology – particularly, evolutionary biology – psychology, or sociology) does not, in itself, seem to have these normative consequences about how we should lead our lives. But such purported empirical facts may indeed be highly relevant to the human function or nature in my *broader*, normative sense – although it should be remembered that such facts are not equivalent to the human nature or function in this broader sense. The human nature or function in this sense is something that many, perhaps even most, humans might fail to instantiate – at least fail to instantiate *fully*.

The term 'function' as used in this context may seem to be a somewhat peculiar choice of terms. As I use the term, it translates the Greek term *ergon*, which literally means 'work'. What perhaps makes the translation 'function' seem peculiar is that, for us, this term usually connotes a sort of means, something that is conducive to achieving some *other* end or purpose. Thus a knife's cutting function is not an 'end in itself' but is typically used to achieve some other end. The heart's function of pumping blood also serves a further purpose in the metabolism of an organism possessing a heart. And even the baker's function, or the brain surgeon's or the nuclear physicist's, is thought of as serving some further personal or social purposes.

But, at the beginning of the third millennium, most of us do not think of human beings, or a distinctive activity or group of activities to be designated the 'human function', as serving some further social or cosmic purpose. Many classical pagan and Christian moral and political thinkers did, although they were often rather vague about what that further purpose is and how humans contribute to it. However, I do not intend that my use of the term function should entail that the human function *must* serve as a means for accomplishing anything else, at either the social or cosmic level. According to some doctrines of the human function, it may be an end in itself and may not contribute to anything beyond itself. But there are two features that *are* central to my conception of the human nature, function, or purpose: (a) while such a nature or function is common to humankind, in general, it is not necessarily to be identified with a purported list of human propensities or needs that might be supplied by an empirical science such as biology, psychology or sociology; (b) this nature or function has normative consequences that would nowadays typically be described as 'moral' or 'ethical', that is, it has consequences about how we human beings should behave, consequences that impose certain obligations on us. In other words, the conception of a human function or purpose or of human nature is a conception of human flourishing. This conception will often have metaphysical and religious elements, as well as 'strictly' ethical/moral elements. And, in many cases, the metaphysical and religious elements are inseparable from – and really motivate or explain – the moral and ethical ones.

Let us call such a conception a 'normative anthropology'. For someone reflecting on large political issues at the beginning of the third millennium of the common era, a fundamental question is whether it is possible to develop a coherent political philosophy apart from a normative anthropology. My own opinion is that it is not. However, I believe that it is fair to say that at least one tradition of central importance within contemporary political philosophy is committed to making the attempt. I also believe that it is not really possible to address this fundamental question without consideration of the history of Western political philosophy, beginning with Greek antiquity. Consequently, I propose to examine, in this short introduction to political philosophy, significant bits of that history – although in a quite selective way. My hope is that this examination will allow the reader to engage, in an informed and thoughtful way, not only the preceding fundamental question about contemporary political philosophy, but also a number of other rather abstract, theoretical issues central to philosophical reflection on political matters, issues to which I return toward the end of this introductory chapter.

My 'story' of political philosophy – and my cast of characters

First, however, I perhaps should attempt to give the reader some idea of what is distinctive (and controversial) about this particular introduction to political philosophy. Political philosophy is one of those divisions of philosophy in which we initially may be inclined to think that there is little more to be done than to trot out our personal beliefs about politics, perhaps with a view to winning over others to our own convictions. As an alternative view of the subject, I propose that an introduction to political philosophy should be an invitation to think in a systematic and coherent way about the fundamental nature of political organization *and* its relation to the nature of human beings. I shall not be presenting a lawyer's brief on behalf of some particular form of government or some particular conception of justice – or, indeed, on behalf of some particular political theory.

However, I do make some basic assumptions that affect the text that follows. Perhaps the most fundamental of these assumptions is built into the idea of a normative anthropology, which I introduced in the preceding section. A basic idea of what I shall call 'classical' political philosophy was developed in Greek antiquity and adopted – but transformed – in the Christian intellectual traditions of late antiquity and the Middle Ages. This is the idea that the philosophical consideration of political concepts naturally presupposes normative ideas connected with some notion of an objective human good, end, purpose, or function (*ergon*). This idea of a human good or *ergon*, as it figures in political theory, was much more radically transformed in European political philosophy of the seventeenth and eighteenth centuries. By the twentieth century, many major political philosophers appeared to believe that it is possible 'to do political philosophy' without reference to such a normative metaphysical, ethical, or religious ideal. My quite controversial thesis is that this belief is illusory.

During the last century, many areas of philosophy have become more technical and narrowly focused – which is by no means an altogether bad thing, in my view. It is not surprising that this tendency toward specialization has affected political philosophy. Consequently, many introductions to political philosophy are analytic and largely ahistorical explorations of such political concepts as justice, rights, equality, political obligation, and democracy, and of such issues as the relation (opposition?) between the individual person and the community, between liberty and equality, or between reward of individual merit and effort, on the one hand, and satisfaction of basic human needs, on the other.

There is certainly nothing wrong with such approaches to political philosophy. They can be highly valuable and, I hope, complementary to my own approach. But my contention is that, at some point in the investigation into such issues, it is highly enlightening – and, indeed, necessary – to step back and think about what metaphysical, ethical, or religious assumptions concerning a normative anthropology are presupposed (or ruled out) by our analysis of such political concepts and our treatment of such paradigmatic political issues. I submit that we shall always find relevant fundamental assumptions.

An additional controversial assumption that I make is that taking an historical view of political philosophy is a particularly effective way of entering into a theoretical consideration of its fundamental issues. In general, it seems to me that there is no better way of learning how to 'do philosophy' than critically examining the way it has been done by others whose excellence in the enterprise has been long recognized. In the particular case of political philosophy, it seems to me that there is at least some truth to the claim of the nineteenth-century German philosopher F.W. Nietzsche that the concepts, categories, and issues of such a 'cultural discipline' can be adequately understood only in terms of their historical 'genealogy'.[1]

Like all historical narratives, mine is a 'story' – it has a plot. I have already given some indication of what that plot is. In very schematic outline, my story begins with Greek political thought and its clear and unequivocal invocation of a normative anthropology, a conception of the human function or *ergon*, as central to political philosophy. Christian normative anthropology is then assimilated into this classical conceptual framework in a variety of ways, introducing new emphases and new problems (e.g., the existence of a special sort of political obligation, the political demarcation of the secular and the sacred). Beginning in about the seventeenth century or a bit before, the distinctively Western tradition of liberalism begins to develop in European political thought. That new style of political thought had conceptual roots in the older traditions of classical political thought but also gave rise to the particular political preoccupations associated with Modernity. Beginning in the eighteenth century, but especially in the nineteenth, various critiques of liberalism appeared. Then, despite the enormous vicissitudes in *practical* politics in the twentieth century, the century ended with the theoretical dominance of liberalism (in various guises). The reasons for the present dominance of liberal political philosophy I take to be broadly cultural (and perhaps economic) rather than strictly intellectual. That is, varieties of contemporary liberal political theory possess unresolved conceptual tensions and, perhaps, inconsistencies.[2]

The appeal of liberal political theory, I think, derives from the fact that it tends to underwrite widely held cultural and secular moral values, particularly those that tend to be accepted by the cultural, socioeconomic, and political elites within the so-called 'first-world' political communities of Europe and North America. It is not so much that contemporary liberal political philosophy has found theoretically successful refutations of critiques that derive either from the early classical tradition of political philosophy (e.g., natural law theory) or from later traditions (e.g., Marxism). Rather, liberal political theory has often adopted the strategy of either ignoring or attempting to steer its way around these criticisms – thus avoiding direct confrontation. Later in this book, however, I shall argue that when the fundamental connection between political theory and normative anthropology is acknowledged, such confrontations are difficult to avoid.

The reader should be alerted to what I take to be several facts about my approach. The first is that my story is certainly not the only story to be told about political philosophy. No matter how compelling or cogent such a story may be, it typically involves historical and conceptual simplification and a somewhat selective use of data or evidence. In some cases, the interpretation of historical figures that I develop in the following pages has been tailored to fit the general lines of my narrative. In many cases, there are alternative scholarly readings and different possible emphases. In some cases, I explicitly flag these alternatives in notes to the text. But the reader should be aware of the phenomenon in general.

The reader should also be aware that my story has affected the cast of historical characters whom I discuss. For example, it has led me to emphasize the influence of Christianity in political theory to a greater degree than some other approaches would have done. The particular narrative that I develop, together with reasonable constraints on the length of a book that purports to be a short introduction to political thought, have also resulted in some notable omissions. Were this book a comprehensive history of political philosophy, it surely should include some extended discussion of the political thought of (among others) Niccolò Machiavelli (1469–1527), Immanuel Kant (1724–1804), G.W.F. Hegel (1770–1831), Friedrich Nietzsche (1844–1900), and J.S. Mill (1806–1873). It might also treat of Marsilius of Padua (ca. 1280–1342) and of a number of twentieth-century political philosophers who are not squarely in the liberal tradition. The omission of these figures from an historical introduction to political philosophy does not constitute any belief on my part that the thought of any one of them is not significant to the development of political philosophy. It is simply that they are not quite as germane to my story as the figures that I do discuss – and the length of this supposedly short introduction to political philosophy is a consideration that I was unable to ignore. Although my approach is historical, this book is not to be construed as a comprehensive history of Western political thought. Rather, it is an attempt to use historical figures and topics to develop a story about political philosophy. I hope that the story is a plausible and interesting one. However, I also hope that it will serve the purpose of engaging readers in such a way that they may wish to read more widely, to think more deeply, and either to develop my story further (or in different ways) or to create some alternative narrative of their own.

Enduring issues in political philosophy

It is, I think, helpful to preface our historical explorations with a brief and schematic consideration of some of these issues, to which we will be returning from time to time in much more historically concrete contexts. These are some (but by no means all) of what we might call the 'enduring issues' in political philosophy. As such, they figure not only in my particular story about political philosophy but in many other stories as well.

1. Is political organization best conceived as a sort of social tool, a system of social relations designed by humans to supply certain definite, limited goods and services for them? According to such a picture, persons can correctly be thought of as existing, with whatever nature or structure of preferences that they possess, quite independently of any system of political organization. Political organization would thus be an extrinsic means for doing certain things for human beings. In that respect, it would not be essentially different from other voluntary associations, despite the fact that it may be expedient to give it coercive powers typically denied to associations that are truly voluntary.[3] Or might political organization better be conceived in 'organic' terms – that is, as a type of natural human relationship much like the family or tribe? According to this alternative model, who we are as human persons – our very nature, our conception of our interests, or our systems of preferences – is at least partly defined by the political organization of which we are members. It would not be surprising that political organization, although 'natural' in this sense, would be malleable – susceptible to alteration by a variety of historical forces. And it might even be questionable whether there would be any plausible criteria that could serve to justify or legitimate one form of polity over another in any way that would not be historically relative and, thus, which *would* be universally valid or 'absolute'.[4]

2. Is the purpose of political organization to give persons what they *need*, in some equitable way, whether or not what they need coincides with what they explicitly desire or prefer? If there is a specific human

end, function, or purpose, which has normative consequences about the way persons *should* act and be treated, then it seems eminently sensible that the principal function of political organization should be to further that end, function, or purpose. This would be a matter of enabling (and encouraging) citizens to become good or virtuous persons, in the sense of persons who live up to that objective purpose or fulfill that function or business well. As Aristotle puts it in his *Politics*, "the end of the *polis* [city-state] is the good life" and "political society exists for the sake of noble actions, and not merely living together."[5] Or, on the contrary, is it the purpose of political organization to give persons what they want – that is, to satisfy, in some equitable way, their desires or preferences? It may transpire that the latter conception of the proper rôle of political organization is particularly attractive if one has given up the idea of some objective human purpose, function, or business that could undergird the *political* project of giving citizens what they need, in the sense of supplying what is needed to make them good persons. Alternatively, one perhaps might develop a theory according to which the 'human good' becomes a subjective matter of 'what is good for the individual person' in such a way that (perhaps with certain restrictions) an individual citizen's preferences really *define* what is 'good for that citizen' and, consequently, what he or she needs.

3. Whether the purpose of political organization is to give persons what they need or what they want (or some combination of both), a virtually universal assumption is that it should fulfill its function in some equitable, fair, or just way. So a third issue is: what principle of distributive justice should be exemplified by political organization? As the term suggests, distributive justice pertains to 'dividing the pie' – to parceling out whatever the state properly supplies to its citizens, as well as whatever obligations or demands it may impose on them. As we shall see, the classical ideal of distributive justice is that for distribution to be equitable, fair, or just, the distribution should be in proportion to the deserts of those to whom distribution is made. So, a distribution of equal shares would be just only if those to whom distribution is made are equally deserving, according to whatever criterion of desert is being employed. Even if one agrees with the classical premise, extending back to Greek antiquity, that distributive justice is the primary virtue of political organization, that very abstract principle of distributive justice answers few questions about political distribution: what sorts of thing are properly distributed *by the state*?[6] What constitutes the relevant kind of desert or worthiness with respect to the way the distribution of these things is to be effected?

A closely related issue pertains to how to conceptualize the distinction between distributive justice, on the one hand, and what was classically termed commutative or rectificatory justice, on the other. According to the classical distinction, commutative justice pertains to relations between private individuals – to the equity of contractual exchanges and to the equity of the retribution or compensation due to individuals when they have been wronged by other individuals. Should the state perhaps concentrate on the enforcement of commutative justice rather than concern itself with matters of distributive justice? In other words, is the principal purpose of political organization not to give persons what they want or what they need in conformity with some principle of distributive justice (as most classical political philosophers believed), but rather to administer and to enforce principles of fair exchange and compensation (as various modern political thinkers have believed)?

4. Does the state's fulfilling its purpose, whatever that may be, *entail* that all the citizens must be somehow involved in the political decision-making or governing of the state? For example, does a distributively just 'division of the pie' include a distributively just division of political power or authority? Or, if the correct political decisions get made, should it be largely a matter of indifference to us who makes them and what the particulars are of the political organization by means of which they are made?

5. Finally, do citizens owe a special kind of allegiance to the political institution(s) of the community to which they belong? If so, and if this allegiance imposes moral obligations beyond the merely prudential, what might be its source or justification? How does such an allegiance, and the obligations it imposes, distribute over (or come in conflict with) subsidiary forms of political organization? With trans-political organizations, such as churches or other cultural or intellectual institutions? With other moral principles?

The preceding questions constitute a sample of the enduring issues of political philosophy. They are also issues about which many readers may already have formed some definite opinions. As I said before, a not uncommon belief of those who are approaching political philosophy for the first time is that it must consist simply in setting forth one's 'personal' political beliefs so as to share those beliefs with others and (if one is sufficiently persuasive) to win them over to one's particular political perspective. But it takes little reflection to make us realize that we usually have rather uncritically absorbed our political beliefs in a piecemeal and perhaps haphazard way – by osmosis, as it were – from various elements of our surrounding social, cultural, and political environment. Political philosophy involves us in systematic (and historical) reflection on these beliefs, the sources of these beliefs, and possible alternatives to these beliefs – and, I maintain, reflection about the relation of political ideas and ideals to conceptions of what human life really should be about (that is, to normative anthropologies). Engagement with political philosophy may leave the particular political beliefs with which we began largely intact; or it may result in a very different political perspective. However, the process should lead to more informed and reflective political commitments and that, it seems to me, is a good thing.

Before concluding this short introduction to a short introduction to political philosophy, I should emphasize the point – which I trust will become obvious, in a more concrete way, in what follows – that political philosophy is neither history, sociology, nor political science. Political philosophy is generally not concerned with concrete issues of public policy or with 'nuts and bolts' issues pertaining to the concrete functioning (efficient or otherwise) of the machinery of government. Such issues are often of immense importance. But they also typically involve empirical considerations, 'matters of fact', which can only be competently addressed – if at all – by thorough factual study by those with special technical expertise. In some rather obvious but difficult-to-define sense, political philosophy is both more fundamental and more abstract.[7] But not necessarily less important. Let us begin with the source of so much of the Western intellectual tradition: Greek antiquity.[8]

2

Classical Greek Political Philosophy: Beginnings

Nature or nurture?

Claims about beginnings in philosophy are usually disputable, but a case certainly can be made that Western political philosophy begins with the Sophistic movement of the fifth and fourth centuries B.C.E. The Greek noun '*sophistês*' (sophist) originally meant simply someone who 'practices wisdom.' As a group, they were paid teachers of the young males of the various Greek city-states (*poleis*, in the Greek plural). Their students generally came from the upper rungs of their respective communities. Although there were differences in the curricula of the sophists, the tuition offered by the sophist Protagoras, as depicted in Plato's dialogue the *Protagoras*, was probably not atypical: "The proper care of [the potential student's] personal affairs, so that he may best manage his own household, and also of the state's affairs, so as to become a real power in the city, both as a speaker and man of action."[1] Sophistic teaching, then, was at least in part focused on the political: its purpose included preparation of the young man of means and position to take a rôle in the affairs of his particular political community or *polis*.

Such teaching would have included rhetoric and debate. Then, as now, debate was often taught by encouraging students to develop the facility of mounting a persuasive argument on either side of a particular question. Then, as now, this procedure can appear to the bystander as opportunistic or cynical – perhaps even as an endorsement of a

12

skeptical or relativistic view of the matter at issue: there is no truth, nothing beyond divergent personal opinions, or, if there is, it seems unlikely that we will be able to come to agreement about what that truth is. It may sometimes also happen that this methodology has the psychological effect of encouraging such relativism or skepticism (or cynicism) in its practitioners and students. Indeed, there is evidence of theoretical relativism and skepticism on the part of some Greek Sophists. Whatever the precise details, the term '*sophistês*' soon acquired the pejorative connotations that its English cognate 'sophist' now possesses: a purveyor, usually a cynical purveyor, of tricky and specious arguments; someone who assumes and advances what he knows to be a false position.

While the sophists have generally suffered from a bad press, some of their modern admirers have advanced the plausible suggestion that the sophistic tradition has had a more lasting influence in Western thought than most other philosophical and scientific traditions of Greek antiquity. "Whatever we may think of the Sophistic movement, we must all agree that ... no intellectual movement can be compared with it in the permanence of its results, and that the questions which the Sophists posed have never been allowed to lapse in the history of Western thought down to our own day."[2] Most of these questions we would now categorize as moral or ethical in nature, and many were political.

One of the most important conceptual tools formulated by the sophists in order to deal with such questions was the first ancient version of the familiar nature versus nurture distinction: the *nomos-physis* antithesis. On the one side of this antithesis, there is *physis* or nature, with its connotations of immutability and necessity. If something exists 'by *physis*' then that is the way that it always was and is and always necessarily will be. On the other side, there is *nomos*, usually translated as 'law', but law in the sense of the term that presupposes a law giver: "an acting subject – believer, practitioner or apportioner – a mind from which the *nomos* emanates."[3] *Nomos* includes the ideas of custom and convention and connotes contingency, or even artificiality: if something exists 'by *nomos*' then it could be (or could have been) different had someone so decided. While the concepts of *physis* and *nomos* may not originally have been incompatible ideas, they soon came to be regarded as antithetical.

A question then considered by the sophists was whether political organization, specifically the Greek *polis* or city-state, exists by *physis* or by *nomos*. The same question was posed about the whole panoply of institutions and principles to which we might apply the terms 'ethical' or 'moral'. In particular, are those human character traits, which the

Greeks sometimes referred to as political 'virtues' (*aretai*, in the Greek plural[4]) and which enable persons not just to cooperate but to live a full social existence, a matter of *physis* or a matter of *nomos?* Not surprisingly, the answers to these questions fall into two principal categories: those that come down on the side of *physis* and those that come down on the side of *nomos*.

Protagoras' democratic traditionalism

Among the partisans of *nomos*, perhaps the most important is Protagoras, the first great sophist. In Plato's dialogue by that name, the character Protagoras develops his account of human acquisition and possession of the political *aretai* in terms of a myth, a version of the story of Prometheus. The gods, having created the various species of mortal creature, charge Prometheus (Foresight) and Epimetheus (Hindsight) with "equipping them and allotting suitable powers to each kind."[5] Epimetheus asks for the job of distributing these powers. While he does a satisfactory job with the brutes, he finds that he has nothing left to apportion to humans. Prometheus helps out by stealing "technical wisdom" and fire from Athena and Hephaestus in order to give them to humans. With their technical skills, humans "discovered articulate speech and names, and invented houses and clothes and shoes and bedding and got food from the earth."[6] While these skills sufficed for their nurture, humans were not able to cooperate to defend themselves from beasts because they lacked 'political skill', "of which martial skill is a part": "when they gathered in communities they injured one another for want of political skill."[7] Fearing the destruction of the human race, Zeus sends Hermes to give to humans two political *aretai*: *dikê* (justice, a sense of right) and *aidôs* (restraint, modesty, a sense of respect for others). When asked by Hermes whether he should distribute these two *aretai* unequally, in the way that the technical skills are distributed, or to all alike, Zeus replies that they should be given to all alike: "There could never be cities if only a few shared in these virtues, as in the arts. Moreover, you must lay it down as my law that if anyone is incapable of acquiring his share of these two virtues he shall be put to death as a plague to the city."[8]

What is the point of Protagoras' story? He proceeds to spell out the main point to the dialogue's other principal interlocutor Socrates:

> Thus it is, Socrates, and from this cause, that in a debate involving excellence [*aretê*] in building, or in any other craft, the Athenians,

like other men, believe that few are capable of giving advice, and if someone outside those few volunteers to advise them, then as you say, they do not tolerate it – rightly so, in my submission. But when the subject of their counsel involves political *aretê*, which must always follow the path of justice and moderation [or temperance, self-control: *sophrosunê*], they listen to every man's opinion, for they think that everyone must share in this kind of *aretê*; otherwise the state could not exist.[9]

From Plato's introduction to this story, as well as what we know of Protagoras, it is clear that he would not intend his tale of divine intervention to be taken literally. He was at least an agnostic about such theological matters. It is indeed true that the gods were thought by some to be the agents providing the authoritative will that constitutes *nomos*. For others, that job fell to quasi-mythical lawgivers such as Solon (for Athens) and Lycurgus (for Sparta).

But according to Protagoras the authoritative will that constitutes *nomos* can be thought of as a combination of "lawgivers of ancient times"[10] along with the accumulated traditions of generations – those practices, principles, and *aretai* that are the result of a long history of cooperation and shared social life. Since these traditions are the common property of all, the political *aretai* belong to all who have been properly acculturated. Protagoras suggests to his skeptical interlocutor Socrates that, because "all are teachers of *aretê* to the best of their ability, you think that no one is. In the same way if you asked who teaches the Greek language you would not find anyone."[11] Protagoras claims that "if we can find someone only a little better than others at advancing us on the road to *aretê*, we must be content,"[12] and makes the 'modest' claim that he, a sophist who professes to teach *aretê*, fits this description.

In a speech from the sixth book of his *History of the Peloponnesian War*, Thucydides represents Athenagoras, a leader of the democratic faction in Syracuse, as making a similar claim about political *aretê* and wisdom:

It will be said, perhaps, that democracy is neither wise nor equitable, but that the holders of property are also the best fitted to rule. I say, on the contrary, first, that the word *demos*, or people, includes the whole state, oligarchy [literally, rule by the few] only a part; next, that if the best guardians of property are the rich, and best counselors are the wise, none can hear and decide so well as the many; and that all these talents, individually and collectively, have their just place in a democracy. But an oligarchy gives the many their share of the danger, and not content with the largest part takes and keeps the whole of the profit.[13]

It is not surprising that advocates of a democratic form of polity, in which there is wide participation by citizens in the political decision-making process, should place a particular trust in the (political) wisdom of the people. We see here two ancient examples of this trust, but only hints of the reasons for it. Let us further explore these hints. What are the political *aretai* that are commonly possessed, according to Protagoras? A sense of justice or what is fair (*dikê*) and restraint or respect for others (*aidôs*). And what are the particular talents of 'the many', according to Thucydides' Athenagoras? Hearing the arguments, perhaps conflicting arguments, of wise counselors and sizing them up. If we assume with Protagoras that *dikê* and *aidôs* are in some sense the common inheritance of all, what further assumptions could justify the claim that these *aretai* give their possessors an equal claim to participation in the governing process?

A plausible response begins with the commonsensical observation that each participant in some particular cooperative enterprise, which issues in a fairly specific benefit, might well appear to be the best judge of whether he or she is sharing fairly in that benefit. Of course, where different participants contribute to different degrees (or in different ways), the situation is complicated, and there might well arise disputes about how the 'pie of benefits' is to be divided. But it is perhaps not unreasonable to assume that fellow citizens, who have acquired the political *aretai* of *dikê* and *aidôs* in a common social and cultural context, could come to some agreement about just distribution of benefits in such cases. It is precisely the lack of any agreed-upon scheme of distributive justice in an oligarchic *polis* to which Athenagoras objects. So we might say, that (i) if political decisions are largely limited to such particular enterprises of joint cooperation and consequent distribution of benefits, and (ii) if participants have internalized the requisite sense of fairness and mutual respect, Protagoras' democratic traditionalism is a rather plausible view. It also would seem that these conditions are most easily satisfied in small and rather primitive societies, where joint-cooperation enterprises are straightforward, where social distinctions (e.g., of class or wealth) are not great, and where the citizens have undergone a common process of socialization.

As we shall see, in his *Republic* Plato uses just such assumptions to introduce a form of democratic traditionalism, but only to transform it into a quite different political theory. However, there were also other

Greek thinkers who disputed not only Protagoras' egalitarian democratic claims but also his foundation of the political *aretai* in *nomos*.

The functionalistic foundation of the political
aretai in nature (*physis*)

In terms of the *nomos-physis* antithesis, the foundation of political
organization and of the political virtues or *aretai* in nature (*physis*) is
the obvious alternative to their foundation in *nomos*. The appeal to
physis often had a normative, rhetorical character: that is, *physis should*
be in control; but *nomos* – conventional mores, customs, human laws –
frequently constitute an unwarranted and morally deleterious
constraint on the operation of nature. We find the appeal to nature conjoined with a particular notion of an unwritten or 'common' (*koinos*)
law. In some cases, this concept of law is no more than what eventually
came to be called the *ius gentium* (Latin for law of peoples), those parts
of written law or of customary and unwritten moral principles that are
held to be shared by all peoples. The *ius gentium* was construed by some
as the commandments of the god(s) and, as such, would seem to be a
matter of *nomos*. However, by the fourth century B.C.E. Aristotle identifies common or universal law, "all those unwritten principles which
are supposed to be acknowledged everywhere,"[14] as "law according to
nature": "For there really is," he says, "a natural justice and injustice
that is common to all, even to those that have no association or
covenant with one another."[15] The explicit opposition to *nomos* (in the
form of "association or covenant") is here obvious. But how, more
explicitly, are political organization, law, justice, and the political *aretai*
grounded in *physis*? At least part of the answer to this question involves
what I shall call the functionalistic conception of *aretai*, the virtues or
excellences of something.

In Plato's dialogue the *Meno*, which pertains to the question of
whether *aretê* is something that can be taught, the character Meno
expresses what was probably a very common Greek conception of *aretê*.
In response to Socrates' question, "What do you yourself say *aretê* is?",
Meno responds as follows:

> But there is no difficulty about it. First of all, if it is manly *aretê* you
> are after, it is easy to see that the *aretê* of a man consists in man-
> aging the city's affairs capably, and so that he will help his friends
> and injure his foes while taking care to come to no harm himself.
> Or if you want a woman's *aretê*, that is easily described. She must

be a good housewife, careful with her stores and obedient to her husband. There is another *aretê* for a child, male or female, and another for an old man, free or slave as you like; and a great many more kinds of *aretê*, so that no one need be at a loss to say what it is. For every act and every time of life, with reference to each separate function [*ergon*], there is an *aretê* for each one of us, and similarly, I should say, a vice [*kakia*].[16]

According to Meno's conception, an *aretê* of something X is a quality or capacity that enables X to fulfill well X's proper *ergon*, its work, business or function. So if X's function is to G, an *aretê* of X, a virtue or excellence of X, makes X a good G-er. This is the essence of what I am calling the functionalistic conception of *aretai*. Meno here makes the traditional and commonsensical assumption that, in the case of human beings, function is relative to gender, age, social status, occupation, and so forth. The function of a man is different from that of a woman, that of a free man different from that of a slave, that of a noble different from that of a plebeian, that of a herdsman different from that of a vine dresser.

Plato's character Socrates is not satisfied with Meno's traditional and commonsensical account, however. He makes the Platonist assumption that there must be some essential nature (*ousia*, in the Greek), which all these different sorts of *aretê* have in common, and that that common nature is what he is interested in. So, in terms of the functionalistic model, what Socrates' response suggests is that there is an essential nature or *ousia* shared by all human beings, that this is a sort of *human* function or *ergon*, common to all members of the species, and that it is this generic function that determines what the human *aretê* or *aretai* are – what the quality or qualities are that enable a person to carry out the distinctive human function well and, thus, to be a *good human being*.

This functionalistic model supplies a framework for grounding the human *aretai*, including the political *aretai*, in nature (*physis*)[17] – as opposed to tradition, convention, or agreement, all gathered together under the concept of *nomos*. However, the functionalistic model also makes it quite imperative to address the issue of what the human function or *ergon* is, since an account of the human *aretai*, the qualities and capacities that makes a person a good human being, will obviously depend on precisely what that human *ergon* is. As we shall see, many thinkers of Greek antiquity implicitly or explicitly accepted the functionalistic model. Consequently, the issue of the human *ergon* looms large in classical moral and political thought. The model becomes so ingrained, however, that it is frequently the case that the nature of the human *ergon* is not so much explicitly discussed as it is presupposed. In other words, a conception of the human *ergon* is often a basic assumption that must be supplied if sense is to be made of the explicit doctrine of a particular thinker.

The functionalistic foundation of *aretai* in *physis* was frequently employed to argue that, because of the fact that the pursuit of self-interest and the domination of others is grounded in the human *physis* or *ergon*, true virtue lies in those strengths (which is what the Latin *virtus* literally means) that facilitate the pursuit of self-interest and domination. This sort of egoistic foundation of *aretai* in *physis* appealed particularly to those of oligarchic or aristocratic sentiment and is deprecated by the Athenian Stranger in Plato's *Laws* as the doctrine that "the height of justice is one who conquers by force." A principal source of faction in cities, he continues, is the doctrine of the "right life according to *physis*, which in truth is a life of dominating one's fellows and not serving others according to *nomos*."[18] Similarly, in Plato's *Republic* the character Glaucon (speaking as devil's advocate) claims that "every [human] nature naturally pursues its own advantage as a good, but it is diverted by the force of *nomos* to the respect of equality."[19] Glaucon, in fact, presents what is no doubt the historically most important political theory that involves an appeal to an egoistic conception of human *physis* as determinative of true virtue. But the doctrine that he presents, which is a form of what later came to be called contractarianism, also accommodates *nomos* after a fashion.

Glaucon's contractarian political theory

In Plato's *Republic* the character Glaucon presents an account of justice (which may be derived from some sophistic source) that he professes, hoping Socrates will refute it. His account is brief and I quote it in its entirety:

> They say that to do wrong is naturally good and to be wronged is bad, but the suffering of injury so far exceeds in badness the good of inflicting it that when they have done wrong to each other and suffered it, and have had a taste of both, those who are unable to avoid the latter and practise the former decide that it is profitable to come to an agreement with each other neither to inflict injury nor to suffer it. As a result they begin to make laws and covenants,

and the law's command they call lawful and just. This, they say, is the origin and essence of justice; it stands between the best and the worst, the best being to do wrong without paying the penalty and the worst to be wronged without the power of revenge. The just then is a mean between two extremes; it is welcomed and honoured because of men's lack of power to do wrong. The man who has that power, the real man, would not make a compact with anyone not to inflict injury or suffer it. For him that would be madness. This then, Socrates, is, according to their argument, the nature and origin of justice.[20]

There is much that is going on in this passage, much that is presupposed, and much that is unsaid. To begin with, we notice the combination of *physis* and *nomos* in the passage. "To do wrong is *naturally* good": this clearly is an assumption concerning human *physis*. But what does it mean and is it a plausible assumption? As we shall later see, Thomas Hobbes, writing in the seventeenth century, elaborates on the meaning of and evidence for a similar assumption. Glaucon appears to identify the impetus "to do wrong" with the natural inclination of "every human nature to pursue its own advantage as a good." The key Greek term in the phrase that I have translated by the rather neutral "pursue its own advantage" is *pleonexia*. It is often translated as 'graspiness', 'greed', 'arrogance', or 'desire for undue gain' and connotes the desire to have the advantage, to have *more* for one's own share – which typically means 'more than others'. So, the underlying picture of the human function or *ergon* is that of unlimitedly acquisitive consumption of satisfactions: the natural human good, goal (*telos*) or *ergon*, is to acquire as many satisfactions as one can. These satisfactions may be the result of the consumption of material goods, of sexual or other sensual activities, or simply of the domination of one's fellow human beings. But the basic idea is that the gaining of such satisfactions constitutes the sum and substance of the human business. It is what life is all about.

Particularly if there is a limited supply of such satisfactions to be obtained, persons are likely to come into conflict over the pursuit of them. Hence there arises the will "to do wrong," to increase one's share of satisfactions at the expense of others' shares, in Glaucon's account. Now, in view of this conception of the human *ergon*, the functionalistic conception of *aretai* would entail that the true and natural human *aretai* would be those qualities that would allow their possessor to maximize his or her satisfactions. To put this point in the language of *conventional* morality sounds paradoxical. The true human virtues are those qualities that enable one successfully 'to do wrong'; more briefly, 'injustice' is a virtue. However, Glaucon's story is more complicated. Since, he holds, human beings all share this same nature or function and since humans are apparently equally vulnerable to having wrong done to them, the forthright practice of the natural, self-aggrandizing *aretai* results in an insupportable social situation. Each of us is continually vulnerable to being on the receiving end of others' pursuit of their interest; and this situation is not at all conducive to the fulfillment of one's own natural human function.

At this point, *nomos* enters the story in the form of a 'social compact' or contract, according to which each person undertakes to restrain himself somewhat in the fulfillment of his own natural human function in return for the exercise of like self-restraint on the part of others. In effect, Protagoras' *dikê* and *aidôs* are the result. But, unlike Protagoras, Glaucon does not consider these *aretai* to constitute a sort of second nature. They cut too much against the natural grain and, indeed, can be considered *aretai* only in a very limited and contingent sense: *if* I am vulnerable, in the sense that the existence of other persons with natures like mine places a limitation on the unfettered pursuit of my self-aggrandizement, *then* the social contract represents making the best of a bad situation. It allows me to pursue my self-interest within the restrictions of *dikê* and *aidôs*, which is not a natural and complete fulfillment of my human nature but is the best I can do in the circumstances.

Of course, as Glaucon proceeds to point out, *dikê* and *aidôs* would not be *aretai* for a person not subject to such vulnerability. He tells the story of a shepherd, an "ancestor of the Lydian Gyges," who discovers a magical ring that makes him invisible – with predictable results. The shepherd is able to pursue his function as a consumer of satisfactions without constraint and does so. *Dikê* and *aidôs* are of no value to him; indeed, according to the functionalistic model, they are not *aretai*. Glaucon concludes that, for those who can get away with it, *apparent* justice, rather than justice itself, is the real *aretê*. That is, if one has that ability (and luck) to secure oneself against the effects of the wrongdoing of others by *their* practice of the conventional *aretai* of *dikê* and *aidôs* while pursuing one's own self-aggrandizement as vigorously as possible, such behavior would certainly seem to allow one to fulfill one's nature as a consumer of satisfactions better than playing by the conventional rules of *nomos*.

Glaucon here is offering an argument for being a 'free rider', that is, for taking advantage of the social cooperation of others while reneging, to the degree one can get away with it, on the conventional constraints on one's behavior. Is there any obvious response to Glaucon's argument? One sort of response, with echoes in contemporary game theory, is prudential. That is, free riding ultimately is not to the advantage of the individual – perhaps because it is destructive of the relations of social and political cooperation which certainly *are* to the advantage of the individual. We shall have occasion to consider such responses in later historical settings. But it is worth pointing out that Glaucon's argument considers an individual who is a *successful* free rider, a person who practices injustice successfully in the sense that his injustice is not detected and does not fatally undermine the system of cooperation that he is taking advantage of. If such a case is possible – and surely it is possible, at least on occasion – it is difficult to see how a prudential response would be effective.

Another sort of response invokes moral restraints on even undetected free riding. But are such moral restraints a matter of *physis* or of *nomos*? Might they be a matter of *physis*? Glaucon's argument has been that free riding, the practice of only apparent justice, is a *natural aretê*, according to the functionalistic conception of *aretai* and Glaucon's conception of human *physis* or nature as unlimited acquisition of satisfactions. In other words, according to Glaucon's application of the functionalistic model, the human virtues or *aretai* would be just those qualities or capacities of character that enable one to be successful in grabbing as many satisfactions as one can. So a moral response grounded in *physis* does not seem to be forthcoming in view of Glaucon's self-aggrandizing conception of human nature. The other option is a moral response grounded in *nomos*, in conventional morality. But, in the picture that Glaucon has constructed, conventional morality will seem quite pointless from the perspective of the successful free rider.

Nonetheless, Glaucon and his brother Adeimantus profess the hope that Socrates (speaking for the author Plato, of course) will refute this argument, as well as the contractarian conception of justice that undergirds it. Whether Socrates does effect this refutation and, if so, how he does so are topics to which we turn in the next chapter.

3

Plato: Government for Corrupted Intellects

Socrates' *polis* of pigs

Plato is too wise to attempt a direct refutation of Glaucon's contractarian account of the state and of justice, which we considered in the preceding chapter.[1] In view of the normative anthropology – that is, the conception of human nature – assumed by Glaucon and his implicit appeal to the functionalistic model of the human virtues or *aretai*, it seems to be virtually impossible to avoid his conclusion concerning the virtue of apparent, as opposed to real, justice. As we shall see, Plato develops a quite different normative anthropology, one that yields a very different picture of the nature and rôle of political organization.

In the *Republic*, his character Socrates[2] makes the first move by constructing an account of political cooperation quite different from Glaucon's, one in which the elements of *physis* and *nomos* appear in a much less antagonistic form than in Glaucon's account:

> I think a *polis* comes to be, I [Socrates] said, because not one of us is self-sufficient, but needs many things. Do you think a *polis* is founded on any other principle? – On no other.
>
> As they need many things, people make use of one another for various purposes. They gather many associates and helpers to live in one place, and to this settlement we give the name of *polis*. Is that not so? – It is.

And they share with one another, both giving and taking, in so far as they do, because they think this better for themselves? – Quite so.[3]

Socrates additionally appeals to a fundamental characteristic of human *physis*: "Each one of us was born not altogether similar to another but differing in *physis*, so that one will be better at one kind of work (*ergon*), another at a different kind. Or does it not seem that way to you? – Certainly."[4] In view of these facts about human *physis*, as well as the additional fact that some tasks will not wait until another task is finished (e.g., the grape harvest cannot be delayed, if the grapes are not to spoil, until I finish building a house), Socrates advocates a system of social cooperation based upon division of labor and mutual exchange of the surpluses produced by each person concentrating on one type of task.

According to Socrates' account, *physis* gives us human beings both our lack of individual self-sufficiency and our differential talents and abilities; *nomos* responds with a system of mutually advantageous economic specialization and exchange of surpluses. It is clear that the resulting *polis* sketched by Socrates is a quite primitive society, even by the standards of the Greek world of the late fifth or early fourth centuries B.C.E. It also appears to be quite egalitarian. That is, there is no mention of a hierarchical political structure – or, indeed, of any formal political structure at all. Since the topic of the *Republic* is the nature of justice (*dikaiosunê*), Socrates does inquire as to where it is to be found in the *polis* he has envisioned and receives the following response: "I do not know unless it is somewhere in a kind of mutual service of these same citizens."[5] Socrates responds only "perhaps you are right," and continues with his description of his *polis*. The Greek term *chreia* in the answer that I have translated 'service' also means 'need', 'familiarity', or 'any relation of business or social intercourse'. And I think that Socrates' interlocutor has indeed given what Plato considers to be the correct answer. The citizens' lack of self-sufficiency and the *polis*' economic and social relations, founded on economic specialization and the principle of reciprocity or fair exchange,[6] represent a form of distributive justice: each citizen contributes a particular product or commodity according to his means and receives what he or she needs for sustenance according to his needs in a way that each judges to be *fair*.

The aristocratic young males who are Socrates' interlocutors (that is, the other characters in the dialogue with whom Socrates carries on his philosophical discussion) are not impressed. Glaucon sarcastically inquires, "If you were founding a *polis* of pigs, Socrates, how else than this would you fatten them?"[7] In the sketch of his *polis*, Socrates has been exclusively concerned with providing his citizens with a healthy but basic ('primitive', his interlocutors would say) biological existence and a system of stable, intimate, simple social relations restricted to the family and somewhat larger 'tribe'. Biological needs are met in his *polis*, but without any frills or luxury; in that ideal city – the *polis* of pigs – there is, for the most part, freedom from want, freedom from disease, and freedom from fear. But is this all there is to human life? Is the human *ergon* or function no more than to live out one's life in its biological, familial (and perhaps tribal) dimensions – ideally in a manner as comfortable as that provided by Socrates' *polis* of pigs? It seems likely that most of humankind has been in a position to aspire to little more than this modest (but, alas, usually unattainable) goal. However, Socrates' interlocutors certainly think that there is more to life than this. So does Plato. Both Plato and Socrates' interlocutors in the *Republic* may be said to have aristocratic ideals of human life. But, as we shall see, these ideals differ dramatically.

The 'republic' of Plato's *Republic*

Glaucon and Socrates' other aristocratic interlocutors are interested in a 'real' *polis*, that is, a civilized, cultivated, materially affluent *Greek* city-state – no doubt one where they could enjoy the amenities to which they are accustomed. It is certainly worthy of note that Socrates says that his *polis* of pigs seems to him to be the "true *polis*, like someone who is healthy."[8] But, he adds, he is willing to consider the case of an "extravagant [or swollen or inflamed] *polis*." What does he mean? The way of life of the *polis* of pigs will not be to everyone's liking, Socrates admits. Some will want more by way of luxuries – "couches and tables and other kinds of furniture ... cooked dishes and unguents and perfumes and courtesans and pastries – various kinds of all these."[9] Increased wants lead to the need for more raw products and land, with the consequence that "we must therefore annex a portion of our neighbors' land if we are to have sufficient pasture and ploughland, and they will want to annex part of ours if they too have surrendered themselves to the limitless acquisition of wealth and overstepped the boundaries of the necessary."[10] This need leads, in turn, to the establishment of a professional soldier class, which is introduced by the same principle of division of labor or economic specialization that underlay Socrates' original *polis* of pigs.

In effect, Socrates has admitted that Glaucon's conception of the human *ergon* as the unlimitedly acquisitive consumption of satisfactions has some basis in our experience: there is considerable inclination, at least on the part of some people, to act that way. And this fact leads away from the *polis* of pigs to the extravagant or inflamed *polis*. To make a long dramatic story short, what Plato does through his character Socrates is to construct an 'inflamed *polis*' with the inflammation under control. This is the famous 'republic' that gives the dialogue its name. The transformation from the *polis* of pigs is subtle but quite substantial – and, some would argue, disingenuous. Perhaps most important are two changes to the class of professional soldiers introduced at the beginning of consideration of the inflamed *polis*. They become responsible not just for dealing with the external security of the state but also become the guardians of its *internal* security and order. And they are divided into a class of rulers, who make the political decisions for the *polis*, and a class of auxiliaries, who faithfully implement these decisions. The remainder of citizens are lumped into the artisan or tradesman class, whom we may think of as the generators of the gross national product (GNP) of the state. Thus we have the famous three classes of Plato's 'republic'. The members of this last class are allowed some luxuries that are denied to the rulers and auxiliaries, who live a communal and – from the point of view of most of us – austere existence. However, members of the class of GNP-generators have no political function within the state and, indeed, no say in the political process by which decisions are made for the common good of the *polis*.

It is important to note that the three classes of Plato's inflamed *polis* with the inflammation under control, i.e., the republic, are introduced and justified by the principle of economic specialization to which Socrates appealed in the founding of his *polis* of pigs. Each of the classes has its own product or commodity to offer to other members of the community, and each receives in turn from the surplus provided by members of the other classes. The rulers provide the political decision-making for the *polis* and the auxiliaries the implementation of those decisions; and each of these classes receive the modest material support needed for the physical sustenance of its members. The class of GNP-generators (still characterized by internal economic specialization, which Plato now regards as less important) provide physical sustenance for themselves and the other two classes – and a bit of limited luxury for themselves; in turn, they receive the rational guidance they are unable to supply for themselves in the form of the political rule by the other two classes. The three classes are not castes in the sense that the descendants of members of one class are forever consigned to membership in it. Indeed, the elaborate education system of the republic sketched by Plato is in large part devoted to the attempt to place each person in the class for which he or she has the aptitude.

There are a number of assumptions involved in this transition from *polis* of pigs to republic. Perhaps the most obvious is that 'ruling' or political decision-making is now regarded as a very specialized task that requires very special (and apparently rare) aptitude and the sort of education that will best develop that aptitude. Political *aretai* are no longer the common possession of all, as they were for Protagoras (and as they perhaps seemed to be in Socrates' sketch of the *polis* of pigs). The result is that Plato's application of the principle of economic specialization has consequences in his republic that are very different from its application in the *polis* of pigs: the political community of the republic is unabashedly hierarchical and not at all egalitarian. In fact, it is Plato's inegalitarian application of the principle of economic specialization that yields the account of distributive justice which he has been searching for. Within the republic justice is a matter of each member of each of the three classes attending to the proper business of that class and not attempting to arrogate the function of a different class.[11]

Plato also claims that those desires that

> are simple and measured and directed by reasoning with intelligence and right belief you will meet with in but few people who are the best by nature and the best educated. – True.
>
> You will see this also in your city; there the desires of the inferior many are controlled by the desires and the knowledge of the fewer and better? – I do indeed.[12]

It is arguable that the principal point of Plato's republic and of the particular principle of distributive justice that it enshrines is to insure that those citizens receive the rational direction that they require. It is desirable that those humans who cannot supply it for themselves receive it from an external source; and it is *just* that, within the *polis*, this important 'commodity' of rational direction be supplied by those most capable of supplying it. To understand more fully why Plato effects the transformation from *polis* of pigs to the hierarchical republic of the *Republic* and to appreciate some fundamental problems with Plato's political philosophy, we must consider Plato's normative anthropology, his doctrine not only of the human nature or *ergon* but also of what might be termed the 'human predicament'. Certain crucial elements of this doctrine are not explicitly found in the text of the *Republic*.

The human *ergon* and the purpose of political organization

The conception of human beings as rational animals is not uncommon in the Western intellectual tradition, of course. Plato, however, adopts a rather extreme version of this conception. By and large, Plato conceives of human beings as intellects: the human *ergon*, function or business, is to understand or know the truth – period. In fact, Plato holds that each human has always been, to a greater or lesser degree, in possession of that truth. The truth in question has two particularly important characteristics. To begin with, it is unchanging, necessary and supra-sensible. That is, it is not fundamentally *about* the physical world of change, accessible to our senses; it is not scientific, in the contemporary sense of that term, nor historical. Second, it is unified. Knowledge in the fullest sense (something that we might perhaps describe as wisdom) is not piecemeal or compartmentalized: to know something in this sense depends on knowing its relations to the rest of what is knowable.

In Plato's view, human beings were once in full possession of this knowledge. However, human nature has been corrupted in the sense that we have been led away from this state of knowing or understanding. Consequently, we now possess knowledge only in an implicit, one might say subconscious, manner. And we are no longer single-mindedly focused on the *ergon* of knowing the truth. This corruption of human nature is Plato's doctrine of the 'fall'. Of course, I am not referring to the story of the expulsion from the Garden of Eden found in *Genesis* and shared by the Judaic, Christian, and Islamic religious traditions. But Plato has his own version of the doctrine and his own supply of myths, not necessarily mutually consistent ones, with which to express it. He sometimes appeals to reincarnation to express the fact that we find humans in various degrees of corruption; and perhaps the same person can either move further away from or progress closer to the ideal of a human as an intellect. We are all of us corrupted intellects, however. Indeed, Plato tends to view the fact that we are *embodied* or 'incarnate' intellects, distracted in varying degrees by the demands (and temptations) of our biological existence, as at least symptomatic of our corrupted, fallen state. It appears that it is not just the sensual pleasures, but also the desire of honor or esteem (*timê*) and the desire to dominate others, that lead us away from our true *ergon* of knowing the truth and make us corrupted intellects.

According to Plato, it is philosophy – in its etymological sense of 'love of wisdom' – that leads us back to our *ergon* and true nature.

Philosophy has both a positive and a negative aspect. On the positive side, the love of wisdom will involve its active and often arduous pursuit through intense study and thought. On the negative side it will involve the assumption of ascetic attitudes and practices to wean us away from concerns not conducive to our function of knowing. It is for this reason that, in the *Phaedo*, Socrates characterizes philosophy as a preparation for "dying and being dead."[13]

Plato is certainly single-minded, if not monomaniacal, in his commitment to his intellectualistic conception of the human *ergon* as understanding or knowing the truth. This is our proper and true Ultimate End; and I think that it is not unfair to say that any aspect of human life that is not directed toward its attainment Plato is inclined to dismiss as, at best, trivial, and at worst, pernicious. As I suggested earlier, it appears that not only human biological existence but also human *social* existence can deflect us from the pursuit of our true *ergon*. This fact makes for an ambivalent attitude on Plato's part to the place of the political in human life.

We might well expect that the purpose of the *polis*, and of political organization in general, would be to enable its citizens best to live up to the distinctively human *ergon* of knowing the truth, since that function is, after all, the sum and substance of what human life is all about. According to such a conception, the better a *polis* is at fulfilling this single task, the better *polis* it will be. But, *in fact* political organization typically seems to be devoted primarily to enabling its citizens to satisfy their biological needs. The Greek *polis* also supplied the setting for the social life of its citizens. These functions were also recognized in Socrates' sketch of his *polis* of pigs. But they are functions that are relevant to fallen human nature, to human beings as corrupted intellects, rather than to the human *ergon* of understanding the truth. Of course, the republic of Plato's *Republic* retains the function of providing for its citizens' biological and social existence. But Plato evidently believes that political organization should do more than pander to the corrupted element of human nature. If political organization is to be relevant to the true human *ergon*, it must somehow further the rationality of its citizens; it must be at the service of the realm of reason. As we saw, Plato holds that his republic does, in fact, do this: in his republic the rational element in the state, that is, the class of rulers, is supposed to serve the realm of reason and to impose rationality on the *polis*. But what, more precisely, does this amount to for Plato?

Furthering rationality by means of the *polis*?

The most obvious sense in which Plato's republic might be said to "further the rationality of its citizens" or "be at the service of the realm of reason" pertains to a central feature of this state: ruling or political decision-making is restricted to the most rational individuals, those persons in whom the capacity for reason is the strongest and whose education has fully developed that capacity. They are not only philosophers ('lovers of wisdom') but persons *possessing* wisdom to a greater degree than their fellow citizens in the other two classes. Plato, as we said, conceives of political decision-making in a most non-Protagorean way – as a particular art or craft with its own set of particular *aretai* or virtues. I suppose that even in contemporary, democratic constitutional states most of us think that at least *some* political functions require particular talents or expertise. But the sort of talent, expertise, or rationality we have in mind typically has to do with the management of people – knowing how to be a charismatic leader, to forge consensus, to organize, and to delegate, etc. Note that the rationality at issue is knowledge how to get things done, that is, rationality directed toward action. However, we also noted earlier that Plato does not see knowledge as compartmentalized; for him, knowledge constitutes a unified understanding of the way things are, a unified realm of reason. Platonic knowledge would seem to be a sort of wisdom, and it is reason in the sense of possession of wisdom of this sort that should characterize the rulers in Plato's republic. Reason or rationality in this sense is fundamentally knowledge that reality (the unified, supra-sensible, realm of reason or of the 'Forms', according to Plato) is of such-and-such a nature. That is, reason, according to Plato's paradigmatic conception of it, would seem fundamentally to be directed toward *understanding* the truth, not toward action.

It is far from obvious that possession of *this* sort of theoretical knowledge or wisdom is directly pertinent to success in ruling or political decision-making. It seems that the primary function of Plato's republic, beyond enabling its citizens to provide for their basic biological needs, is to inculcate this sort of knowledge in its citizens. But the knowledge and skills required to do this successfully, we might plausibly suppose, is not itself really this sort of theoretical knowledge. What is needed evidently is a sort of *practical* rationality. But Plato does not seem really to have a conception of practical reason – that is, knowledge or wisdom directed toward action – as distinguished from his conception of theoretical reason, knowledge or wisdom directed simply toward the understanding of the truth about reality.[14]

Plato's lack of a distinct conception of practical rationality leads us back to the issue of *how* political organization (and, in particular, the 'republic' of his *Republic*) is supposed to "further the rationality of its citizens" or "be at the service of the realm of reason." One might assume that furthering the rationality of the citizens of the republic would be a matter of enabling or encouraging the citizens of the *polis* to *act* rationally. But this would be a matter of furthering practical rationality, and I have just suggested that Plato has no clear conception of a distinctively practical rationality. About the only doctrine of what it would mean to behave rationally in our everyday affairs that can be gleaned from Plato's works is the entirely negative, ascetic idea of suppressing our appetites and desires, which Plato seems to regard as intrinsically opposed to reason. This is the *Phaedo*'s ideal of philosophy as practice for dying and being dead. It appears that, for the members of the class of GNP-generators (and perhaps even for the class of auxiliaries), practice of asceticism in the form of restraint of desires and appetites is the only possible way of acting rationally. And, at least for the GNP-generators, Plato seems to believe that this restraint must be externally applied. The republic can further the rationality of these citizens only in a quite minimal and negative way.

A similar problem exists for what is usually considered a central feature of the *Republic*'s argument on behalf of justice. Plato argues that analogous to justice in the republic, which is a matter of members of each of the three principal classes attending exclusively to the function of that class and not attempting to interfere with the functions of the other classes, is justice within the individual person's *psychê* or soul. This is a matter of each of the three parts or faculty of the soul – the rational part (*nous*), the courageous or spirited part (*thymos*), and the appetitive part (*epithymia*) – attending to its own function and not interfering with the functions of the other parts. According to Plato, the result is a sort of psychic health or harmony, which is surely worth possessing for its own sake: the rational faculty should be in charge of the person's interior and exterior life and its decisions should be faithfully put into effect by the will or spirited faculty (*thymos*). And, it seems, the basic job of the appetitive faculty is to be subservient to the other faculties; its desires apparently should be indulged only insofar as doing so is of aid to the temporary (and unnatural, degraded) embodied state of the soul. A perennial criticism of Plato's analogy is that it is far from obvious that his conception of 'justice' as psychic health or harmony has much to do with justice in the more usual political or social sense. However, it also seems that only the philosopher- or ruler-type of person is capable of achieving this internal order that Plato identifies with 'justice' in the individual. For those who are not ruler-types, it appears that this order, this discipline, would need to be imposed from without. But Plato never really addresses the issue of whether such an *internal* state or disposition could be externally imposed.

For members of the class of rulers, the prospects are perhaps better. These are the least corrupted intellects in the *polis*, the citizens who are best equipped to achieve the human *ergon* of knowing. But it seems that the best way that the republic could further the rationality of these citizens would be to provide them with (modest) material support and free them as much as possible from the demands normally associated with human biological and social existence so that they might withdraw for solitary study and reflection – or perhaps withdraw into an elite school or research institute not dissimilar to the 'Academy' founded by Plato in Athens. Indeed, Plato *might* have developed a political doctrine according to which the proper rôle of political organization is precisely to support such activity on the part of the select few capable of engaging in it. However, this does not seem to be his conception of the proper function of the *polis*. Such a conception would obviously make the state 'elitist' in the following sense: political organization would exist in order to promote the good or *ergon* of only the relatively few who are most able – the 'least corrupted intellects'. Other humans in the community would have only instrumental value insofar as they are of use in this task. *Their* individual goods would not, in themselves, be of concern to the *polis*. Consequently, there is a sense in which this majority of human beings in the community would not be citizens – that is, full and equal associates – in such a *polis*.

Plato may be an 'elitist' with respect to his convictions about who should be in charge, who should be making the political decisions in his republic. But his political philosophy does not seem to be elitist in this stronger sense. The citizens of all three classes in his republic, although they have different rôles in the state, all matter – the *polis* is supposed to exist for the good of all of them. In particular, the political function of the rulers is to *rule*; they are not to be allowed to withdraw from the social and political life of the republic in order to spend their time in understanding, or coming to understand the truth – whether singly or in a scholarly community such as Plato's Academy. But, in view of Plato's conception of the human *ergon* and his apparent acceptance of the functionalistic conception of human *aretai*, what obligation do ruler-types have to concern themselves with political matters? Plato considers this question in a very famous passage from the seventh book of the *Republic*, the allegory of the cave.

Why should anyone return to the cave?

The allegory of the cave is surely one of the most striking and famous passages in the *Republic*. Prisoners (representing the human race) are confined to a dark cave and chained so that they can see only the cave wall in front of them. A fire burns behind them and a 'puppet show' is provided for them with the puppet figures casting their shadows, which is all the prisoners see of this procedure, on the wall that they face. Understandably, the prisoners take what they see to be the sum and substance of reality. There are certain patterns of regularity to the passing shadows and the more attentive of the prisoners can, by purely empirical means, come to discern something of these patterns of regularity. They "have praise and honours for each other, and prizes for the man who saw most clearly the shadows that passed before them, and who could best remember which usually came earlier and which later, and which came together and thus could most ably prophesy the future."[15]

In this allegory of enlightenment, when one of the prisoners is set free he begins to discern the general illusion afflicting humankind. He first sees what is really going on in the cave and then ascends "by a rough and steep path" to the reality of daylight. Plato suggests that if someone who had undergone such enlightenment were to return to the cave he would have little interest in the prisoners' pastime of discerning empirical regularities in the shadows and making predictions on the basis of these patterns. Nor would he be very good at this activity "while his sight was still affected [by the light of reality] and his eyes had not settled down."[16] The unenlightened prisoners would maintain that the returning prisoner "had returned from his upward journey with his eyesight spoiled, and that it was not worthwhile even to attempt to travel upward. As for the man who tried to free them and lead them upward, if they could somehow lay their hands on him and kill him, they would do so."[17] So, as an empirical matter, Plato is not optimistic that the masses that need rational direction will really appreciate the services of the enlightened. Nor, as a psychological matter, will the enlightened have much interest in supplying these services.[18] Yet, Socrates insists that in his republic it is essential "to compel the best natures to reach the study which we have previously said to be the most important, to see the Good and to follow that upward journey."[19] But they are not to be allowed "to stay there and be unwilling to descend again"[20] to the cave-*polis*.

At this juncture, Socrates' interlocutor Glaucon raises a most pertinent objection: "Are we then to harm them [the philosopher- or ruler-types] and make them live a worse life, when it is possible for them to live a better one?"[21] Socrates responds that it is not the concern of the law to make one part fare well but, rather, to make the whole *polis* fare well and to make the members of each part "share with each other the benefits which each group can confer upon the community."[22] He denies that his republic does any injustice to "those who have become philosophers" (i.e., ruler-types who are the most able to fulfill the human *ergon* of understanding the truth and who have made most progress in doing so):

> Those who have become philosophers in other cities are justified in not sharing the city's labours, for they have grown into philosophy of their own accord, against the will of the government in each of those cities, and it is right that what grows of its own accord, since it owes no debt to anyone for its upbringing, should not be keen to pay it to anyone. But we have made you in our city kings and leaders of the swarm, as it were, both to your own advantage and to that of the rest of the city; you are better and more completely educated than the others, and you are better able to share in both kinds of life. Therefore you must each in turn go down to live with other men and grow accustomed to seeing in the dark.[23]

Socrates' response to Glaucon's objection is not, I think, an adequate one – at least in terms of Plato's framework for treating of moral and political issues. Recall that, in terms of the functionalistic conception, what constitutes human virtues or *aretai*, what makes a person a good person, are those capacities and qualities that enable their possessor successfully to fulfill or live up to an objective human function or *ergon*. According to Plato, this *ergon* is, simply, to understand, to know the truth; we humans are essentially intellects. So a quality will count as a virtue, an *aretê*, for Plato, only if it somehow contributes to our knowing, or coming to know, the truth. Now, if what we nowadays call a moral obligation has essentially the same source – if I, as an intellect, am (morally) obliged to do precisely those things that contribute to my fulfilling my understanding-function and if I am obliged to refrain from doing those thing that are inconsistent with or detract from my fulfilling this function – it seems that Glaucon is correct. Philosopher- or ruler-types have no obligation to rule; and it seems plausible to say that we are harming them in insisting that they do. Plato's conception of the human *ergon* does not have any essential *social* component. Though it may, as a matter of fact, be of some use to have study groups, teachers and fellow students, in coming to know the truth, this would appear to be a contingent fact about human nature as we find it. The act or state of understanding seems to be essentially solitary. Thus, it is very difficult for him to give an account of what we think of as typical social *aretai* and obligations.

In his response to Glaucon's objection, Plato clearly appeals to a notion of reciprocity or fair play. It simply would be unfair for a philosopher-type, having received the benefits of the republic, to with- hold his or her ruling services. Plato, in effect, appeals to a principle of distributive justice as 'fairness' that would seem to be grounded in Protagorean *nomos*: deeply ingrained, traditional notions of *dikê* and *aidôs* are invoked to justify a social obligation. As we saw, the Protagorean element was present in the *polis* of pigs, and it is not entire- ly absent from the republic either. In fact, it may turn out that any plau- sible political theory must appeal to such notions as foundational. However, it is not at all clear that this appeal to fairness can be success- fully integrated with what appears to be Plato's *theoretical* mechanism: his strictly intellectualist account of the human *ergon* or *physis*, and his normative use of that *physis* to ground the human *aretai* and, deriva- tively, human (moral) obligations.

In the following chapter, I shall maintain that Plato's sometime pupil Aristotle gives a more coherent account of human social obliga- tions and, consequently, is able to develop a more adequate political philosophy. To make a long-ish story short, he is able to do so because he possesses a more complex conception of the human *ergon* – one that includes a social component.

4

Aristotle: Politics as the Master Art

The human good: intellectual *and* political

A fundamental and quite Greek assumption made by Aristotle[1] is the claim that what gives human life its significance is the fact that there is an objective 'chief good' to which all human action ideally should be directed. In the second chapter of the first book of his *Nicomachean Ethics*, Aristotle specifies political knowledge or science as being concerned with this chief human good:

> If, then, there is some end of the things we do, which we desire for its own sake (everything else being desired for the sake of something else), and if we do not choose everything for the sake of everything else (for at that rate the process would go on to infinity, so that our desire would be empty and vain), clearly this must be the good and the chief good. Will not the knowledge of it, then, have a great influence on life? ... If so, we must try, in outline at least, to determine what it is, and of which of the sciences or capacities it is the object. It would seem to belong to the most authoritative art and that which is most truly the master art. And politics appears to be of this nature; for it is this that ordains which of the sciences should be studied in a *polis*, and which each class of citizens should learn and up to what point they should learn them.[2]

Since Aristotle proceeds to assert that the political art or science "legislates what it is necessary to do and to abstain from,"[3] it is eminently sensible for him to claim that the execution of this political function should always refer to this chief human good – if there is one. He also identifies, with relatively little argument, the chief human good with the human function (*ergon*), purpose or nature.[4] However, we may well wonder (a) whether there is in fact such a chief human good (and whether it is to be identified, as Aristotle identifies it, with successfully performing a distinctive human function or living up to a distinctive human nature). We may also wonder (b) whether, if there is such a chief human good (function or purpose), *what* exactly it is.

Question (a) is perhaps the more difficult question, to which I shall later return. With respect to question (b), Aristotle gives an initial and none too informative answer in the first book of the *Nicomachean Ethics*: the chief human good is, in the Greek, *eudaimonia* (or, in its verbal form, *to eudaimonein*). The traditional English translation for the Greek is 'happiness' or 'being happy', but most contemporary commentators agree that this translation is misleading. The English word happiness connotes something like an affect or emotion, which may come and go in the life of a human agent and over which the agent often seems to have limited control. Aristotle's *eudaimonia* is certainly not an emotion; it is a much more settled, stable way of life that is to be identified with a pattern of behavior or activities of a human agent. For this reason, many scholars now prefer a translation such as 'faring/doing well', 'flourishing', or 'prospering'. Such a translation makes it quite clear that to say, as does Aristotle, that the objective, chief good of human existence is *eudaimonia* does not really address the question of what, substantively, this 'flourishing' consists.

Aristotle is well aware of this feature of his account. He maintains that although there is virtually universal agreement that the chief human good is *eudaimonia*, there is much disagreement concerning what sort of life instantiates it – what, that is, constitutes human flourishing. Aristotle has three primary candidates for the lifestyle or mode of life (*bios*) that instantiates *eudaimonia*: the life directed toward pleasure, the political life, and the contemplative life (that is, the life directed toward understanding or knowing the truth).[5] Aristotle has no more respect than does Plato for the conception of the chief human good or function as the pursuit of pleasure or the consumption of satisfactions. However, his attitude toward the remaining two candidates, the political life and the contemplative life, is considerably more complex.

At the conclusion of the preceding chapter I mentioned that Aristotle, unlike Plato, explicitly includes a social component in his conception of the human *ergon* or function. However, the manner in which he does this is still a topic of scholarly dispute, and Aristotle may, in fact, not have a single unambiguous and consistent account of the dual nature of human beings. Yet he does seem to attribute such a dual nature to humans. One part of this nature or function, discussed in chapters seven and eight of the tenth book of the *Nicomachean Ethics*, is fundamentally the same as Plato's account of the human nature: to understand or know the truth, *theôria* (contemplation) in Aristotle's terminology. His model for this activity (or state of being) seems pretty clearly to be drawn from his non-anthropomorphic conception of gods. Aristotle's deities bear little relation to the Olympian deities of Greek mythology and literature. In his cosmology, they are responsible for the motions of the celestial spheres, which in turn are responsible for the diurnal revolution of the 'fixed stars' (the stars whose positions relative to each other does not vary and whose apparent diurnal revolution we now attribute to the spinning of the earth) and the periodic motions of the 'wandering stars' or planets (which, for Aristotle, would include Mercury, Venus, the moon, the sun, Mars, Jupiter, and Saturn). For Aristotle, the deities move the celestial spheres as 'unmoved movers': that is, they do not exert their effect by pushing, pulling or any other sort of physical contact but rather by a sort of attraction like that exerted on a sentient being by an object of desire. He also holds that what is definitive of the form of life of these deities, which are indivisible substances without physical magnitude and without parts, is knowing, *theôria*; indeed, the 'head-honcho' deity that is responsible for moving the outermost sphere of fixed stars is described as "thought thinking itself."[6]

Exactly what this characterization entails about the object(s) of divine intellection is not clear, nor is the relation between the intellection of the gods and their function as cosmological movers. But it is fairly evident that Aristotle believes that the gods have no concern with the lives of human beings, and they certainly are not creator-gods in the manner, say, of the Judaeo–Christian–Islamic God. Nor do they have any social or communal existence. Consequently, he holds that the moral and political virtues (*aretai*) and vices simply do not apply to them. Aristotle's gods are simply intellects or knowers. Nonetheless, Aristotle believes them to be *living* – indeed, preeminently living, although obviously not in anything like the contemporary biological sense of living.[7]

In *Nicomachean Ethics* 10.7–8 Aristotle makes it clear both that (at least some) humans are able to partake in this function of knowing or *theôria*, although in a quite limited and imperfect manner, and that this activity or state of knowing represents the highest aspect of the human *ergon*. Although this activity is hyper-human (he says that "it is not in so far as he is man that [a human being] will live so, but in so far as something divine is present in him"[8]), we should nonetheless try to fulfill this aspect of our function and, "so far as we can, make ourselves immortal, and strain every nerve to live in accordance with the best thing in us."[9] Aristotle's gods are continuously in the state of knowing or contemplating the truth, naturally and without effort. For us humans, however, much preliminary effort in the form of study and research is required. This study and research is not an end in itself but is directed toward giving us brief glimpses, so to speak, of the sort of state or activity of knowing which the gods continuously experience.

The preceding account sounds much like the Platonic conception of human beings as intellects. Where Aristotle differs from Plato is in his explicit endorsement of another kind of life, the 'political life', as an aspect of the human function or *ergon* and, also, as an instantiation of *eudaimonia*:

> But in a secondary degree the life in accordance with the other kind of *aretê* is *eudaimôn*; for the activities in accordance with this befit our human estate. Just and brave acts, and other excellent acts, we do in relation to each other, observing what is proper to each with regard to contracts and services and all manner of actions and with regard to passions. Practical wisdom, too, is linked to *aretê* of character, and this to practical wisdom, since the principles of practical wisdom are in accordance with the *aretai* of character, and rightness in the *aretai* of character is in accordance with practical wisdom. Being connected with the passions also, the *aretai* of character must belong to our composite nature; and the *aretai* of our composite nature are human; so, therefore, are the way of life and the *eudaimonia* which correspond to these.[10]

This other aspect of the human function Aristotle sometimes describes as the political life and sometimes as activity in accordance with the *aretai* of character or 'moral virtues', such as justice, temperance, courage, generosity, friendliness, honesty, etc. (which he discusses at length in his *Eudemian* and *Nicomachean Ethics*).

But what does this 'political' function, good, or mode of life amount to? It obviously is not the life of a politician or public servant in the contemporary sense of these terms. Nor is it a life directed toward the end of winning public fame or honor (*timê*). The adjective, political, is of course derived from the Greek *polis*, the city-state. It seems best to interpret Aristotle's conception of the political life quite broadly. It is the life of a citizen, the 'social life' lived in community with one's fellows, with all that that conception entails. And it entails a great deal for Aristotle: having been reared in a community and having absorbed a certain (Greek) culture, with its ideals of virtuous behavior and of noble or fine (*kalon*) conduct – and then proceeding to live one's life with one's fellows in a *polis* in a way that exemplifies this culture and these ideals. This is the import of Aristotle's famous claim that "man is a *zô(i)on politikon*, a political animal."[11] Aristotle typically conceives of such a 'political life' in the broadest and most general terms: it is simply conduct in accordance with the virtues of character, which is undertaken 'for its own sake' or (apparently equivalently, in Aristotle's view) because such behavior is noble (*kalon*).

Aristotle agrees with Plato that one part of our human function or good – which indeed exemplifies the godlike aspect of our nature – is to understand, to know the truth. But we are not *simply* intellects. Part of our function is to live the life of the *polis*, and the *aretai* of character are of preeminent importance in doing so; the life of the *polis*, in other words, provides the social context for the exercise of these virtues. This characteristic sort of human social life requires the right sort of moral training and the development of the right sorts of habit of character. But it is not instinctual in the way that the life of non-rational social animals is. According to Aristotle's ideal, it is rational and reflective. It requires a nicety and soundness of judgment that Aristotle identifies as *practical* rationality or intelligence (*phronêsis*, in the Greek). However, Aristotle warns that we should not expect the same degree of precision in practical or ethical reasoning as we find in application of theoretical reasoning: "now fine and just actions, which political science investigates, exhibit much variety and fluctuation, so that they may be thought to exist only by *nomos* (convention), and not by *physis* (nature).[12]

Exactly what comprises Aristotle's conception of practical rationality and what is the precise nature of its interaction with the *aretai* of character in directing human behavior are notoriously difficult (and disputable) scholarly topics. But it is clear that Aristotle recognizes that the rationality characteristic of human beings comes in two varieties. The higher, godlike sort is directed, as Plato recognized, toward understanding the truth. But there is another sort of distinctively human rationality that is directed toward action and is implicated in the characteristically human way of existing, which is social (i.e., political) life. For Aristotle, this social life is *praxis* (action), which is undertaken for its own sake and is typically contrasted by him with *poiêsis* (making), which is directed toward some resultant product or state of affairs distinct from the making-behavior itself. Aristotle thus explicitly 'builds into' the human *ergon* a distinctive social component. However, we may wonder whether his way of doing so is at all plausible. In particular, let us further consider the closely related issues of whether it is reasonable to maintain that there is such a thing as the 'chief human good' and whether Aristotle's broad and inclusive conception of the political life could be a candidate for even an aspect or part of that chief good.

'Successful political activity' (*eupraxia*) as a grand end?

One possible interpretation of Aristotle's version of the nature and rôle of the human *ergon* (function) goes as follows. What determines the *eudaimonia* of a person, considered simply as a human person, is that person's success in living his or her life. Success in living a human life essentially involves fixing on the correct conception of the chief human good – which amounts to a correct conception of the human *ergon* – and acting to achieve or live up to that conception. Insofar as a person possesses the correct conception of the human good/*ergon* and insofar as he is able (and circumstances allow him) to order the conduct of his life in conformity with that conception, the person can correctly be characterized as a good person. The chief human good or human *ergon* is here being thought of as what S. Broadie terms a 'grand end':

> an explicit, comprehensive, substantial vision ..., a vision invested with a content different from what would be aimed at by morally inferior natures. This blueprint of the good guides its possessor in all his deliberations, and in terms of it his rational choices can be explained and justified.[13]

In a similar vein D. Bostock speaks of a 'dominant aim' or 'dominant activity': "a career, an occupation, a goal that organizes and structures all the rest of one's life."[14]

It is not unreasonable, I believe, to think of Plato's conception of the human *ergon* as knowing the truth or of Aristotle's quite similar conception of the contemplative aspect of the human *ergon* as a grand end or dominant aim, in this sense. But what of Aristotle's conception of the social aspect of the human *ergon*, the practical or political life of living in society with one's fellows? Broadie does not believe that Aristotle really conceives of the correct exercise of practical rationality – that is, of *eupraxia*, which may be translated as 'successful practical activity' – as being directed toward any grand end. Bostock is less certain that Aristotle does not hold a grand end/dominant aim conception of *eupraxia*, but he thinks that such a conception would be wrong. Bostock reminds us that Aristotle frequently characterizes the political/social aspect of the human *ergon* simply as conduct in conformity with the moral virtues (which Bostock terms 'practical virtues') and adds:

> But [actions exemplifying] the practical virtues are not them-selves a career, an occupation, a goal that organizes and structures all the rest of one's life. One who sets out simply to cultivate the practical virtues has not yet chosen any dominant activity for his life, and has so far no definite direction in which to aim. That is not how the practical virtues function.[15]

But what is *Aristotle's* view of the political aspect of the human func-tion? There seem to me to be at least two alternative interpretations. One interpretation does indeed make Aristotle's 'political' *ergon* a grand end or dominant aim – even a career or occupation. But to many contemporary readers, it will seem to be a quite elitist and very parochial conception of what human life should amount to. The basic idea is that the political life, conduct in conformity to the *aretai* of char-acter undertaken for its own sake (or because of its nobility), is the idealized life of a Greek gentleman of the fourth century B.C.E. Like perhaps the majority of thoughtful persons up until the twentieth cen-tury, Aristotle believes that "leisure [*skolê* in the Greek, whence comes 'scholar', 'school', etc.] is necessary for the development of *aretê* and for political actions":[16]

> And any occupation, art, or science, which makes the body or soul or mind less fit for the practice or exercise of *aretê* is artisan-like; wherefore we call those arts artisan-like which tend to deform the body, and likewise all paid employments, for they absorb and degrade the mind.[17]

"It is not possible," Aristotle says, "for anyone who is living the life of an artisan or of a hireling to practice conduct in conformity with *aretê*."[18]

As Bostock says, "one who is forced for financial reasons to engage in [such a life] is automatically debarred from *eudaimonia*."[19]

The person fulfilling the political aspect of the human *ergon* thus will be a man of leisure and at least moderate wealth. He will manage his own household or estate, with its dependent women, children, slaves, and other retainers. He will interact with a group of similarly situated male friends. And he will share in the social and cultural life of his *polis*, and the management of its affairs, with these friends and other more-or-less equal (male) fellow citizens. Insofar as such a person can be said to have an occupation, profession, or career, this is it. This sort of life provides the context or arena – indeed, the only really possible arena – for the exercise of the moral virtues or *aretai* of character, according to this interpretation of Aristotle. And the man engaged in *eupraxia* or 'successful practical activity' will really have no grand end or dominant aim/activity in his life *other than* leading this sort of aristocratic life – a life that will require a number of dependents and auxiliaries (women, slaves, free servants, resident aliens) who apparently are not themselves achieving *eudaimonia* in the form of successful practical/political activity.

Of course, Aristotle holds that the social/political aspect of the human *ergon*, while distinctively human, is inferior to the intellectual aspect: understanding or knowing the truth. If the preceding interpretation of Aristotle's understanding of *eupraxia*, successfully fulfilling the political aspect of the human *ergon*, is at least approximately correct, it is easy to see how such a public life of a man of affairs could conflict with the life of assiduous study and research, which would seem to be necessary for fulfilling the higher function of contemplation or understanding. It is also easy to understand, according to this account, Aristotle's claim that the political life of *eupraxia* is relatively less self-sufficient than the life of knowing, of *theôria*. While it may be correct, as Aristotle claims, that "it is possible to do noble acts without ruling the earth and sea,"[20] it seems that fulfilling the political function of *eupraxia* would at least require the good fortune of being born a free Greek male into a family of at least some means and social position – and the good fortune of sustaining that social position throughout one's life. It is also clear that if *this* is the principal aspect of the chief good and human *ergon* that it is the business of the *polis* to further, there are many members of the human species resident in the *polis* whose good is of no political concern. Or, more accurately, the *polis* will be concerned with such persons only insofar as their welfare is instrumental to the *eupraxia* of those citizens who are capable of achieving it.

I shall return to this issue a bit later in this chapter. For the moment, however, I wish to turn to an alternative view of Aristotle's conception of the political aspect of the human *ergon*, one which perhaps is rather more attractive from the contemporary perspective. This interpretation – which I shall term the 'multiple ends' (as opposed to the 'grand end') interpretation and which owes much to the thought of S. Broadie – is built upon a particular conception of Aristotelian practical rationality. According to this conception, the exercise of practical rationality or wisdom (*phronêsis*) is *not* to be conceived in terms of a 'craftsman' model, according to which practical rationality is oriented to a chief human good, a good that is conceived of as a grand end – "a grand substantial vision of the good which remains constant from one situation to another and thereby acts as the deliberator's lodestar."[21] Rather, human agents will be motivated by many different goods, ends, or purposes, which may (but need not) fit togther into a more or less coherent life plan. Practical rationality, which evidently is peculiar to human agents, is a matter of deciding what is the all-things-considered best thing for the agent to do in a particular circumstance. This is a matter of taking into account considerations of quite disparate kinds and, for such a consideration, either balancing it with those of other kinds or else deciding that it is, in the given circumstances, irrelevant. As Broadie explains it,

> Hence when Aristotle says that practical wisdom, and all practical deliberation, is concerned with 'living well in general', he has to be thinking of this unrestricted good in terms of an unrestricted openness to any kind of consideration when deciding what to do. The physician's deliberations admit only medical pros and cons, the professional runner's only those concerned with running. ... Hence the practical agent differs not by being focused on another special sort of good that is special because unrestricted and categorically demanding, but by being focused on a restricted good (not always the same one, either) with a focus that sets no limit on the considerations that could affect which way he goes with regard to that good or to the points of view that might make a difference.[22]

According to such an interpretation, the exercise of practical rationality, in conjunction with the moral virtues, by a human agent within the context of the *polis* (i.e., *eupraxia* or 'living in society with one's fellows with all that doing so entails') would not constitute any grand, overarching aim or *purpose* of that agent. Such an agent is simply going about his business or, rather, variety of businesses, pursuing a variety of goods.

But in what sense, then, might such a life be termed political and how does the exercise of practical rationality and the *aretai* of character constitute one aspect of the human function or *ergon*? I do not believe that the answers to these questions are obvious. But the following are perhaps possible answers. It is certainly true that Aristotle believes that the *polis* provides the setting in which *all* human activities transpire and all endeavors are played out. As Aristotle puts it in the *Politics*,

> When several villages [each one of which is a sort of extended family] are united in a single complete community, large enough to be nearly or quite self-sufficing, the *polis* comes into existence, originating in the bare needs of life, and continuing in existence for the sake of the good life ...
>
> Hence it is evident that the state is a creation of nature, and that man is by nature a political animal. And he who by nature and not by mere chance is without a *polis* is either worthless or higher than human.[23]

So, whatever the private aims, purposes, or goals of a human being are, they are political in Aristotle's broad sense of the term: they are pursued within the social context of the *polis*.

Moreover, if a person has been properly enculturated into a *polis* (that is, if the person is fully a human being [*anthrôpos*], in Aristotle's social sense of *anthrôpos*), one of the kinds of consideration involved in the exercise of that person's practical rationality in the pursuit of his or her various goals and ends will be what we call *moral* considerations. Nowadays we might be most inclined to think of such considerations in terms of prescriptive and proscriptive rules ('thou-shalts' and 'thou-shalt-nots'). Aristotle is more inclined to think of them in terms of the exercise of the various moral virtues or *aretai* of character: acting justly, acting courageously, acting temperately, etc. But, according to the interpretation we are considering, the force of Aristotle's claim that a virtuous human agent's activity in conformity with these virtues is undertaken 'for its own sake' is merely the one, irreducible consideration that a moral agent brings to bear in pursuing whatever ends that he has is that he should do so justly, that he should do so honestly, that he should do so courageously or forthrightly, etc. By 'irreducible' I mean that the properly socialized or enculturated agent will not have ulterior motives (for example, "justice pays" or "courage will make me admired") in pursuing his various ends and goals in a moral fashion – in conformity with the *aretai* of character. Such an agent will conduct his affairs morally simply because that is the right way to go about one's business, whatever that business, in all its details, may be.

According to this conception, what does Aristotle mean when he says that the distinctively human aspect of the human *ergon* or function is *eupraxia* or 'successful practical activity' or the 'exercise of practical rationality in conformity with the moral virtues and undertaken for its own sake' or the 'political life' (living in the *polis* with one's fellows, with all that such a concept entails)? It would not be that the virtuous agent will have such an activity or such a mode of life as an overarching, conscious (or 'intentional' in contemporary philosophical jargon) aim or purpose – a grand end or dominant aim that is distinct from his many, diverse everyday aims or purposes. Rather, it means that what is distinctive about human beings is that they employ practical rationality in the pursuit of their various individual, private goals and ends within the social context of the *polis*, in community with other humans. And this employment of practical rationality is guided and constrained by moral considerations that, for Aristotle, are built into the conception of conduct in conformity with the *aretai* of character. *Why* do humans do things this way? Simply because that is the kind of creature we are: it is our function or *ergon* as human beings, as members of the human species, to go about our individual businesses in a social context constrained by moral considerations. Later philosophical traditions influenced by Aristotle will use the term 'essence' for this general idea. For Aristotle (as well as for many other Greek thinkers), this species-*ergon* has normative force, that is, implications about how we *should* conduct ourselves. And it is also a consequence of the fact that we are the kind of creature that we are – in particular, that our behavior is guided by (practical) *reason* as opposed to instinct – that we can individually do either better or worse jobs of fulfilling this function.

I believe that Aristotle himself probably did not clearly distinguish between the grand-end and multiple-ends versions of his conception of the distinctively human, political aspect of the human *ergon*. Yet, he certainly holds that it is the business of the *polis* to promote the fulfillment of this function on the part of its citizens; and it is not surprising that these different conceptions of the human political function suggest different pictures of the rôle of the *polis* in carrying out this task. I shall return to this issue later in this chapter. A prior issue, however, is the nature of the relation between the *polis* and the lives of its citizens.

The *polis* as a complete community

As we saw, Aristotle holds that "the *polis* is a creation of nature, and that man is by nature a political animal."[24] He says that the family or household (*oikos, oikia*) "is the association established by nature for the supply of men's everyday wants."[25] "But when several households are united, and the association aims at something more than the supply of daily needs, the first society to be formed is the village (*kômê*)."[26] And, as we saw, Aristotle sees the *polis* as formed from several villages. The *polis* is described by Aristotle as 'complete', *teleios*, and as "by nature prior to the household and to each of us."[27] The primary sense of both complete and prior here is that of self-sufficiency:

> The proof that the *polis* is a creation of nature and prior to the individual is that the individual, when isolated, is not self-sufficing; and therefore he is like a part in relation to the whole. But he who is unable to live in society, or who has no need because of self sufficiency is not part of a *polis*: so he is either a beast or a god.[28]

Aristotle's account of the relation between a person and the *polis* may seem to resemble the lack of individual self-sufficiency and consequent impetus to economic cooperation undergirding Socrates' *polis* of pigs. However, Aristotle makes it clear that what we may call lack of economic or biological self-sufficiency is not what leads to the *polis*. The chief purpose of the *polis* is not to provide for the economic or biological welfare of its citizens: he says,

> the *polis* exists not for the sake of only living [i.e., being sustained in the biological sense] but rather for living well: if only living were the object, slaves and brute animals might form a *polis*, but they cannot, for they have no share in *eudaimonia* or in living in conformity with moral choice. Nor does a *polis* exist for the sake of alliance, that is, so that the citizens may be wronged by no one, nor yet for the sake of exchange and mutual usefulness. ... Whence it may be further inferred that *aretê* must be the care of the *polis* which is truly so called, and not merely one that enjoys the name: for without this end the community becomes a mere alliance which differs only in place from alliances of which the members live apart; and law (*nomos*) is simply a convention and, as the sophist Lycrophron says, a guarantor of mutual rights – but is not able to make the citizens good and just.[29]

So, it is clear that Aristotle holds that the nature of a human person depends on the social setting supplied by the *polis*. The very possibility that a biological entity coming from its mother's womb might fulfill the human function and thus might truly exemplify the natural species 'human person' depends upon that entity's being enculturated in the *polis*. Of course, this state of affairs is not surprising since Aristotle has explicitly built a social or political component into his conception of the human *ergon*. He also obviously believes that a consequence of man's *ergon* is that the primary purpose of the *polis* is to inculcate *aretai* – that is, to facilitate the citizens' coming to fulfill the human function as well as they can.

All of this suggests a very comprehensive rôle for the *polis*. It is probably a mistake to think that Aristotle's doctrine of the priority of the *polis* to the individual (and family and village) entails that he thinks of the 'state' as a sort of organism for the sake of which individual persons exist and function. But the *polis* certainly is constitutive of the very identity of its citizens as human persons and supplies the necessary conditions for their living up to that identity – fulfilling their human *ergon*. It would seem that Aristotle believes that there is no aspect of the lives of its citizens that, in principle, should be excluded from the political realm, that is, from concern of the *polis*.

The 'in principle' is an important qualification in the preceding statement for at least three reasons. First, the claim applies to the ideal *polis* or, as Aristotle puts it, the *polis* "in accord with our prayers, when no external considerations present impediments."[30] It seems that the more a *polis* diverges from the ideal, the less able it will be to inculcate *aretê* in its citizens; and the less it should attempt to do so. On a note of realism, Aristotle admits that "the best is often unattainable, and therefore the true legislator and statesman ought to be acquainted, not only with that which is best in the abstract, but also with that which is best relatively to circumstances."[31] In *Nicomachean Ethics* 10.9, Aristotle allows that it is best that there is "common and correct attention" to issues of the upbringing of the young and the pursuits of citizens. But, in the absence of such correct public attention, "it would seem right for each man to help his children and friends to *aretê*."[32] A second and related qualification is that, at least in some situations and to some degree, social institutions subsidiary to the *polis* are best able to carry out some of the enculturation necessary for citizens successfully to fulfill the political aspect of their human *ergon*:

For as in *poleis* laws and customs have force, so in households do the injunctions and habits of the father, and these have even more because of the tie of blood and the benefits he confers; for the children start with a natural affection and disposition to obey. Further, individual education has an advantage over education in common, as individual medical treatment has.[33]

The final qualification pertains to Aristotle's extremely inclusive sense of political and his concept of the *polis* as the *teleios* or complete (perfect) form of human social organization. The contemporary moral and political philosopher J. Finnis elaborates on this ideal of a complete community:

So there emerges the desirability of a 'complete community', an all-round association in which would be co-ordinated the initiatives and activities of individuals, of families, and of the vast network of intermediate associations. The point of this all-round association would be to secure the whole ensemble of material and other conditions, including forms of collaboration, that tend to favour, facilitate, and foster the realization by each individual of his or her personal development.

Such an ensemble of conditions includes some co-ordination (at least negative co-ordination of establishing restraints against interference) of any and every individual life-plan and any and every form of association. So there is no aspect of human affairs that as such is outside the range of such a complete community.[34]

However, another contemporary commentator on Aristotle, F. Miller, objects that Aristotle's concept of the *polis* as complete involves a confusion due to the fact that two notions are

fused together in his conception of a polis: viz., the state and society. A state in the modern sense is an association which possesses a monopoly over the legitimized use of coercive force within a definite geographical area. It discharges narrowly political functions (those of deliberation, officiation, and adjudication in Aristotle's theory), maintains internal order, and defends against external enemies. In contrast, a society includes the full range of associations which human beings need to meet their basic needs and to flourish: including households, personal friendships, fraternal clubs, religious cults, schools (including Plato's Academy and Aristotle's Lyceum), and business relations organizations. This all-inclusive community contains an intricate web of relationships, voluntary as well as coercive, private as well as public, through which individuals can find sustenance, companionship, and happiness.[35]

Thus, according to Miller, Aristotle's famous claim should be understood as the claim that man is a *social* animal, rather than a *political* one, in the modern and proper sense of political. Miller's point, I believe, will have considerable resonance with many contemporary readers. However, it may suggest that, were Aristotle simply to have been clearer about the state/society distinction, he would have endorsed a much more limited rôle, even in the theoretical, ideal case, for the *polis* (in the narrow, political, and coercive sense of *polis* as state).

Aristotle, however, seems to assume that in order for human persons to flourish, for them to fulfill their function, some overall coordinating social structure is needed; and he obviously finds that in the *polis*. As Miller's description of society ("an all-inclusive community [that] contains an intricate web of relationships, voluntary as well as coercive, private as well as public") makes clear, it does not have this sort of co-ordinating capacity – largely because it does not have any formal structure itself. Perhaps the most usual contemporary assumption, at least in the so-called developed Western states, is that it is the *individual citizen* (aided, when he or she is young by parents or other legal guardians) who should be responsible for constructing such a 'cafeteria-style' social structure in order to further his or her conception of what is important in life. Society, it is assumed, is simply a collection of the various aids and options, some of them incompatible, which are available to the individual citizen for this constructive enterprise.

It is worth noting here the rather obvious fact that contemporary life is much more complex than the life of the fourth-century B.C.E. *polis* with which Aristotle was familiar. And, at least for us denizens of Western constitutional democracies, part of this complexity lies in the existence of various sorts of basic options open to us concerning how we are to live our lives. So it is perhaps natural for us to see Aristotle's assumption of the need for a political structure for society – in other words, his assumption of the necessity for the *polis* as a complete community – as foreign to our notion of the political, and foreign in an unpleasantly restrictive or even totalitarian way.

However intrusive we might find it, Aristotle contrasts this political coordination of the lives of the citizens within the *polis* (which should be carried out by established laws, customs, and procedures) with the personal dependency or subjection of citizens to the will of a particular person or group of persons. Perhaps somewhat facilely, he remarks that "while people hate *men* (*anthrôpôn*) who oppose their impulses, even if they oppose them rightly, the law in its ordaining of what is good is not burdensome."[36] We have here an early appearance of one of those perennial themes in political philosophy, one which will be developed by later thinkers (such as Rousseau). Nonetheless, for Aristotle himself the political making and administering of law remains in fact quite personal: he envisions a *polis* in which not only do the citizens know one another but also in which their interactions are characterized by civic friendship and *homonoia* (literally, unanimity – the sharing of fundamental values, ideals, and concerns):

> friendship seems to hold *poleis* together, and lawgivers to care more for it than for justice; for unanimity seems to be something like friendship, and this they aim at most of all, and expel faction as their worst enemy; and when men are friends they have no need of justice, while when they are just they need friendship as well, and the truest form of justice is thought to be a sort of friendship.[37]

For Aristotle, at least in the ideal case, there is no real distinction between society and the state. We might say that the apparatus of the state supplies the *form* for a particular society or community. And the direction supplied by the political structure of the *polis*, its laws, institutions, and administrators, to the citizens in terms of their fulfilling their human *ergon* will be personal and intimate. Of course such a picture is quite closely tied to the size and other particular characteristics of the *polis*, the Greek city-state. While we may wonder how much of Aristotle's political thought can be exported to political units of different sizes and characters (e.g., much larger, geographically extended, and ethnically diverse nations), it is far from obvious that Aristotle would have shared this worry. He is concerned primarily with the *polis* 'of our prayers' and secondarily with the types of constitution or regime (*politeia*) that he actually found in the Greek world.

The rôle of politics: the master art?

Aristotle does, of course, recognize a particularly political aspect of the *polis*, which he locates in its constitution or regime (*politeia*, which he identifies with *politeuma*, government[38]): "a constitution is the organization of offices in a *polis*, and determines what is to be the governing body, and what is the end (*telos*) of each community."[39] In his discussion (in the *Politics*) of the variety of constitutions found in the Greek world, he distinguishes them on the basis of how widely active participation in political decision-making is shared among the populace: "The true [or correct] forms of government, therefore, are those in which the one, or the few, or the many, govern with a view to the common interest (*koinon sympheron*); but governments which rule with a view to the private interest, whether of the one, or of the few, or of the many, are perversions."[40] Aristotle characterizes a (true or correct) constitution as a "form of justice."[41] He also in several places identifies the common interest with justice.[42] So the idea of the state's furthering the common interest or good of its citizens entails that it does so justly.

In the fifth book of the *Nicomachean Ethics* Aristotle notes that there is a sense of justice (*dikaiosunê*) in which it is *arête* or virtue in general – in relation to others.[43] However, in the narrower and proper sense of justice, Aristotle makes the distinction between the two kinds of justice I distinguished in the first chapter: distributive and rectificatory (or commutative) justice. The former kind of justice is

> that which is manifested in the distribution of honour or money or the other things that fall to be divided among those who have a share in the constitution (for in these it is possible for one man to have a share either unequal or equal to that of another), and another kind is that which plays a rectifying part in transactions. Of this there are two divisions; of transactions some are voluntary and others involuntary – voluntary, such transactions as sale, purchase, usury, pledging, lending, depositing, letting ..., while of the involuntary some are clandestine, such as theft, adultery, poisoning, procuring, enticement of slaves, assassination, false witness, and others are violent, such as assault, imprisonment, murder, robbery with violence, mutilation, abuse, insult.[44]

Aristotle proceeds to explicate the former notion of distributive justice in terms of a mathematical metaphor: a distribution (of benefits or burdens) is distributively just in cases where 'geometrical proportionality' is maintained – that is, just in cases where distribution is made 'in proportion' to the degree of possession of the appropriate sort of merit or worth by those to whom distribution is to be made. It is, I believe, important to remember that this is a metaphor, and to remember Aristotle's caution against expecting more precision in a matter than its subject matter permits. However, the concept of fairness of distribution of both the benefits and burdens of political cooperation is of immense importance in the later development of political philosophy. And the idea of the centrality of this conception of distributive justice to the political order is an idea that has persisted (with challenges from those who maintain the political centrality of the idea of commutative justice) into the twentieth century. Despite his commitment to the political centrality of distributive justice, Aristotle admits that there may be disagreement about *how* to apply the concept – in particular, what the relative sort of merit is in determining who should be the political decision-makers: "For all men agree that what is just in distribution must be according to merit in some sense, though they do not all specify the same sort of merit, but democrats identify it with the status of freeman, supporters of oligarchy with wealth (or with noble birth), and supporters of aristocracy with *aretê*."[45]

For Aristotle, the state's pursuit of distributive justice and the common interest of its citizens does *not* entail that all the citizens will actively participate in 'ruling' the *polis* or making the political decisions that are intended to further, justly, the common good of its citizens. Aristotle's general position is that it is best (evidently both most just – in terms of a conception of distributive justice that allots political decision-making responsibility in accord with *aretê* of character – and the most effective way to pursue the common interest of the citizens) that those who excel in *aretê* (evidently moral virtue or *aretê* of character) should rule:

> We maintain that the true forms of government are three, and that the best must be ruled by the best, and in which there is one man, or a whole family, or many persons, excelling all the others in *aretê*, and both rulers and subjects are fitted, the one to rule, the others to be ruled, in such a manner as to attain the most choice-worthy life. We showed at the commencement of our inquiry that the *aretê* of the good man is necessarily the same as the *aretê* of the citizen in the best *polis*. Clearly then in the same manner, and by the same means through which a man becomes truly excellent, he will frame a state that is to be ruled by an aristocracy or by a king, and the same education and the same habits will be found to make an excellent man and a man fit to be a statesman or king.[46]

This passage alludes to one of the more important issues in Aristotle's political thought. If we assume, as does he, that politics (that is, the making of political decisions for the common good of the citizens of the state) is the 'master art' within the state, what sort of skills or *aretai* should a politician (a political decision-maker) have? As we have seen, Aristotle holds (1) that *eupraxia*, or successful practical activity, is the distinctively human aspect of the human function or good; (2) that this function can be fulfilled only within the *polis*; and (3) that the fulfilling of this function on the part of the citizens must be encouraged, coordinated, and facilitated by the political decision-makers of the *polis*. Exactly *how* this is to be done depends on how we conceive of the *ergon* or function of *eupraxia*. If we conceive of this function substantively, as consisting in particular kinds of activities directed toward a 'grand end' or 'dominant aim' (as high an end as the endowments of each individual citizen permits), then a good deal of technical expertise will be required on the part of the politician. He or she will, as it were, be involved in the micro-management of the lives, the education and the pursuits of the citizens. And in such a case, it is not obvious that this technical expertise has much to do with the moral virtues, the *aretai* of character (activity in conformity with which is another, favorite Aristotelian characterization of *eupraxia*). So Aristotle's claim above identifying (what it takes to make) a good person and a good politician is certainly open to serious objection.

However, as we saw, another possible interpretation of Aristotle is that *eupraxia* is not to be interpreted substantively: it is not a particular kind of activity directed toward a particular grand end or dominant aim. Rather, it is simply the distinctively human characteristic of pursuing our various ends or aims within the social context of the *polis* and, most importantly, within the context of the practice of the *aretai* of character discussed by Aristotle in the *Eudemian* and *Nicomachean Ethics*. So the politician's principal rôle would be the inculcation of the moral virtues in the citizenry. In this case, it seems quite plausible that the politician attempting this task needs to be a morally excellent man (a *spoudaios*, in Aristotle's Greek) himself. Such a person must be well enculturated, must recognize and understand the values of his community and practice them. As Broadie puts it, we find Aristotle taking for granted "a shared commitment to good upbringing in qualities standardly accepted as fundamental human excellences."[47] We see here some continuity with Protagoras' democratic traditionalism, which we discussed in an earlier chapter. According to the present interpretation of Aristotle, he – like Protagoras – understands the moral or political *aretai* to be the common possession of the community. For Protagoras, a 'good Sophist' such as himself (who is really an outsider in the *polis*) possesses a greater ability than most citizens to inculcate these *aretai*, and he is willing to do so, for a price. For Aristotle, this task should fall to the more virtuous of the citizens, and the political machinery of the *polis* should be designed to permit (and require) them to attend to it.

Broadie notes the lack of any great impetus on Aristotle's part to question the validity of the traditional, social assumptions about *aretai* of character:

How moral evaluations can be rationally justified at all is the leading problem of classical modern ethics. In this regard, Aristotle's moral philosophy is remote and offers no answers, for he does not confront that radical question. This may seem a severe limitation, and there is a temptation to seek to explain it by the assumption that Aristotle speaks in and for a morally homogeneous circle unriven by dissensions that lend credibility to moral scepticism and moral relativism.[48]

There is, in Broadie's view, some reason to resist this temptation. In fact, she believes that there are indications that Aristotle realizes that being a paragon of traditional values is perhaps a *necessary* but not *sufficient* condition for the excellent practice of the master art of politics. She further suggests that Aristotle may realize that a more philosophical, reflective attitude toward moral goodness is necessary for success in inculcating such goodness in citizens. We may well agree that, whether Aristotle would admit the point or not, it seems that *something* beyond moral goodness, perhaps even something that is a sort of technical expertise, would seem to be needed for great statesmanship. But is moral goodness even a *necessary* condition for such greatness? As I hope that readers will by now have realized, the answer to that question must depend on what the rôle of the political decision-maker is. The answer to that question will then depend on what the proper rôle of political organization is in human lives. And, in turn, the answer to that question will depend – I have claimed and will continue to argue – on what I have termed a normative anthropology. It is a fundamental virtue of his political thought, in my view, that Aristotle realizes so clearly that political philosophy is inextricably connected to what he calls *anthrôpeia philosophia*, the 'philosophy of human nature'.[49] And such a philosophy of human nature will certainly include or presuppose a normative anthropology.[50]

Epilogue

I suppose that it is often assumed that the most important contribution of Greek antiquity to political thought was its development of the concept of democracy, or rule by the 'people'. I further suppose that, as an historical fact, the Athenian democratic tradition has played an inspirational rôle in the thought of some classical modern and contemporary democratic theorists – despite the fact that ancient Greek democracy was such a different thing from the modern forms of polity to which the term 'democracy' has been applied.

However, from a more *philosophical* political perspective, the contribution of the ancient Greeks, while certainly momentous, lies elsewhere. The Greeks (especially Aristotle, with particular clarity and explicitness) introduced a number of fundamental assumptions: (a) political structure, whether a matter of nature or convention, has a purpose, either a purpose that is simply cooperation in pursuit of individual security or biological sustenance or a purpose that transcends such concerns; (b) a normative anthropology, an account of human nature and of what human flourishing is all about, is directly relevant to addressing the rôle of political structure; and (c) in whatever way these features of a political theory are worked out, the ideas of distributive justice and a common good will play complementary rôles in the resulting theory. As we shall see, these basic assumptions persist – although they certainly do not go unquestioned or unchallenged – in later developments of political thought.

There is also another fundamental issue in political philosophy that, as we have seen, arises in Greek thought. An assumption common to many varieties of normative anthropology is that what it means (in part or whole) to be a non-defective adult human person is to be a moral agent who is capable (perhaps to a relatively less or greater degree than other persons) of bringing a moral perspective to bear on our momentous and not-so-momentous decisions. Let us call this assumption the thesis of human moral worth. Aristotle, in particular, finds for such worth a sort of conventional or *nomos*-based source – being enculturated into a *polis*. In its paradigmatic sense, *full* enculturation is restricted to full citizens. Thus, the thesis of human moral worth, at least in the sense of fullest moral worth, is not applied universally to human beings: it is withheld or restricted, for example, in the case of 'natural' slaves, of women, and even of common laborers. As we shall see, the tendency of much later Western moral and ethical thought has been toward the increasing universalization of the thesis of human moral worth. In this later thought, human moral worth has also not always been so closely tied to enculturation or socialization into a moral community.

Consequently, a central but, I believe, still quite unresolved issue in the history of Western political philosophy is the import of the thesis of human moral worth with respect to two questions concerning political decision-making: who should be making decisions directed toward the common good and how should the content and scope of those decisions respect this thesis?

5

Christianity: A Political Religion?

The rise of Christianity to a position of religious dominance within the Roman empire from the time of Augustus at the beginning of the first century C.E. to that of the first Christian emperor Constantine early in the fourth century, certainly had immense political consequences, theoretical as well as practical. In this chapter, I shall consider some of the theoretical consequences.

The social and political success of Christianity brings to the foreground, in particular, questions about the source of political authority and the legitimacy of political institutions. The concept of the Christian *ecclesia*, the church or community of the faithful, can confront the secular *polis* or state in a variety of ways: as a political rival; as an authoritative but benevolent senior partner (or subservient junior partner) of the secular state in the enterprise of attending to the welfare of the state's citizens; as embodying a moral (or political) ideal against which that secular state may be measured; or as a spiritual community set apart from all secular states, the concerns of which are of an order entirely different from the concerns of such states.

The nature of the allegiance owed by citizens to the political institutions to which they belong also comes to be conceptualized in a way generally unlike that of pagan antiquity. This fact is perhaps the principal source of an enduring issue in later Western political thought: the presence or absence of a special sort of moral obligation owed to the state, which is not to be reduced to considerations of individual self-interest or even to the promotion of the common good.[1]

At a yet more fundamental level, Christianity postulates a human nature, function, or purpose more complex and, indeed, more 'extravagant' than that postulated by the various naturalistic normative anthropologies of Greek antiquity – one that privileges the eternal, celestial or spiritual nature of human beings (as well as perhaps taking into account their transitory, terrestrial or biological nature). If, then, the fundamental rôle of political organization is to secure the common good of its citizens, one might expect that this more complex, extravagant conception of the human function – and, hence, a more complex, extravagant conception of the common human good – will yield a more complex (or ambivalent) conception of the rôle of the political in human life. And, indeed, we do seem to find this consequence in political philosophy after the rise of Christianity.

The New Testament and beyond

Any consideration of the influence of Christianity on political thought must surely begin with the Christian scriptures. It is obvious that the canonical New Testament is not even in part a work of political philosophy. However, there are passages in the *New Testament* that traditionally have been taken to be particularly relevant to political matters – although the message that they convey certainly appears to be a mixed one. I begin with several of these passages.

Jesus in his appearance before Pontius Pilate

> Jesus replied, 'Mine is not a kingdom of this world; if my kingdom were of this world, my men would have fought to prevent my being surrendered to the Jews. But my kingdom is not of this kind.' 'So you are king then?' said Pilate. 'It is you who say it,' answered Jesus. 'I was born for this, I came into the world for this: to bear witness to the truth; and all who are on the side of truth listen to my voice.' (*St. John* 18:36–37)[2]

The attempted entrapment of Jesus by the Pharisees

> 'Master, we know that you are an honest man and teach the way of God in an honest way, and that you are not afraid of anyone,

because a man's rank means nothing to you. Tell us your opinion, then. Is it permissible to pay taxes to Caesar or not?' But Jesus was aware of their malice and replied, 'You hypocrites! Why do you set this trap for me? Let me see the money you pay the tax with.' They handed him a denarius, and he said, 'Whose head is this? Whose name?' 'Caesar's,' they replied. He then said to them, 'Very well, give back to Caesar what belongs to Caesar – and to God what belongs to God.' (*St. Matthew* 22:16–21)

St. Paul on the duty of civil docility

You must all obey the governing authorities. Since all government comes from God, the civil authorities were appointed by God, and so anyone who resists authority is rebelling against God's decision, and such an act is bound to be punished. ... The state is there to serve God for your benefit. If you break the law, however, you may well have fear: the bearing of the sword has its significance. The authorities are there to serve God: they carry out God's revenge by punishing wrongdoers. You must obey, therefore, not only because you are afraid of being punished, but also for conscience' sake. ... Pay every government official what he has a right to ask – whether it be direct tax or indirect, fear or honour. (*Romans* 13:1–7)

St. Paul's exegesis of the commandment to love one's fellow man

Avoid getting into debt, except the debt of mutual love. If you love your fellow men you have carried out your obligations. All the commandments ... are summed up in this single command: *You must love your neighbor as yourself.* Love is the one thing that cannot hurt your neighbor; that is why it is the answer to every one of the commandments. (*Romans* 13:8–10)

The early Christian community as described in *Acts*

The faithful all lived together and owned everything in common; they sold their goods and possessions and shared out the proceeds among themselves according to what each one needed. They went as a body to the Temple every day but met privately in their houses for the Breaking of the Bread; they shared their food gladly and generously; they praised God and were looked up to by everyone. Day by day the Lord added to their community those destined to be saved. (*Acts* 2:44–47)

These passages suggest the political options, so to speak, for Christianity, options that can be set forth in neat but ahistorical opposition. Is Christianity a political or apolitical religion? And, irrespective of the answer to this question, is its message a cosmopolitan or a sectarian one? A good case can be made that what came to be regarded as orthodoxy (literally meaning 'correct belief') in Christianity involved the attempt to maintain some sort of balance, however precarious, among all these options. The history here is messy, as is usually the case. However, for the moment, I shall consider the options in a somewhat schematic way.

The idea that the essential focus of Christianity is on individual spiritual regeneration or salvation can easily yield an interpretation of Christianity as an apolitical religion. Did not Jesus, in the passage from the *Gospel of St. John* quoted above, deny that his kingdom is of this world and did he not disappoint many Jewish potential followers by refusing the role of a political Messiah? The otherworldly aspect of the Christian message can hardly be ignored – and, historically, it certainly has not been ignored. This strand in Christianity is clearly and succinctly summed up by the contemporary theologian and political philosopher E.L. Fortin:

[Christianity] is essentially a nonpolitical religion. Unlike Judaism and Islam, the two other great monotheistic religions of the West, it does not call for the formation of a separate community or provide a code of laws by which that community might be governed. It takes for granted that its followers will continue to live as full-fledged citizens of the political society to which they belong and share its way of life as long as they are not forced to indulge in practices that are directly at odds with their basic beliefs, as were, for example, idolatry and emperor worship.[3]

There is a sense in which the issue of cosmopolitanism versus sectarianism arises even for an essentially apolitical conception of Christianity. By sectarian, I here mean a conception of Christianity as pertaining only to the select few and emphasizing the status of Christian believers as constituting a community 'set apart', both from humankind in general and from particular political orders. An apolitical form of sectarianism would, of course, conceptualize this community set apart as a purely *spiritual* community, one existing on a completely different plane from concrete political structures – *poleis*, kingdoms, or empires – and in that sense apparently not in competition with such concrete secular political structures. It seems that the apolitical sectarian option found vigorous expression in various forms of gnostic Christianity in the second century; and Christian gnosticism seems to have issued in Manichaeanism in the third century. According to gnostic doctrine, elect souls are quite special: they are bits of divinity temporarily imprisoned in matter. The world of matter – including, of course, all human political and social arrangements – is evil. And, according to Manichaean doctrine, worldly pursuits and possessions are forbidden to elect souls.[4]

Cosmopolitan versions of apolitical Christianity are more orthodox and can trace their origins at least back to St. Paul: "there are no more distinctions between Jew and Greek, slave and free, male and female, but all of you are one in Christ Jesus" (*Galatians* 3:28). An apolitical form of cosmopolitanism would seem to present little threat to the established political order. This theme is supported by the several recommendations of civil docility found in the Christian scriptures. The passage from *Romans* previously quoted underlines the strand of political conservatism in Christianity – as does an admonition of St. Peter: "For the sake of the Lord, accept the authority of every social institution: the emperor, as supreme authority, and the governors commissioned by him to punish criminals and praise good citizenship. God wants you to be good citizens, so as to silence what fools are saying in their ignorance" (*1 Peter* 2:13–15). The doctrine that political structures are divinely instituted and that rulers are (more or less directly) divinely commissioned presents the believer with a particularly weighty reason for submitting to legitimate political authority, *whatever form it may assume*. The doctrine also greatly increases the importance of the criterion of *legitimacy* in assessing political structures. It is not unfair, I think, to characterize the political thought of Greek and Roman pagan antiquity as emphasizing, in the assessment of a political structure, its efficiency and justice in bringing about whatever end or ends the assessor believes political structures are supposed to effect. The idea of a sort of political legitimacy that is not to be identified with the just and efficient fulfillment of a political *function* was not a very prominent idea in Western political theory before the advent of Christianity. After Christianity achieved social dominance, 'top down' theoretical accounts of the source of political legitimacy – that is, accounts that trace a particular lineage of political legitimacy directly from the action of God or of his designated agents – were popular for a long time but did not fare very well subsequent to Robert Filmer's seventeenth-century defense of the 'divine right of kings' (in particular, the divine right of the Stuart monarchs of England).[5] However, concern with political legitimacy, as distinct from political justice and efficiency, persists in modern and contemporary political theories, and its prominence in such theories probably owes much to the 'new' Christian focus on political legitimacy.

One might think that Christian apolitical cosmopolitanism should largely have prevented conflict between Christianity and secular political authority – and also have prevented Christianity from winning any great political influence. But, of course, history tells a quite different story on both scores. To begin with, Christians generally proved to be quite adamant in resisting certain civil obligations, such as the emperor worship mentioned by Fortin. Even an apolitical stance had it limits. Also, there certainly are political strands in the Christian message. It is difficult not to interpret the fundamental Christian moral imperative of love of one's neighbor as having social – even political – implications. The egalitarian communistic life of the apostolic church in Jerusalem, described in the passage from the second chapter of the book of *Acts* previously quoted, clearly indicates the general direction of those implications.

Such a social existence seems practicable only for relatively small societies of the devout. Yet, it is clear that the point of the parable of the good Samaritan (*St. Luke* 10:29–37) is that love of neighbor is not to be confined to those near and dear – nor to the closed circle of the devout. And the following injunctions are obviously not limited to one's dealings with fellow Christians:

> Love your enemies, do good to those who hate you, bless those who curse you, pray for those who treat you badly. To the man who slaps you on one cheek, present the other cheek too; to the man who takes your cloak from you, do not refuse your tunic. Give to everyone who asks you, and do not ask for your property back from the man who robs you. Treat others as you would like them to treat you. If you love those who love you, what thanks can you expect? Even sinners love those who love them. ... Even sinners lend to sinners and get back the same amount. Instead, love your enemies and do good, and lend without any hope of return. You will have great reward, and you will be sons of the Most High, for he himself is kind to the ungrateful and the wicked. (*St. Luke* 6:27–35)

The problem here is a perennial one within Christianity, one in which the sectarian versus cosmopolitan options come squarely into focus. What we may call the ethical demands of Christianity are stringent. It may also seem that, in order to fulfill those demands, a rather particular sort of social and political context is needed. What sort of political structures, if any, are appropriate for large numbers of persons who practice, in a serious and quite literal way, the dictates of apostolic charity described in the preceding passage (the practice of which would seem to involve apostolic poverty, as well)? Perhaps not the common political structures found either in the ancient pagan world or, later, in the (nominally) Christian and post-Christian secular world.

As the influence of Christianity increased in the Greco-Roman world, that is, as Christianity began to achieve the status of a world religion, the problem of the sectarian versus cosmopolitan option became of greater practical significance. Orthodox Christianity, as usual, tried to have it both ways. On the one hand, there are 'counsels of perfection', to which many may be called but for which few seem to be well suited. The result was the establishment of communities set apart (as, for example, monastic communities), which, ideally, were non-sectarian in the sense of being in communion with the 'catholic' (meaning literally 'universal') church and at the service of the larger social-political community, at least through the office of prayer and sacrifice. On the other hand, there were increasing numbers of Christians – from East and from West, Greek and Jew (although increasingly the former), slave and free, male and female, rich and poor – who were perhaps less fitted to the pursuit of Christian perfection or the practice of 'radical' apostolic charity but who were not therefore necessarily less serious in their faith. We might perhaps call these folk the 'cosmopolitan clientele' of the Church. The problem that thus becomes increasingly important is how Christianity is to reconcile its rather extravagant normative anthropology with a social morality suitable for its cosmopolitan clientele. Some scholars believe that tools sufficient for accomplishing this task were already in the possession of St. Paul.

Pauline cosmopolitanism

In characterizing Christianity's normative anthropology as 'extravagant', I mean to point out the fact that Christianity holds two doctrines concerning the true function, end, or good of human persons: (i) that function is the attainment of a kind of existence (salvation: eternal life in communion with God and in the fellowship of the saved) that transcends any sort of state or activity achievable in this mortal, biological life; and (ii) that function is not something that human beings can achieve or attain by their own (individual or social) efforts but, rather, is a gift bestowed by the grace of God. I believe that it is rather obvious that such a normative anthropology, together with the classical assumption that the rôle of political organization is to facilitate the attainment of the human end or function by its citizens, will have some non-classical political consequences. I return to some of these consequences later in this chapter. The attentive reader may also detect a certain political paradox in connection with doctrine (ii) above. If the fulfillment of the true human function is simply a divine gift bestowed on some persons but not on others, it may seem that theoretical concern about how political organization can or cannot facilitate the fulfillment of this function or the attainment of this good by its citizens is misplaced. God's will in this regard is simply done and that is the end of the matter – irrespective of the political context in which a person finds him- or herself. I do think that this political paradox is an important problem in Christian political philosophy and return to a consideration of it in the next chapter. However, for the moment, I wish to consider St. Paul's development of the Christian normative anthropology.

Paul's normative anthropology is constituted from a number of interrelated parts. First of all, there is the eschatological emphasis on human destiny, where 'eschatological' (from the Greek for ultimate or 'last' things) signifies an ultimate state of existence, subsequent to biological death, of human beings. In Athens, Paul tells his pagan audience that "now [God] is telling everyone everywhere that they must repent, because he has fixed a day when the whole world will be judged, and judged in righteousness, and he has appointed a man to be the judge. And God has publicly proved this by raising this man from the dead" (*Acts* 17:30–31). Moreover, observance of moral and religious law, embodied in the Mosaic law, is of no help in preparing oneself for this judgment: "no one can be justified in the sight of God by keeping the Law: all that law does is to tell us what is sinful" (*Romans* 3:20). Salvation, the attainment of the ultimate human end, involves internalizing the spirit of Christ, which is characterized by Paul in terms of the death of the 'old man' – that is, one's corrupted, 'natural' self – and the birth of a 'new man' – that is, one's regeneration as a Christlike person:

If in union with Christ we have imitated his death, we shall also imitate him in his resurrection. We must realise that our former selves have been crucified with him to destroy this sinful body and to free us from the slavery of sin. When a man dies, of course, he has finished with sin.

But we believe that having died with Christ we shall return to life with him. ... When he died, he died, once for all, to sin, so his life now is life with God; and in that way, you too must consider yourselves to be dead to sin but alive for God in Christ Jesus. (*Romans* 6:5–11)

And, says Paul, "we know that when the tent that we live in on earth is folded up, there is a house built by God for us, an everlasting home not made by human hands, in the heavens" (*2 Corinthians* 5:1). The ultimate end, the ultimate function, of human life is an eternal sharing in the perfect life of God. Paul recognizes that we do not know exactly *what* the nature of that life is, but Christian tradition has generally conceived it as having some sort of intellectual, some sort of affective, and some sort of social dimension. This end is attainable, for 'circumcised' (Jews) and 'uncircumcised' (gentiles) alike only by faith (*pistis*),[6] but such faith is a gift of God, the fruit of grace given to God to those whom he chooses:

Everyone moved by the Spirit is a son of God. ... The Spirit himself and our spirit bear united witness that we are children of God. And if we are children we are heirs as well: heirs of God and coheirs with Christ, sharing his sufferings so as to share his glory. (*Romans* 8:14–17)

Several recent scholars have emphasized the connection between St. Paul's thought and that of secular, Hellenistic philosophical schools.[7] In particular, T. Engberg-Pedersen has argued for a similarity between Paul's conception of conversion to Christ and the Stoic theory of *oikeiôsis*, "the theory of how a person will or may undergo a change in his or her understanding of the good, from taking it to be constituted of what basically amounts to possession of ordinary, material goods on the part of the individual him- or herself to a quite different understanding of it."[8] For the Stoics, the "different understanding" of the human function, end, or good in which *oikeiôsis* issues is *homologia* – 'living in conformity with nature'. *Homologia* is an identification of oneself with the divine reason that pervades and orders the *cosmos*; it is a matter of "*using one's reason* for the purposes for which it is designed, that is, for reaching *truth about* the world."[9] Knowledge of this truth includes knowledge of "what particular things in it are valuable for oneself. *That* is what 'preserves' one's *new, rational* 'constitution'."[10] As Cicero notes, *homologia* yields the central insight that "the good to which everything else is referred are acts in conformity to moral rectitude and in moral rectitude (*honestum*)"[11] itself. As Engberg-Pedersen puts it,

> There is only one thing [according to the Stoics] that may properly be called good: *homologia*, getting things right about the world. For that alone has the character that qualifies it for being what the *telos* [end of human action] consists in, the character of self-sufficiency. If you have grasped that the human *telos* is *homologia*, then you are in possession of a 'valuable thing' to which nothing can be added and from which nothing can be removed. Indeed, it is a valuable thing that in a sense 'includes' all other particular valuable things under it because it alone *determines* their value.[12]

Analogously, Engberg-Pedersen argues, for Paul "the grasp of Jesus as the Christ and Lord (with *all* that this in effect means) is the *only* thing of ultimate importance."[13]

For the Stoics, the identification of self with the 'cosmic reason' and, for St. Paul, identification of the self with Jesus Christ involve a sort of transformation of oneself – and, indeed, a transformation where one identifies oneself not just with reason and with Christ, respectively, but also with all other persons who have received similar insight. For both the Stoics and St. Paul, this ontological transformation – that is, transformation in one's 'being' – will (ideally) have profound moral implications about one's behavior: one simply will treat others in a different way because one sees them, and oneself, in a different way.

The normative anthropologies of both Paul and the Stoics possess inherent cosmopolitan political possibilities. For Aristotle (and for Protagoras before him), *nomos* – that is, the customary, the conventional, and the *cultural* – plays a large rôle with respect to the pursuit and fulfillment of a supposed human function, end, or good. Fulfilling the human function, achieving the human good, is something that requires the local *political community* (the *polis*). And the customs, mores, and culture of the local political community, in turn, help to determine the concrete content of the human function. Thus, there is a sense in which, for Aristotle and Protagoras, morality and politics are local affairs. The case of Paul and the Stoics is quite different. For both, fulfilling the human function is a matter of gaining the right sort of insight about the world, about human beings, and about the place of the latter in the former: "everything hangs on coming to *see* the good, on getting a proper rational grasp on it. Then [ideally] all 'passions' will be blotted out. There will be no weakness of the will. And one will always and only *act* on one's (new) insight."[14] In principle, at least, recognition of the true human function and the appropriate accompanying behavior do not require a certain sort of socialization or enculturation; they do not, in other words, require that one has been brought up in the right way.

The normative anthropologies of Paul and of the Stoics, then, yield what one might term '*potential* cosmopolitanism'. For Paul, all are called to rebirth in Christ and, *in principle*, each person, irrespective of the peculiarities of his or her personal, social, or cultural status, is capable of such rebirth. For the Stoics, all are called to the 'full rationality' of *homologia* and, *in principle*, each person, irrespective of the peculiarities of his or her personal, social, or cultural status, is capable of such *oikeiôsis*. It is clear that we have, in both cases, a 'potential *cosmopolis*', that is, a non-local community of those united by their common recognition of the true human function, end, or good and their common resolve to conform their behavior to implications of that recognition. But is there a concrete political dimension, so to speak, to this *cosmopolis*? And how does the fact that, at any given historical juncture, there apparently will be only a limited number of persons who have gained such insight and undergone such regeneration affect the answer to this question?

In the case of the Stoics, there was an apparent tension between a strain of political radicalism, which certainly seems to possess sectarian implications, and a much more moderate, accommodating political stance, which could be presented in a more cosmopolitan light. Although we know relatively little about the *Republic*, a book on political theory by the founder of Stoicism, Zeno of Citium (334–262 B.C.E.), the work was notorious for its unconventionality. According to the ancient historian of philosophy Diogenes Laertius, the ideal community described by Zeno would consist only of those excelling in virtue (*spoudaioi*), while all others should be regarded as "foes, enemies, slaves, and aliens to one another."[15] Women would be 'held in common'; there would be no temples, courts of law, or gymnasia; currency would not be used for purposes internal or external to the community; men and women would wear the same sort of clothes and no part of the body would be entirely concealed.[16] Although such a notion is obviously a philosopher's ideal (in the tradition of Plato's *Republic*), it is also obviously a very concrete conception of social, if not political, existence. In the words of Engberg-Pedersen,

> what Zeno envisaged was what has aptly been called an anarcho-syndicalist state, or rather not exactly a state; for the point of abolishing temples, lawcourts, gymnasia, currency and the institution of marriage seems precisely to have been that there should no longer *be* a state. Instead, there apparently would be cities of some sort, probably communities at a very low level scattered in a landscape of no very clear limits. ... Moreover, in spite of the obvious differences between Zeno's conception and Paul's idea of a Christ-believing congregation – one more or less a dream, the other very much a reality – the way they relate to the rest of society is closely similar. Both, are, basically outworldly [i.e., otherworldly, or 'sectarian', in my sense] entities.[17]

By the time of Chrysippus (*c.*280–208 B.C.E.), the so-called 'second founder' of Stoicism, this radical strain in Stoic political thought had begun to be replaced by a more accommodating cosmopolitanism. The ideal *polis* is no longer an (ideal) community set apart, as for Zeno, but rather "a community of all those people who are morally good wherever they live on earth. They all belong to the same community (so there is only one such community) just by being morally good."[18] It is this cosmopolitan ideal that is described by Cicero:

> they [the Stoics] hold that the universe (*mundum*) is governed by the divine will; it is a city or state of which both men and gods are members, and each one of us is a part of this universe; from which it is a natural consequence that we should prefer the common advantage to our own. For just as the laws set the safety of all above the safety of individuals, so a good, wise, and law-abiding man, conscious of his duty to the state, studies the advantage of all more than that of himself or of any single individual. The traitor to his country does not deserve greater reprobation than the man who betrays the common advantage or security for the sake of his own advantage or security.[19]

Here the ideal of the *cosmopolis* has become an essentially moral ideal, rather than a distinctively political one. The virtuous constitute a *polis* only in a rather metaphorical sense. But because of their virtue, they will be able to act in conformity with the primary political virtue of civil cooperation, which is really a form of justice: they will be able to direct their behavior in terms of fulfilling the common good, rather than their own private good. And the reason they will be able to do so, is that the *oikeiôsis* that they have undergone allows them to see that fulfilling the human function, which is their *true* good, consists in such virtuous activity. So the Chrysippean *cosmopolis*, although a source of general civic virtue in its members, does not, as Engberg-Pedersen comments, provide a "recipe for direct social and political action. Rather, [Chrysippus] will have seen it as a kind of limiting construct, which might then be put to use in actual social and political practice in a number of ways."[20] I shall suggest that it is possible to discern analogues of both the Zenonian and the Chrysippean political perspectives in St. Paul's letters.

When we turn to those letters, we see, I believe, the limits of Paul's 'potential cosmopolitanism': all may be called to rebirth in Christ. For those given the grace to respond to that call, there is a transformation of behavior that, in a sense, renders traditional, 'nuts-and-bolts' politics otiose. "Do not model yourselves," says Paul, "on the behavior of the world around you, but let your behavior change, modeled by your new mind" (*Romans* 12:2). Much of the *paraenesis* (moral exhortation) in Paul's letters is directed specifically toward the conduct of Christians within the new Christian *ecclesiai* or churches. Thus he rebukes a 'brother' of the church of Corinth for bringing a "court case against another in front of unbelievers" (*1 Corinthians* 6:6): "how dare one of your members take up a complaint against another in the lawcourts of the unjust instead of before the saints? As you know, it is the saints who are to 'judge the world'; and if the world is to be judged by you, how can you be unfit to judge trifling cases? Since we are also to judge angels, it follows that we can judge matters of everyday life" (*1 Corinthians* 6:1–3). Some of these passages certainly suggest an 'anarcho-syndicalist'[21] ideal not unlike that of Zeno's *Republic*, which is being concretely instantiated in the Christian churches.

However, much Pauline *paraenesis* also seems to be an exhortation to (very high) standards of conduct that would be applicable to a Christian's dealing with the wider, not necessarily Christian world. In *Galatians*, Paul specifically identifies reprehensible behavior with the 'flesh' (*sarks*: in some contemporary translations, 'self-indulgence'):

> Let me put it like this: if you are guided by the Spirit you will be in no danger of yielding to the flesh. ... If you are led by the Spirit, no law can touch you. When the flesh is at work the results are obvious: fornication, gross indecency and sexual irresponsibility; idolatry and sorcery; feuds and wrangling, jealousy, bad temper

and quarrels; disagreements, factions, envy; drunkenness, orgies, and similar things. I warn you now, as I warned you before: those who behave like this will not inherit the kingdom of God. What the Spirit brings is very different: love, joy, peace, patience, kindness, goodness, trustfulness, gentleness, and self-control. There can be no laws against things like that, of course. (*Galatians* 5:16–23)

St. Paul here is suggesting that the same 'fruits of the Spirit' that serve Christians in the intimate social communities of the *ecclesiai* or churches should not prejudice their position in the larger cities or states in which they find themselves but, rather, should make them ideal citizens of these (still pagan) political communities.

Yet, while Paul exhorts the members of the church in Rome to "deal with one another, to the glory of God, as Christ dealt with you" (*Romans* 15:7), he recognizes that what is an appropriate expression of believers' 'new life in Christ' within the Christian churches may not always be appropriate in a wider social context. He makes this point with particular force in *1 Corinthians*:

When I wrote in my letter to you not to associate with people living immoral lives, I was not meaning to include all the people in the world who are sexually immoral, any more than I meant to include all usurers and swindlers or idol-worshipers. To do that, you would have to withdraw from the world altogether. What I wrote was that you should not associate with a brother Christian who is leading an immoral life, or is a usurer, or idolatrous, or a slanderer, or a drunkard, or is dishonest; you should not even eat a meal with people like that. It is not my business to pass judgment on those outside. Of those who are inside, you can surely be the judges. But of those who are outside, God is the judge. (*1 Corinthians* 5:9–13)

Here Paul certainly assumes that the Christians in Corinth are *not* expected to "withdraw from the world altogether." And it seems plausible that this assumption will apply to most other Christians as well. So, it seems to me, there is a sort of political ambivalence in St. Paul's thought, an ambivalence between the sectarian and the cosmopolitan. There is the 'potential cosmopolitanism' of the universal call to Christian discipleship. But there is the concrete, 'anarcho-syndicalist' political sectarianism of life within the (small and local) Christian *ecclesiai*. While the virtues to which all Christians are called serve, first of all, the small and local Christian churches, Paul makes the cosmopolitan assumption that these same virtues make for exemplary citizenship in the wider, pagan political world.

But is it not the case that this ambivalence between the cosmopolitan and the sectarian represents a certain weakness in Paul's thought? That is, is there not a Christian moral imperative to transform not just individual lives but to transform society – to make society, in the wider sense, more like the (ideal) small and local Christian *ecclesia*? And is it not the case that this imperative requires a more thorough integration of the sectarian and the cosmopolitan elements in Christian moral thought than that achieved by Paul? It is, I hope, not unfair to St. Paul to suggest that this ambivalence between the sectarian and the cosmopolitan was not as worrisome to him as it might otherwise have been because of his eschatology – that is, because of his conviction that the *parousia* or 'second coming' of Christ in glory was immanent. In Paul's view, it was really only *God's* action in the *parousia* that would bring to full fruition Christian cosmopolitanism.

However, with the passing of several centuries – without the *parousia* but with the growth in numbers and influence of Christians – it became virtually inevitable that the cosmopolitan strain in Christianity would be reconceptualized. It is not surprising to find the topic of the Christian cosmopolitanism becoming quite important with the advent of Christian Roman emperors in the fourth century C.E. I turn next to that crucial period in Christian political thought.

The Roman empire Christianized

Many Christian writers of the second and third centuries C.E., such as Justin Martyr and Tertullian, did not believe that Christianity was destined to be adopted by the Roman emperors. In 312 C.E., however, Constantine proved them wrong. In preparing to go into battle with his political rival Maxentius at the Milvian Bridge, Constantine had a vision (or dream) of the Christian cross along with the inscription "*In hoc signo vinces*" ("By this sign thou shalt conquer") – or something similar. He in fact did conquer and, as a result, removed various political disabilities (including persecution) from which Christians had suffered. Constantine himself seems to have sincerely accepted the Christian faith, although he did not actually receive baptism until shortly before his death. During his reign, the influence of Christianity steadily increased. Legislation of 318 C.E. denied competence of civil courts in cases where appeal was made to the court of a Christian bishop, while legislation of 333 required that state officials enforce decisions of Christian bishops and decreed that a bishop's testimony should be held by all judges to be sufficient, without the need of corroborating testimony.

With the exception of the brief reign (360–363 c.e.) of Julian, who apostatized from Christianity to monotheistic paganism, the imperial influence of Christianity generally continued to grow in the fourth century. During the reign of Theodosius (who first came to power in 379 c.e. as Gratian's fellow emperor of the East), both paganism and the Arian Christian heresy[22] were repressed in favor of Catholic Christianity. Within this political context, it is not surprising that a new conception of Christian cosmopolitanism should arise – one in which a very close connection is established between the Roman empire and the messianic hope of a *universal ecclesia*, a kingdom of Christ. A contemporary of Constantine, Eusebius of Caesarea, was quick to develop what E.L. Fortin has aptly termed an 'imperial theology'[23] reflecting this connection. Eusebius develops a synoptic view of history in which God operates through certain social and political institutions and his adversary Satan operates through opposing institutions. The ultimate victory belongs to God, of course, but the faithful have had much to suffer along the way. Eusebius comes very close to viewing the Christianized Roman empire as the culmination of history:

> Their [the Jews'] law became famous and spread among all men like a fragrant breeze. Beginning with them the minds of most of the heathen were softened by the lawgivers and philosophers who arose everywhere. Savage and unbridled brutality was changed to mildness, so that deep peace, friendship, and mutual intercourse obtained. Then, at last, when all men, even the heathen throughout the world, were now fitted for the benefits prepared for them beforehand, for the reception of the divine and heavenly Logos of God, the teacher of all virtues, the minister of the Father in all good things, appeared at the beginning of the Roman Empire through man. In nothing did he change our nature touching bodily substance; his acts and sufferings were such as were consistent with the prophecies which foretell that man and God shall live together to do marvelous deeds, and to teach all Gentiles the worship of the Father.[24]

This prophecy has apparently been fulfilled by the Christian emperors: "choosing unto Himself the souls of the supreme Emperors, by means of these men most dearly beloved of God, He cleansed the whole world of all the wicked and baneful persons and of the cruel God-hating tyrants themselves."[25]

In a long passage describing the fate of the church, Eusebius seems virtually to identify the church with the theocracy of Israel in pre-Christian times and, in more recent times, with the Christianized Roman empire. In an elaborate metaphorical passage he compares the structure of the *community* of the church (= empire?) with the structure of a church *building*. Even those of very modest spiritual development have their place: "Building verily in righteousness, he duly divided the whole people according to their several abilities; with some he fenced the outer enclosure and this alone, surrounding it with a wall of un-erring faith (and this was the great multitude of people who were unable to support a mightier structure); to others he entrusted the entrances to the house, setting them to haunt the doors and guide the steps of those entering ..."[26] Eusebius is here simply elaborating on the view of his master Constantine, who regarded himself as something like a bishop (meaning literally, 'overseer') and addressed himself to Christian bishops in these terms: "you are bishops of those inside the Church, while I have been appointed by God as bishop of those outside."[27]

Eusebius ends his *Ecclesiastical History* on a triumphal note. Subsequent to the defeat of his last political foe Licinius,

Constantine, the most mighty Victor, resplendent with every virtue that godliness bestows, together with his son Crispus, an Emperor most dear to God and in all respects like unto his father, recovered the East that belonged to them, and formed the Roman Empire, as in the days of old, into a single united whole, bringing under their peaceful rule all of it. ... So then, there was taken away from men all fear of those who formerly oppressed them; they celebrated brilliant festivals; all things were filled with light, and men, formerly downcast, looked at each other with smiling coun-tenances and beaming eyes; with dancing and hymns in city and country alike they gave honour first of all to God the universal King, for this they had been instructed to do, and then to the pious Emperor and his sons beloved of God; old ills were forgotten and oblivion cast on every deed of impiety; present good things were enjoyed, with the further hope of those which were yet to come. And, in short, there were promulgated in every place ordinances of the victorious Emperor full of love of humanity, and laws that betokened munificence and true piety.[28]

Thus, in Eusebius' imperial theology, Christian cosmopolitanism triumphs – in a very concrete political form. Even Eusebius recognizes that Constantine has not transformed the empire into a large-scale replica of the small and local (ideal) Christian *ecclesia*. That is, Constantine has not succeeded in constructing an empire constituted exclusively of reborn Christians, all living an 'anarcho-syndicalist' communal life of apostolic charity and poverty, like that depicted in the second chapter of *Acts*. Not only are there nominal and lukewarm Christians; there remain pagan subjects of the empire. So, it is not even strictly true that the empire has become – to repeat my earlier description – a non-local community of those united by their common recognition of the true human function, end, or good and their common resolve to conform their behavior to implications of that recognition. However, there is now in place a formal, hierarchical Christian empire; and according to Eusebius – at least, in his more optimistic moments – there now exists, for the first time, the very real potentiality for movement in the direction of a genuinely Christian society. In the meantime, those who have not yet accepted or not yet fully actualized the Christian normative anthropology can be accommodated in the 'outer enclosure' of the Christianized empire.

The advent of *tempora Christiana* (the Christian era)

It is perhaps not surprising that the triumphalistic optimism of Eusebius was short lived. Various forms of immorality and crime did not disappear from the empire; neither did paganism. Catholic Christianity was plagued with a variety of heresies and schisms. Social and political dissensions and factions continued within the empire; and, certainly by the early fifth century c.e., there was increasing pressure from the barbarian masses outside the empire. Particularly traumatic was the sack of Rome in 410 c.e. by Goths under the command of Alaric. After not quite a century of mostly Christian emperors, there still existed a pagan social and cultural elite, many of the members of which blamed the empire's contemporary woes on Christianity. The phrase '*tempora Christiana*' ('Christian times' or 'the Christian era') became a phrase of reproach and abuse. Not only was the wisdom of forsaking the old gods questioned. The perennial issue of the compatibility of Christianity and good citizenship was once again raised.

Against this social background, St. Augustine of Hippo[29] began the composition of his monumental *City of God*, which will receive more attention in the following chapter. However, Augustine also commissioned a young *protégé*, the Spanish priest Paul Orosius, to write a history of *past* calamities of the world. The rhetorical idea seems to have been to demonstrate, against those pagans carping against the supposedly disastrous new *tempora Christiana*, that the good old pagan times were not at all good but, in fact, were much more dreadful than are the current times. According to the characterization of Fortin,

> Whereas Augustine's main concern was with the city of God, Orosius concentrated on what may fairly be called the city of the devil. His relatively short work [*Seven Books of History against the Pagans*], which enjoyed enormous popularity during the Middle Ages, is a catalogue of all the evils known to have been perpetrated or endured by human beings since the beginning of recorded time. Even a superficial reading of the book reveals, however, that in discharging his mandate Orosius went well beyond the call of duty. His simpleminded thesis is that, far from boding ill for the Empire, Christianity was responsible for the untold favors that had accrued to it in recent times. Its auspicious birth under Augustus had coincided with an era of unprecedented peace and held out the promise of even greater benefits in the future. Indeed, all of human history up to that moment could be seen as a lengthy preparation for the advent and eventual triumph of the Christian faith.[30]

In other words, Orosius develops Eusebian imperial theology to such an extreme that it becomes almost ridiculous. His rhetorical strategy frequently leads him to minimize the seriousness of contemporary social, political, and military developments. It was during the reign of the particularly feeble emperor Honorius (Theodosius' younger son, who was sole Western emperor from 395–423 C.E.) that the sack of Rome occurred, that Spain was occupied by the Vandals, that the empire lost the control of Britain, and that a variety of imperial usurpers rose and fell. Nonetheless, Orosius writes as follows:

> Observe how, under Christian rulers and in Christian times, civil wars are settled when they cannot be avoided. The victory was won, the city stormed, the usurper was seized. And this is not half the story. Look elsewhere and see a hostile army vanquished, a count in the service of that usurper [Maximus] – he was more

violent than the usurper himself – forced to take his own life, many ambuscades broken up or evaded, countless preparations rendered useless. Yet no one planned stratagems, no one drew up a line of battle, and lastly, no one, if I may use the expression, even unsheathed his sword. ... Now, to prevent anyone from regarding this as a result of chance, let me produce testimony to God's power, which orders and judges the universe, so that its revelation may either confound the objectors or force them to believe. I mention, therefore, a circumstance unknown to all and yet known to all. After this war in which Maximus was slain, many wars, both domestic and foreign, have indeed been the lot of Theodosius and his son Honorius up to the present day, as we all recollect, and yet almost all have ended either without bloodshed or, at least, with very little, as a result of decisive victory due to divine influence.[31]

Following Eusebius, Orosius sees the Christian cosmopolitanism of the (tottering) Roman empire as something close to the penultimate stage in salvation history – the stage immediately prior to the 'end of the ages' and the *parousia*, Christ's second coming in glory.

St. Augustine, it seems, was none too pleased with the doctrine developed by his *protégé*. The imperial theology of Eusebius and Orosius is, in his view, simply too good to be true. If faced squarely, historical facts certainly do not seem to support the view that a secular political institution (such as the Roman empire) can be, in effect, *identified* with the Christian *ecclesia*. It follows that a person's Christian life cannot plausibly be *identified* with his or her life as a citizen of some secular *polis*. The old question then reemerges: what rôle can a secular political institution have in promoting the *Christian* conception of the human function, end, or good? Or, in other words, what are the proper implications, with respect to political theory, of a distinctively Christian normative anthropology? In the following chapter, I turn to two profound, historically influential, but quite different answers to this question – that of St. Augustine and that of St. Thomas Aquinas.

6

Augustine and Aquinas: Politics for Saints and Sinners

In this chapter I consider the political philosophy of two Christian saints, St. Augustine (354–430 c.e.) and St. Thomas Aquinas (1224–1274 c.e.). When we bear in mind that almost nine hundred years separate their births, it is not surprising that their political theories should be quite different, despite the fact that they are perhaps the two preeminent theologians of the Western or Roman Christian Church. They lived in quite different worlds: Augustine in north Africa (and, relatively briefly, in Italy) during a time of social upheaval towards the end of the Roman empire; Aquinas in Italy, Germany, and France during a period of intellectual upheaval occasioned by the introduction of pagan and Islamic thought into the life of the educated, Latin-speaking class of Europe (which, at the time, was mainly a class of clerics).

At the conclusion of the preceding chapter, I suggested that Augustine and Aquinas developed two profound, historically influential, but quite different answers to the following question: what are the political implications of a distinctively Christian normative anthropology, that is, of a distinctively Christian conception of the proper human nature, function, or purpose? They certainly agree that the *ultimate* nature, function, or purpose of human beings is "to know [God our Creator and Redeemer], to love Him, and to serve Him in this world, and to be happy with Him for ever in heaven."[1] Thus, they both subscribe to a Christian anthropology that is extravagant in the following sense: it postulates a human *ergon* – a human work or function – (i) which transcends any state or activity that is fully achievable in this mortal, biological, and social life, and (ii) which is not achievable by human beings at all without specific divine assistance. The question, then, is "what is the rôle of the state, or of political organization more generally, in helping human beings to fulfill this function or attain this end?"

It stands to reason that the answer to this question will depend, at least in part, on one's conception of the relation between this *ultimate* human function or end and other, more everyday or mundane natural human activities, goods, ends, and purposes (which, from the Christian perspective, evidently will be in some sense subsidiary to the ultimate human function). Augustine and Aquinas have a rather different theoretical conception of this relation between the ultimate, supernatural function of human beings and their subsidiary natural activities and ends. This difference – which I shall explore in some detail in this chapter – in part explains their different conceptions of the proper rôle of politics in human affairs.

These different conceptions can be characterized quite simply. Augustine holds that the most that one can reasonably expect from a political structure is that it should promote, to a greater or lesser degree, peace. And he tends to view this central political task negatively – as the suppression of anarchy and of those forms of evil that most disturb civil tranquility. For Aquinas, on the other hand, political organization, chiefly through the instrumentality of human law, has the capacity of furthering, in a more direct or positive way, at least the natural aspects of the human function. In Aquinas' own words,

> it is manifest that what is proper to law is to lead those subject to it to their proper virtue. Since virtue is what makes that possessing it good, it follows that the proper effect of law is to make those to whom it is given good, either absolutely or in some respect. So, if the intention of the one making the law is directed toward the true good, which is the common good regulated according to divine justice, it follows that through the law men may become good in an absolute sense.[2]

I shall suggest that Aquinas' more positive conception of the rôle of secular political organization is related to the fact that he sees a greater degree of continuity than does Augustine between the praeternatural ('beyond the natural') aspect of the human function or good and the natural aspects of that function. However, as the following sections of this chapter will attest, this simple account of the difference in the political theory of Augustine and of Aquinas scarcely does justice to the interest and complexities of the political thought of these two great theologians and philosophers.

St. Augustine

The two rationales of Augustine's *City of God*

One of the greatest (and longest) of Augustine's many writings is the *City of God*, a work of twenty-two 'books' that was begun in 413 C.E., a few years after the fall of Rome to the Goths, and not completed until 425. The *City of God* is not a work of political philosophy, and there is good reason to agree with E.L. Fortin's description of Augustine as exhibiting a "lack of interest in politics."[3] In Augustine's own words, "as for this mortal life, which ends after a few days' course, what does it matter under whose rule a man lives, being so soon to die, provided that the rulers do not force him to impious and wicked acts."[4]

However, there are two principal motivations, which might plausibly be termed political, that seem to be crucially important to the development of Augustine's thought in this work. One is to reply anew to the old pagan charge that the serious, devout practice of Christianity is incompatible with discharging one's civic duties as a member of a secular political society. As I noted in the preceding chapter, this charge reasserted itself with some force after the fall of Rome. The second motivation was to wean his 'noble pagan' readers (as well as those Christians who had been attracted to the imperial theology of Eusebius and Orosius) away from the idea that any secular social or political structure could ever provide the sufficient means for attaining true human nobility – that is, for successfully fulfilling the human function or achieving the human good. In effect, Augustine is committed to a portrayal of Christianity as radically 'counter-cultural' – but as counter-cultural in a politically unthreatening way. Fortin comments on the tension between these two goals: on the one hand, "only by downplaying the merits of Roman political life and exaggerating its shortcomings could Augustine hope to persuade the pagan 'holdouts' of his day that the time had come to embrace the new faith." Thus, according to Augustine, "Rome was never a republic, the pagan virtues are nothing but vices, all rulers are pirates in disguise," and so forth.[5] But, on the other hand, by elevating patriotism to the level of a religious duty, Christianity serves the city more effectively than the moribund pagan religion that his adversaries were trying to revive had ever done. True, Christianity makes a stronger claim on the allegiance of its followers than does the temporal society of which they are members, but, as a religion that transcends all temporal societies, it does not abrogate their citizenship in any particular temporal society.[6]

Augustine's *City of God* serves as a plausible example (we shall see other perhaps even clearer examples in later chapters) of how social circumstances and an author's fundamental commitments can mold theoretical doctrine. But, at the same time, it serves as an outstanding example of the fact that such social and intellectual contextualization of a theoretical work need in no way detract from its philosophical interest or historical importance.

The two cities

There are *two* states or cities (*civitates*) that figure in the *City of God*: the city of God or heavenly city of the title and the earthly city. Augustine proposes to treat of the former "both as it exists in the world of time, a stranger among the ungodly, living by faith, and as it stands in the security of its everlasting seat."[7] The earthly city, in contrast, is a "city that aims at dominion, which holds nations in enslavement, but is itself dominated by that very lust of domination."[8] From the earthly city "there arise enemies against whom the City of God has to be defended, though many of these correct their godless errors and become useful citizens of that City [of God]."[9] The first point to emphasize about the two cities is that they are not, in any literal sense, cities: that is, they are not to be identified with any specific social or political institutions of human history. In particular, the earthly city is not to be identified with the Roman empire (or any other secular state), and the heavenly city is not to be identified with the (Catholic) Church. "In this wicked world," Augustine writes, "in these evil times, the Church through her present humiliation is preparing for future exaltation. ... In this situation, many reprobates are mingled in the Church with the good, and both sorts are collected, as it were, in the dragnet of the gospel ... and enclosed in nets until the shore is reached. There the evil are to be divided from the good."[10]

Augustine uses the figure of the two cities to describe two radically different sorts of person, who are distinguished by their fundamentally different orientation or ultimate motivation. This division depends on Augustine's distinction between *enjoyment* (*fructus*, in the Latin) and *use* (*usus*). The basic idea underlying the distinction is that enjoyment pertains to those things in which lies our happiness. Augustine maintains that it is an *objective* fact that human beings have a certain nature, purpose, or function, and that only the 'enjoyment' of fulfilling that function or living up to that nature constitutes true human happiness. In contrast, those things that are the proper object of use "assist, and (so to speak) support us in our efforts after happiness, so that we can attain the things that make us happy and rest in them."[11] The problem is that, due to the corruption of human nature resulting from the Fall, human beings often try to enjoy what should be only an object of use; and, not infrequently, they attempt to enjoy what should be avoided altogether – both as an object of enjoyment and as an object of use. Not surprisingly, Augustine holds that the "true objects of enjoyment, then, are the Father and the Son and the Holy Spirit,"[12] or as he more famously puts it at the beginning of his *Confessions*, "Thou hast made us for Thyself, O Lord, and our heart is restless until it repose in Thee."[13] But,

> suppose, then, that we were wanderers in a strange country, and could not live happily away from our fatherland, and that we felt wretched in our wandering, and wishing to put an end to it, determined to return home. We find, however, that we must make use of some mode of conveyance, either by land or by water, in order to reach that fatherland where our enjoyment is to commence. But the beauty of the country through which we pass, and the very pleasure of the motion, charm our hearts, and turning these things which we ought to use into objects of enjoyment, we become unwilling to hasten the end of our journey; and becoming engrossed in a factitious delight, our thoughts are diverted from that home whose delights would make us truly happy. Such is the picture of our condition in this life of mortality.[14]

To shorten a rather long story, the heavenly city is constituted of those who love God correctly, who find their enjoyment only in him, and who are destined to eternal beatitude in the company of God and the saints after this mortal, biological life is ended. These are the persons who have accepted and internalized the 'extravagant' Christian normative anthropology of which I earlier spoke. Before the Fall, our first parents (Adam and Eve) belonged to the City of God; indeed, God's purpose in making "a single individual the starting-point for all mankind ... was that the human race should not merely be united in a society by natural likeness, but should also be bound together by a tie of kinship to form a harmonious unity, linked together by a 'bond of peace'."[15] However, "so heinous was [the first parents'] sin that man's nature suffered a change for the worse, and bondage to sin and inevitable death was the legacy handed on to their posterity."[16] There is more than a little mystery concerning the reason for our first parents' fall if they were true members of the city of God. Of course, this is a central mystery of the Christian faith and not just an issue for Augustine. But, in common with the orthodox Christian tradition he holds that because of the "undeserved grace of God," some are rescued from the corruption that, in a sense, now makes us all members of the earthly city. These persons are reincorporated by adoption, as it were, into the city of God. The result is that "there is one city of men who choose to live by the standard of the flesh, another by the standard of the spirit. The citizens of each of these desires their own kind of peace, and when they achieve their aim, that is the kind of peace in which they live."[17]

The earthly city is constituted of those who have *not* been reincorporated into the city of God. Consequently, they are persons who seek their happiness in the enjoyment of things that ought to be only objects of use. Their conception of the human function, or ultimate purpose or good, is faulty – or, if they have some inkling of the truth in this matter, they do not manage to conform their behavior to this insight. They have not, in other words, internalized the extravagant Christian normative anthropology. Whereas the heavenly city was created "by the love of God carried as far as contempt of self," "the earthly city was created by self-love reaching the point of contempt of God." The earthly city "glories in itself," "looks for glory from men," and "lifts up its head in its own glory." In it, "the lust for domination lords it over its princes as over the nations it subjugates." In the earthly city, "its wise men who live by men's standards have pursued the good of the body or of their own mind, or of both."[18] The "citizens of the earthly city are produced by a nature which is vitiated by sin, while the citizens of the Heavenly City are brought forth by grace, which sets nature free from sin. ... In one case we are shown man's customary behavior, in the other we are given a revelation of the goodness of God."[19]

The customary behavior of which Augustine speaks is typically fractious. "For the human race is," he says, "more than any other species, at once social by nature and quarrelsome by perversion."[20] Now, among the "quarrelsome" members of the earthly city, Augustine is willing to draw what we might call commonsensical moral distinctions. Some members of that city, in effect, adopt what Augustine regards as a particularly ignoble hedonistic normative anthropology, a conception of the human function as the pursuit of pleasure and avoidance of pain. Consequently, such persons attempt to find their enjoyment in sensuality. Others are primarily motivated by the desire of domination of their fellows. Less ignoble still are those primarily motivated by the desire for human glory, which is not the same thing as the desire of domination. Indeed,

> there are many good moral qualities which are approved by many, though many do not possess them. And it is by those moral qualities that glory, power, and domination are sought by the kind of men who, as Sallust says, 'strive for them in the right way'. But if anyone aims at power and domination without that kind of desire for glory which makes a man fear the disapprobation of sound judges, then he generally seeks to accomplish his heart's desire by the most barefaced crimes.
>
> Thus the man who covets glory either 'strives by the right way' for it or 'struggles by trickery and deceit', desiring to seem a good man without being so.[21]

However, in some tension with Augustine's 'commonsensical' recognition of better and worse kinds of orientation or 'ultimate objects of love' among the citizens of the earthly city is his theory of the nature of evil, a theory that seems to downplay these distinctions. Evil, according to Augustine, typically lies not in the nature of the object of desire but in the very fact that such desire is 'disordered': that is, what should be desired and sought only as an object of 'use' – and should be of only instrumental service to human beings – becomes an object of enjoyment.[22] Such defection of the will, Augustine says,

> does not consist in defection to things which are evil in themselves; it is the defection in itself that is evil. That is, it is not a falling away to evil natures; the defection is evil in itself, as a defection from him who supremely exists to something of a lower degree of reality; and this contrary to the order of nature. ... By the same token, anyone who perversely loves the goodness of any nature whatsoever, even if he obtains the enjoyment of it, becomes evil in the enjoyment of the good, and wretched in being deprived of a higher good.[23]

"Thus, when man lives 'by the standard of man' and not 'by the standard of God', he is like the Devil."[24] And the "nature of the flesh is good, in its own kind and on its own level. But it is not good to forsake the

Creator good and live by the standard of the created good, whether a man chooses the standard of the flesh, or of the soul, or of the entire man, who consists of soul and flesh and hence can be denoted by either term, soul or flesh, by itself."[25] The ethical consequence, so to speak, of this doctrine is that the pursuit, *as 'ends in themselves' or ultimate ends*, of any 'natural' human functions or goods – for example, biological life, health, security, pleasure, family or social life, knowledge, or even the practice of virtue – is evil. It involves an attempt to enjoy what should be only instrumentally useful. Moreover such strategies are usually vain, since Augustine believes that, as a matter of psychological fact, attempts to enjoy (as ultimate ends) what should only be used do not ordinarily produce lasting enjoyment even in this mortal life. The political consequences of the doctrine, to which I turn in the next section, all derive from the fact that this Augustinian viewpoint allows little room for commonality of interests between citizens of the heavenly city and citizens of the earthly city, a commonality of interests that is frequently assumed to be the rational basis of political cooperation.

Theoretical political consequences

All political institutions will forever be constituted of both citizens of the city of God and citizens of the earthly city. It is only after this age or *saeculum*, which comprises the complete history of the human race on earth, that there will be a final and complete winnowing of citizens of the two cities, a separation of the 'saints' from the 'sinners' (in the sense of the damned or reprobate). It would be presumptuous and sinful to think that anyone other than God himself could, at any time in this age, determine who belongs to which city. There then arises for Augustine a theoretical problem concerning the rôle of political entities. We normally think of such entities as supplying some sort of necessary or useful structure that facilitates cooperation among human persons in their common pursuit of shared goals or purposes – whether such goals and purposes be thought to derive from their common possession of an objective human function, nature, or purpose or whether it be assumed that they simply represent some desires or preferences that, as a matter of fact, a number of humans happen to share in a given place and given time. But Augustine's theory of the two cities suggests that there is strikingly little that the citizens of the heavenly city and those of the earthly city have in common by way of such goals and purposes. The *ultimate* motivations (*fructus* or enjoyments) of the two kinds of person are of entirely different orders; and Augustine suggests that this difference in ultimate motivation will thoroughly color their attitudes to subsidiary goals and purposes – their conceptions, in other words, of what is *useful* and of how it is so. Therefore, there would seem to be very little an *actual* city, state, or kingdom could do to further the ends of its thoroughly mixed citizenry. Indeed, insofar as it furthers the (disordered) ultimate ends of its citizens that are members of the earthly city, it would seem merely to contribute to a continuance of their error, evil, and misery.

It is not surprising, therefore, that Augustine develops a thin or minimalist conception of the proper rôle of the state (or of political organization, more broadly). What political organization rightly contributes to human existence is peace. And, as I said earlier, he generally thinks of the kind of peace that the state can supply simply as the suppression of anarchy and of those forms of evil that most disturb civil tranquility. So there is a significant sense in which the state is (usually) not in a position to do much to assist directly, as it were, its citizens in achieving what they take to be the human function or attaining what they take be their 'enjoyment' or ultimate good. The maintenance of peace, according to Augustine, does include the suppression of the worst forms of vice, which can certainly detract citizens from attaining what they take to be their ultimate good. That is, peace is at most of instrumental value – perhaps in some instances a necessary condition – with respect to the citizens of a state attaining their ends. But the *sort* of instrumental value that it possesses is very different for citizens of the heavenly city as contrasted to citizens of the earthly city.

It might seem that citizens of the city of God would have little if any need for politics at all. In a sense this is true, and in a sense it is not. Augustine, of course, is known for his strong predestinarian doctrine: that is, it is essentially the work of God's grace that incorporates those whom he chooses into the city of God. Without entering into the theological and philosophical subtleties of this doctrine, it is sufficient to note that Augustine holds that God's grace is not coercive but, rather, works through the wills of its recipients; and, in that sense, the acceptance by citizens of the heavenly city of the normative Christian anthropology and their consequent behavior in conformity with that conception of the human function is voluntary.[26] In other words, even though there may be a sense in which divine grace determines its effects, this determination is not *fatalistic* in the sense of making human action otiose or 'meaningless'. Augustine avoids the following old fallacy: if human action is determined, then it does not matter what we do. This is a fallacy because, determination or no determination, certain human actions may be *necessary conditions* for things turning out as they do. Consequently, participation in certain political institutions may be a necessary part of the process of some citizens of the heavenly city working out their divine destiny. And, in fact, Augustine emphasizes the point that the peace and stability supplied by the state may be of *use* to the citizens of the city of God who are also members of such a state. This fact supplies a motivation for cooperation by members of the heavenly city in secular political institutions:

> Meanwhile it is important for us also that this people [the people of the earthly city, who are "alienated from God"] should possess this peace in this life, since so long as the two cities are intermingled we also make use of the peace of Babylon [i.e., the earthly city] – although the People of God are by faith set free from Babylon, so that in the meantime they are only pilgrims in the midst of her. That is why the Apostle [Paul] instructs the Church to pray for kings of that city and those in high positions, adding these words: 'that we may lead a quiet and peaceful life with all devotion and love'.[27]

Yet, Augustine suggests that the sort of peace that can be obtained from political cooperation is not of pressing concern to members of the heavenly city. In contrast, the peace that is the "special possession [of the members of the heavenly city] is ours even in this life, a peace with God through faith; and it will be ours for ever, a peace with God through open vision."[28] This peace is not perfect in this life due to the struggle of the 'flesh' of even members of the heavenly city with their reason and will. But it is far superior to the peace that can be attained through politics.

For one thing, the ultimate destiny of members of the earthly city is not peace at all but an everlasting wretchedness that Augustine describes as a state of war, the very antithesis of peace.[29] The fact that members of the earthly city are always also members of secular states, and are more motivated than are members of the heavenly city to seek positions of power in such states, means that the peace which is the *raison d'être* of secular politics is a terribly fragile thing:

> [the earthly city] has its good in this world, and rejoices to participate in it with such gladness as can be derived from things of such a kind. And since this is not the kind of good that causes no frustrations of those enamoured of it, the earthly city is generally divided against itself by litigation, by wars, by battles, by pursuit of victories that bring death with them or at best are doomed to

death. For if any section of that city has risen up in war against another part, it seeks to be victorious over other nations, though it itself is the slave of base passions; and if, when victorious, it is exalted in its arrogance, that victory brings death in its train. Whereas if it considers the human condition and the changes and chances common to mankind, and is more tormented by possible misfortunes than puffed up by its present success, then its victory is only doomed to death. For it will not be able to lord it permanently over those whom it had been able to subdue victoriously.[30]

According to Augustine, then, members of the city of God will properly expect relatively little from politics. Members of the earthly city may, in fact, expect more but they should not do so. Even the apparently most noble goals of furthering human welfare are corrupted by the will to dominate and love of glory of members of the earthly city: such corruption is the inevitable consequence of the fact that members of the earthly city attempt to find their enjoyment – that is, locate their ultimate function or end – in goods other than the love of God, subsidiary goods that should be, at most, objects of use, not enjoyment. There is good reason to accept the conclusion of the scholar J. van Oort that "Augustine did not see temporal goods separately as neutral goods, but according to the use man makes of them. That use is either good or evil, and in the way temporal goods belong to one of the two cities, either that of God or that of the devil. Not once did Augustine mention an independent, neutral area between the two cities."[31] This claim would appear to hold true for the good of temporal peace, as well as for the more concrete 'benefits' supplied by secular states.

A corollary that Augustine explicitly draws in one of his letters is that the *bad use* of temporal possessions amounts to their *unjust possession*. From the perspective of most legal and political theory, this is a doctrine that is radical to the point of seeming absurd. At the very heart of most doctrines of positive or civil law is some version of a distinction between the 'commands' of that law and the counsel of moral virtue that exceeds the requirement of law. But Augustine's theory seems to undermine that distinction. So, it is perhaps not surprising to find him advancing, in the same letter, the following characterization of civil law: "In this life," he says, "the wrong of evil possessors is endured and among them certain laws are established that are called civil laws, not because they bring men to make a good use of their wealth, but because those who make a bad use of it become thereby less injurious."[32]

This doctrine is, I think, less a matter of the cynicism that a contemporary reader may be tempted to read into it than a corollary of Augustine's doctrine of the two cities. The upshot is that there is relatively little that we can expect from politics in advancing the human good. As long as members of the earthly city control politics, which they inevitably largely will, corruption is all but certain. A bit more may perhaps be expected when members of the heavenly city insinuate themselves into the picture. But, when they attain positions of political authority, such persons will be cautious and skeptical about the possibility of using political means to address human problems.

Some contemporary commentators have seen in Augustine the foreshadowing of a contemporary liberal conception of politics according to which the state does not assume an 'all-encompassing world view' or have ultimate ends of its own; it merely provides neutral means that assist its citizens in achieving their own private ultimate ends, whatever those ends happen to be.[33] However, as we shall have opportunity to consider later in this book, most contemporary liberal political theory mandates such political neutrality as a matter of justice. Augustine certainly has no such doctrine. In fact, as I have argued in an earlier essay, rather than a normative political doctrine about what the rôle of political organization *should* be, Augustine possesses a "radically pragmatic attitude toward the exercise of political authority": "political authority is to be *used* by the citizens of the *civitas peregrina* [the heavenly city in its earthly sojourn], as circumstances permit to further the ends of the heavenly city ... But the details of such use can, it seems, greatly depend upon various contingencies: what is an appropriate use in one set of circumstances may not be appropriate in other circumstances."[34] This pragmatic stance is certainly consistent with the fact that Augustine is willing to make moral judgments concerning worse and better regimes, as well as the fact of his undoubted belief that political authority should "be exercised in non-capricious, legal, just, and moderate ways by righteous men."[35] But his theory of the two cities explains why such exercise of political power is the exception rather than the rule.

Christians as good citizens of secular states?

Thus far I have concentrated on the counter-cultural aspects of Augustine's thought. Perhaps more important from an historical perspective, however, is his attempt to render those counter-cultural features of his version of the Christian normative anthropology politically non-threatening. This undertaking, as I mentioned earlier, is certainly a central rationale of the *City of God*, but it is not limited to that work. There are two principal argumentative strategies that Augustine employs in this undertaking. One is to argue that various 'radical' Christian moral injunctions, such as those found in the so-called Sermon on the Mount, are to be interpreted as pertaining primarily to inner dispositions or attitudes. Consequently, a variety of prudential considerations can be brought to bear in determining exactly what external behavior is appropriate, in the circumstances, as a manifestation of such dispositions. The second strategy is to argue that what would not be morally licit behavior for the Christian who is a private citizen sometimes is permissible if that Christian holds a position of political authority.

In a letter of 412 C.E. written to the Christian tribune Marcellinus (who was later executed, without trial, as a result of political intrigue), Augustine responds to pagans who say that "Christ's preaching and doctrine are not adaptable in any way to the customs of the state, and they give as an example the precept that we are not to return evil for evil to anyone; that we should turn the other cheek when anyone strikes us; that we should let go our cloak when anyone takes our coat; and when anyone forces us to go with him we should go twice as far."[36] Augustine responds that there is certainly nothing detrimental to the state in the disposition to suffer "the loss of temporal goods with patience, in order to show how far these goods are to be despised for the sake of faith and justice."[37] The right time for explicitly acting in conformity with the gospel counsels "is when it seems likely to benefit the one for whose sake it is done, in order to bring about correction and a return to agreement."[38] And, he says,

> finally, those precepts refer rather to the interior disposition of the heart than to the act which appears exteriorly, and they enjoin us to preserve patience and kindly feeling in the hidden places of the soul, revealing them openly when it seems likely to be beneficial to those whose welfare we seek. This is clearly shown in the case of the Lord Christ Himself, a unique model of patience, who was struck on the face and answered: 'If I have spoken evil, give testimony of the evil, but if well, why strikest thou me?' If we look at the words literally, He obviously did not fulfill His own precept, for He did not offer His other cheek to the striker.[39]

A striking example of Augustine's second strategy for arguing for the compatibility of Christian moral counsels with good citizenship – that what may not be morally licit, or at least not morally preferable, for the private Christian can be acceptable 'public behavior' for the Christian holding a position of political authority – is the saint's several discussions of homicide committed in self defense. I concentrate on this particular illustration of Augustine's conception of the relation between private and public morality both because it is typical of his thought on this topic and because it is so much at odds with what later became a more standard view. According to a more standard view, homicide committed in self-defense is a paradigmatic example of morally licit homicide. In fact, it is not unusual to see 'political homicide' – for example that committed by soldiers in war – justified as a sort of delegated extension of the right of self-defense. As we shall see, Augustine's doctrine is almost the opposite. In a letter of 398 c.e. Augustine writes in response to an inquiry about the licitness of self-defense as follows: "In regard to killing men so as not to be killed by them, this view does not please me, unless perhaps it should be a soldier or public official. In this case, he does not do it for his own sake, but for others or for the state to which he belongs, having received the power lawfully in accord with his public character."[40]

In his *De libero arbitrio* (*On Free Choice*), Augustine gives a rather more complete account of this doctrine. There are two reasons that are given for Augustine's reluctance to endorse a 'right' to self-defense. The first is that he (or, rather, the character Evodius in the *De libero arbitrio*, which is written partly in dialogue form) doubts whether "an open enemy or a secret assassin can be killed without any passion in defence of life, liberty, or honour."[41] The assumption seems to be that it is extremely difficult, and perhaps impossible, to kill in self-defense without acquiescing in the affect of anger or some other passion implying the preference of one's own life to the life of someone else; and Augustine's (or Evodius') moral rigorism evidently leads him to view any such acquiescence as sinful. Secondly, the character Evodius argues that "some may perhaps doubt whether the soul's life is by any means taken away when the body perishes, but, if it can be taken away it is of no value, while if it cannot, there is no reason to fear."[42] Here, the operative assumption seems to be the rather Stoic-seeming one that, if something (for example, whether we retain our *biological* life or not) is not within our power, it is not really 'ours' and, hence, we are not warranted in taking a life in the attempt to retain it: "whatever the man who is killed [in self-defense or in resistance to rape] was going to take away is not wholly in our power, and so I do not understand how it can be called ours."[43]

As extreme (even by orthodox Christian standards) as these strictures against self-defense may seem, they are presented in such a way as to minimize worrisome political implications. First, there is a qualification based upon the distinction between public and private status of the agent:

> When a soldier kills the enemy he is enforcing the law, and so has no difficulty in carrying out his duty without passion. The law itself, which is issued to protect its subjects, cannot be convicted of passion. If its author issued it in obedience to God's will, that is to fulfill eternal justice, he may have done so without any passion at all. Even if he issued it out of passion, it does not follow that the law need be carried out with passion, because a good law can be issued by a man who is not good.[44]

One may doubt the psychological accuracy of the claim about the ease with which soldiers (and executioners, jailors, etc.) can perform their duties 'disinterestedly' – without accompanying evil passions. But Augustine's point is clear. When acting in a truly 'public' capacity, one is not primarily acting in a self-interested, self-serving, or egoistic way. Augustine's further assumption seems to be that sinful interior states or passions are typically, in one way or another, connected with such self-serving egoism – although, again, the truth of this assumption may be a matter of moral and psychological dispute.

Second, Augustine (again through the character Evodius) is willing to allow the legitimacy (and even virtue) of laws permitting and regulating self-defense. "I see pretty well," Evodius says, "that a law which gives its subjects permissions to commit lesser crimes in order to prevent greater ones, has a good defence against an accusation of this kind" – namely, that no law that permits behavior that may be unjust or immoral really is a law, in the full and proper sense of the term. With respect to the particular case of legislation allowing homicide in self-defense, he concludes that "I do not, therefore, blame the law which allows such men [e.g., attackers, rapists] to be killed, but I do not see how I am able to defend their slayers." Although it is not clear that Augustine is prepared fully to endorse the doctrine of self-defense he puts into the mouth of Evodius, he *does* endorse the underlying doctrine of the moral licitness of laws (and other public behavior) that accommodate a less than morally perfect world:

> I thoroughly approve of this distinction of yours; although it is incomplete and imperfect, yet it is full of faith and of ideals. The law which is decreed to govern states seems to you to permit much and to leave it unpunished, though it is punished by Divine

Providence. Rightly so. Because a law does not do everything, it does not follow that what it does do is to be blamed.[45]

One might say that Augustine leaves little room for a 'positive' political or legal *theory* that can be divorced from the 'extravagant' Christian normative anthropology that he embraces and that, consequently, can also be divorced from some of the more radical moral implications of that normative anthropology. But, at least in part because of his pessimistic – some might say 'cynical', others 'realistic' – conception of the limitations of political solutions to human problems, he leaves much room for prudential, pragmatic accommodation between believers and the secular state. As I mentioned earlier, the result is that certain themes from contemporary, liberal political theory are foreshadowed in Augustine's thought: the distinction between (private) morality and (public) law; the doctrine of the state as a supplier of 'neutral means', which can be used by a variety of citizens with quite disparate ultimate concerns; a certain caution (to say the least) about the ideal of the state as a 'teacher of virtue'. But, unlike the case of contemporary liberal political theory, Augustine does not construct a political theory in which these conditions figure as desiderata or virtues of the state. Rather, they are corollaries of a quite fundamental Augustinian political doctrine aptly summarized by E.L. Fortin: "Christian wisdom and political power are not only distinct but always more or less at odds with each other in accordance with the vicissitudes of history and the inclinations of our 'restless hearts'. Some regimes are obviously superior to others but nothing suggests that any of them will ever be able to fulfill our deepest longings."[46] According to Augustine, in other words, there is an important sense in which human beings are *not* 'political animals'. The city of God, the '*polis*' to which all humans are called and of which some are destined to be members, is far removed not only from Aristotle's ideal of a *polis* but from any actual human political community. St. Thomas Aquinas tries to bridge this gap.

St. Thomas Aquinas

From about the middle of the twelfth century C.E., Latin translations of Arabic works of philosophy and science, as well as of Greek texts of ancient thinkers, began to appear in Europe. The translation of the Greek texts of Aristotle was completed by a thirteenth-century contemporary of Thomas Aquinas and Dominican friar, William of Moerbecke.[47] Of course, Aquinas himself was a member of the

Dominican order (Order of Preachers), at the time a relatively new mendicant (meaning, literally, 'begging') order, an order of priests who practiced evangelical poverty and who devoted themselves primarily to study, preaching, and teaching – both study and teaching of biblical theology and of secular philosophy and science. As the twentieth-century philosopher and Aquinas scholar J. Pieper puts it,

> the intellectual dynamics of the early thirteenth century was ... determined chiefly by two forces, both revolutionary and both of tremendous vitality: on the one hand the radical evangelism of the voluntary poverty movement, which rediscovered the Bible and made it the guide to Christian doctrine and Christian life; and on the other hand the no less fierce urge to investigate, on the plane of pure natural philosophy, the reality that lay before men's eyes. This latter movement in the direction of a hitherto unknown and novel "worldliness" found ammunition in the complete works of Aristotle, which were at that time just beginning to be discovered.[48]

It may be a bit difficult for us now to comprehend the fact that this ancient pagan learning constituted philosophy and science that was then considered to be – in the contemporary phrase – at the cutting edge. Not all reaction to it was favorable, however. There was a religiously conservative movement, particularly dependent on Augustine and the other Church fathers, that was gravely suspicious of any attempt to assimilate or otherwise to come to terms with pagan (or Muslim) learning. At the other extreme, there was a movement that saw intellectual progress as consisting in the complete acceptance of the scientific view of the natural world developed by Aristotle and later Greek and Muslim commentators on him. Adherents to this view tended to deprecate any religiously motivated attempt to resist, constrain, or modify this secular philosophy and science as reactionary and obscurantist.[49]

It is something of a truism (although a true one, I believe) that St. Thomas Aquinas attempted to steer a middle course between these two extremes. His admiration for the thought of Aristotle is obvious. Of course, he certainly has no intention of jettisoning the theological tradition of the Christian Bible, Augustine, and the Church fathers. Nor does he wish to develop a doctrine of 'two realms', in which this theological tradition is confined to private religious devotion (or restricted to church buildings, convents, and monasteries) and not allowed to color the conception of nature and society to be developed within the secular sciences. The fine details of Aquinas' synthesis of Aristotle and Christianity, which are beyond the scope of this book, are both complex and subtle. However, in our concern with the political thought of Aquinas we must engage his wider world view, beginning with his conception of the human nature, function or purpose – a concept that the reader will recognize as the inevitable starting point in all our discussions, up to this point, of 'classical' political philosophy.

The human function: nature and praeternature

It is no exaggeration to say that Aquinas accepts more or less wholesale the *conceptual framework* of Aristotle's normative anthropology. In fact, Aquinas uses Latin translations of the Greek terminology introduced by Aristotle to develop his theory of the essence, properties, and actions of human beings. Following Aristotle, Aquinas maintains that a human being is naturally a composite of soul and body (with the soul the 'form' of the body – identified with certain active capacities of a human being – rather than an incorporeal substance that moves the body). He also agrees with Aristotle that the preeminent characteristic of a human being is his or her intellectual or rational capacity (designated as 'intellective' soul), but that human beings also have subsidiary, distinctive capacities for 'living' in a biological sense and for sensing their environment (capacities that are designated as 'vegetative' and 'sensitive' soul, respectively). More generally, he follows Aristotle in adopting the functionalistic conception of human nature. That is, human beings have a proper function or business, an ultimate end (*finis*) or good, which is designated as 'happiness' (*beatitudo*, in Aquinas' Latin). Happiness, for Aquinas (as for Aristotle), consists in something objective – the perfection of our human nature; and we human beings all possess a desire and natural inclination directed toward such a perfection. There is no one who does not want to be happy. But human beings have a variety of views (many of them mistaken) about what possessions, states, or activities *instantiate* happiness:

> So, then, as to the aspect of last end, all agree in desiring the last end: since all desire the fulfilment of their perfection, and it is precisely this fulfilment in which the last end consists, as stated above. But as to the thing in which this aspect is realized, all men are not agreed as to their last end: since some desire riches, as their consummate good; some pleasure; others, something else. Thus to every taste the sweet is pleasant; but to some, the sweetness of

wine is most pleasant, to others the sweetness of honey, or some-thing similar. Yet that sweet is absolutely the best of all pleasant things, in which he who has the best taste takes most pleasure. In like manner that good is most complete which the man with well-disposed affections desires for his last end.[50]

This passage contains a particularly clear statement of the *normative* element of Aquinas' version of an essentially Aristotelian anthropology. Human beings have an objective nature which they *should* desire to ful-fill as the ultimate end of all their diverse actions and behavior. But, in fact, not all persons *do* recognize this end and desire to fulfill it. For Aquinas, as for Aristotle, morality pertains to certain kinds of action and traits of character (*virtutes* in Aquinas' Latin; *aretai*, as we earlier saw, in Aristotle's Greek) that are conducive to attaining our happiness in this sense – that is, fulfilling our function or perfecting our nature. Perhaps more than Aristotle, Aquinas emphasizes the distinctive char-acter of *human* virtues. Other natural kinds of things have their own natures with functions and ends that are perfected by their particular virtues or excellences. In things with non-rational natures, such virtues typically operate in a determinate, fixed way so as to invariably and 'automatically' bring about a single sort of result, which contributes to the perfection of the thing in question. However, the human nature is a rational nature and, according to Aquinas, "the rational powers, which are proper to man, are not determinate to one particular action, but are inclined indifferently to many; and they are determinate to acts by means of habits, as is clear from what we have said above. Therefore, human virtues are habits."[51] In other words, the distinctively human virtues (especially what Aristotle called the moral virtues) are acquired habits, which allow their possessor to use his or her reason in the right away – to achieve the objective final end or fulfill the proper ultimate function of human beings. However, human reason in itself is quite capable of going astray, that is, of initiating kinds of behavior that are not conducive to – and, indeed, may be detrimental to – the attainment of the ultimate human end.

So far, in terms of the conceptual tools he employs, my account of Aquinas' normative anthropology applies equally well to Aristotle. This is no surprise, since the source of much of Aquinas' account simply is his reading of Aristotle. However, there are two especially significant points of departure. To consider the first, we should recollect that Aristotle held a naturalistic, bipartite conception of what the human function or good is – and, thus, of what constitutes happiness (*eudaimonia*, in Aristotle's Greek). One aspect of the human function, according to Aristotle, was much like Plato's: knowing the truth. But the other was that quite general and comprehensive but rather nebulous-seeming *social* or *political* function of *eupraxia*, which I earlier attempted to explicate in several (for Aristotle, seemingly equivalent) ways: 'successful practical activity' = 'exercise of practical rationality in conformity with the moral virtues for its own sake' = 'political life' or 'living in the *polis* with one's fellows, with all that that concept entails'. Despite the problematic nature of this second aspect of Aristotle's conception of the human function, it seems clear that both elements of the human function or end (i) are attainable, in varying degrees, by some combination of natural innate and developed human capacities (*aretai*), and (ii) in no way transcend our mortal human biological and social life. The obvious question is how Aquinas manages to accommodate this naturalistic Aristotelian normative anthropology with the 'extravagant' Christian normative anthropology, which we encountered in our discussion of the New Testament, St. Paul, and St. Augustine. The short answer to this question is that Aquinas grafts an account of what we termed human praeternature, in the sense of something that is *beyond* unregenerated human nature, onto a more Aristotelian, naturalistic account of human nature.

This conceptual maneuver, which we shall later consider in more detail, represents the central point of departure of Aquinas from a strictly Aristotelian normative anthropology. However, I wish first to say something about the second point of departure, which derives from what may be regarded as a problem in Aristotle's moral theory. There is an allusion to this problem in a sentence from Aquinas' *Summa Theologica*, which I quoted above: "In like manner that good is most complete which the man with well-disposed affections desires for his last end."[52] What is the import of employing "the man with well-disposed affections" as the *standard* of judgment concerning the "good [that] is most complete"? In the case of Aristotle, this question has led to an argument that his normative anthropology (that is, moral theory or 'ethics') is circular. The argument goes as follows: the moral virtues or *aretai* are, by definition, those character traits that enable their possessor successfully to fulfill the 'social' part of the human function or, in other words, to achieve the social component of the "last end" of human persons. But what is this social component of the last end? To behave as the virtuous, excellent or "well-disposed" (*spoudaios*) person would – that is, to undertake action in conformity with the moral virtues "for its own sake." A quite traditional tactic for escaping the circle has been to enlist an elaborate interpretation of Aristotle's conception of the virtues as means (that is, 'middle ways' between deficiency and excess in actions and passions) in order to provide an independent, objective account of them – that is, an account that does not simply identify the virtues as those character traits that a virtuous person possesses. For readers of Aristotle (such as myself) who do not think that the Aristotelian doctrine of the mean is sufficient for this purpose, there is considerable reason to conclude that Aristotle ultimately relies on *nomos* or convention, in the form of the customary moral ideals of his culture, to furnish him with an account of the moral virtues. According to the characterization of S. Broadie that I quoted in an earlier chapter, Aristotle seems simply to take for granted "a shared commitment to good upbringing in qualities customarily accepted as fundamental human excellences [i.e., virtues or *aretai*]."[53] From the contemporary perspective, such a 'foundation in *nomos*' of the moral virtues leaves Aristotle 'unprotected' from the danger of ethical relativism: if someone were to demand of him some sort of independent grounding of or rational justification for the correctness of his account of the "qualities standardly accepted [by a somewhat idealized Greek culture of the fourth-century B.C.E.] as fundamental human excellences," Aristotle would seem to have little to say by way of reply.

Aquinas does have something more to say, however. And, not surprisingly, it is related to his Christian conception of the universe. At the cosmic level, Aquinas' conception of God as creator, ruler, and preserver of the universe bridges the old Greek antithesis between *physis* (nature) and *nomos* (law, in the sense that presupposes a lawgiver). God's rational design and governance of the universe is conceptualized by Aquinas as a kind of law, eternal law:

> A law is nothing else but a dictate of practical reason emanating from a ruler who governs a perfect [i.e., self-sufficient] community. Now it is evident, granted that the world is ruled by Divine Providence, as was stated in the First Part, that the whole community of the universe is governed by the Divine Reason. Wherefore, the very Idea of the government of things in God the Ruler of the universe, has the nature of law.[54]

"All things," Aquinas says, "partake somewhat of the eternal law, in so far as, namely, from its being imprinted on them, they derive their respective inclinations to their proper acts and ends."[55] In other words, the characteristic ways of existence of *natural* kinds of things, as well as the characteristics (*virtutes*) that makes something a good thing of its kind, are regarded as effects of divine 'legislation'.

In the case of rational beings such as human persons, however, our nature is such that we are to attain to our "proper acts and ends" by the use of (practical) reason. The application of practical reason to this task – that is, our intellectual discernment of what the proper human function or end is, as well as of the virtues that enable us to fulfill that function – is termed 'natural law' by Aquinas:

> Now among all others, the rational creature is subject to Divine providence in the most excellent way, in so far as it partakes of a share of providence, by being provident both for itself and for others. Wherefore it has a share of the Eternal Reason, whereby it has a natural inclination to its proper act and end: and this participation of the eternal law in the rational creature is called the natural law.[56]

According to Aquinas there is a sort of hierarchy of ends to which human beings are naturally inclined. Natural law enjoins what promotes those ends and forbids what is detrimental to them. But it also belongs to practical reason, and thus to natural law, to prioritize these ends. Aquinas gives a general but rather extensive account of this hierarchy in a section of the *Summa Theologica* that has come to be referred to as the "Treatise on Law":

> Wherefore, according to the order of natural inclinations, is the order of precepts of the natural law. Because in man there is first of all an inclination to good in accordance with the nature that he has in common with all substances: inasmuch as every substance seeks the preservation of its own being, according to its nature: and by reason of this inclination, whatever is a means of preserving human life, and of warding off its obstacles, belongs to the natural law. Secondly, there is in man an inclination to things that pertain to him more specially, according to that nature which he has in common with other animals: and in virtue of this inclination, those things are said to belong to the natural law, which nature has taught to all animals, such as sexual intercourse, education of offspring and so forth. Thirdly, there is in man an inclination to good, according to the nature of his reason, which nature is proper to him: thus man has a natural inclination to know the truth about God, and to live in society: and in this respect, whatever pertains to this inclination belongs to the

natural law; for instance, to shun ignorance, to avoid offending those among whom one has to live, and other such things regarding the above inclination.[57]

Aquinas' claim is that, in case of conflict, the latter, more specific ends generally take precedence over the former, more general ones. But the general point to be emphasized here is that, for Aquinas, the virtues or qualities customarily accepted as fundamental human excellences are not dependent upon the *nomos* – the mores, customs, or conventions – of any particular culture, community, or *polis*. Rather, the *nomos* or law that establishes them as virtues is the eternal law of the Creator, a 'law' that establishes the objective natures or functions of all natural kinds of things in the universe and that is thus equivalent to *physis*.

Let us now return to the first and most perhaps significant point of departure of Aquinas from Aristotle: the fact that, as a Christian, Aquinas cannot accept as the sum and substance of normative anthropology Aristotle's naturalistic account of the human function or ultimate end, which of course also serves as Aristotle's account of *eudaimonia* or happiness. The question, again, is how Aquinas manages to accommodate the Aristotelian normative anthropology with the extravagant Christian normative anthropology, which we encountered in our discussion of the New Testament, St. Paul, and St. Augustine. The answer, in brief, is that Aquinas sees the *ultimate* human function or end, and *perfect* happiness, as transcending the Aristotelian naturalistic account of the human function and of human happiness but also as being continuous with that natural function. The details of this answer, however, are more complicated.

Aquinas distinguishes perfect from imperfect human happiness. The latter, which is described by him as a "certain participation of happiness," can be had in this mortal life:

> but perfect and true happiness cannot be had in this life. This may be seen from a twofold consideration.
>
> First, from the general notion of happiness. For since happiness is a perfect and sufficient good, it excludes every evil, and fulfils every desire. But in this life every evil cannot be excluded. For this present life is subject to many unavoidable evils; to ignorance on the part of the intellect, to inordinate affection on the part of the appetite, and to many penal ties on the part of the body; as Augustine sets forth in *De Civ. Dei* xix. 4. Likewise neither can the desire for good be satiated in this life. For man naturally desires

the good, which he has, to be abiding. Now the goods of the present life pass away; since life itself passes away.[58]

Following Aristotle, Aquinas holds that the imperfect happiness attainable in this life is instantiated by the act of knowing ('contemplation') and the 'active life' of *eupraxia*, which he tends to conceive (as Aristotle sometimes does) as behavior in conformity with the moral virtues. Aquinas' conception of imperfect happiness is largely naturalistic in the expected, Aristotelian way. Thus, the sort of knowledge attainable by our natural powers, which finds expression in the "speculative sciences," "cannot extend further than knowledge of sensibles can lead,"[59] and always involves the body with properly functioning sense organs as the supplier of the corporeal 'phantasms' (sense images) necessary for even the most abstruse knowledge. Also, for the sort of imperfect happiness identified with *eupraxia*, the active life of behavior in conformity with the moral virtues, the right sort of social context is necessary. This context typically includes, for example, appropriate "external goods" (for example, sufficient wealth, health, social position) and a "community of friends" (*societas amicorum*).[60] It is in the fulfillment of these *natural* ends that we find imperfect happiness.

Perfect happiness, which "can consist in nothing else than the vision of the Divine Essence,"[61] and which is achievable only in heaven subsequent to biological death, is viewed by Aquinas as the perfection of the intellectual component of the human function. But there is an aspect of this intellectual experience of the 'Beatific Vision' that also perfects the social component of the human function. The contemplation of God (and of all truth through God) is not a 'cold' or 'disinterested' intellectual experience. Rather, the relationship thus established with God (and with the saints and other members of the heavenly kingdom of God) represents the perfect satisfaction of the will, which yields an attendant "delight" (*delectatio*), which "is caused by the appetite being at rest in the good attained. Wherefore, since happiness is nothing else but the attainment of the Sovereign Good, it cannot be without concomitant delight."[62] While we can attain, to varying degrees and as circumstances admit, to happiness by our natural powers (in particular, the natural moral and intellectual virtues), attaining the perfect happiness of the Beatific Vision is beyond our natural powers and requires the direct assistance of God's grace – particularly in the form of "infused virtues," of which the three so-called theological virtues of faith, hope, and love (or charity) are preeminent.

Imperfect happiness is instantiated by the fulfillment or perfection of our human nature, while perfect happiness is found in the fulfillment of our human praeternature. In other words, the continuity between imperfect and perfect happiness represents the marriage of an essentially Aristotelian normative anthropology with the extravagant Christian normative anthropology to which Aquinas remains fully committed. However, it is arguable that the continuity between nature and praeternature is not seamless; consequently, the marriage of the two normative anthropologies is perhaps not a perfect union. The moral virtues are, in general, those capacities or character traits that enable human persons to perform well the social component of our function – that is, those traits that enable us to perfect the social aspect of our nature. But it seems that the sort of 'social functioning' that is part of the mortal, biological life of human persons is very much tied to the contingencies of that mortal, biological life and, consequently, is quite different from whatever might count as the social aspect of our praeternatural end, the eternal contemplation of God in the Beatific Vision. Consequently, it is not obvious how many of the moral virtues that contribute to our mortal social functioning in fairly transparent ways would count as 'virtues' when they are referred to whatever is social about our praeternatural end. To consider several examples, the virtues of courage or fortitude and of temperance no doubt contribute much to our normal, mortal functioning. But would they fulfill any analogous rôle for us once we have achieved the Beatific Vision of heaven?

Aquinas is himself not unaware of this problem and sometimes has to admit that some of the natural moral virtues have, at most, analogous states that count as virtues once we attain our heavenly end. He also maintains that, even if we confine our attention to this mortal life, the moral virtues sometimes function differently (in fact, are *different virtues*) when referred to our natural ends attainable in this life and when referred to our praeternatural end attainable only in the life to come. Aquinas holds that it is not only the theological virtues of faith, hope, and charity that are infused but also that the moral virtues *may* be infused (as opposed to acquired naturally by training and 'habituation'). It seems that it is primarily the moral virtues – or the forms of moral virtues – as directed toward the fulfillment of our praeternatural end that he thinks of as infused. For example, with respect to the virtue of temperance Aquinas writes:

> now it is evident that the mean that is appointed in such like concupiscences [roughly, any sort of desire or passion in which the agent is attracted toward an object] according to the rule of

human reason, is seen under a different aspect from the mean which is fixed according to the Divine rule. For instance, in the consumption of food, the mean [in which temperance lies] fixed by human reason is that food should not harm the health of the body, nor hinder the use of reason; whereas, according to the Divine rule, it behooves man [as a matter of temperance] to *chastise his body, and bring it into subjection* (1 Cor. ix. 27), by abstinence in food, drink and the like. It is therefore evident that infused and acquired temperance differ in species; and the same applies to the other virtues.[63]

The latter, more rigorous form of temperance is directly relevant to attaining our praeternatural end and is thus the more perfect form of the virtue. But that fact does not entail that the 'natural' form of temperance is not a true virtue. Moreover, Aquinas' account of the natural form of temperance does not in any direct and obvious way depend on the extravagant Christian normative anthropology.

We can now understand, I believe, how Aquinas can carve out a sort of space for the secular *polis* – that is, envision a legitimate, 'positive' rôle for political organization in furthering the imperfect happiness that he identifies with the fulfilling of our natural human functions. The state can do very little that could constitute a positive aid to our achieving the perfect happiness that lies in our fulfillment of our praeternatural end; that task falls principally to the Church as the dispenser of the sacraments and minister of what he calls the divine law. But Aquinas' conception of the relation between our natural and our praeternatural end, between perfect and imperfect happiness, leaves plenty of theoretical scope for secular politics. As we shall see in the next section, according to Aquinas' ideal, the human or positive law of the state should concretize and supplement natural law in such a way as to promote the common good of its citizens, where that common good is understood in terms of the promotion of our shared natural ends. In the fulfillment of those natural ends lies our imperfect (but not therefore unimportant) happiness.

The 'parts' of the eternal law: divine, natural, and human law

What Aquinas terms the divine law, which is ministered on earth by the Church, exists because of the existence of the human praeternatural end. Divine law pertains to the sacraments and theology of Christianity and, in general, to what is *particular* to the Christian dispensation with respect to moral and social matters. To quote Aquinas:

It is by law that man is directed how to perform his proper acts in view of his last end. And indeed if man were ordained to no other end than that which is proportionate to his natural faculty, there would be no need for man to have any further direction on the part of his reason, besides the natural law and human law which is derived from it. But since man is ordained to an end of eternal happiness which is inproportionate to man's natural faculty, as stated above, therefore it was necessary that, besides the natural law and the human law, man should be directed to his end by a law given by God.[64]

Aquinas proceeds to state three further reasons for the need of the divine law.

1. Because of the "uncertainty of human judgment, especially on contingent and particular matters, different people form different judgments on human acts; whence also different and contrary [human] laws result." Therefore, so there should be no doubt about what a person "ought to do and what he ought to avoid" with respect to achieving the ultimate human end, "it was necessary for man to be directed by a law given by God."[65]

2. Human laws should be made only with respect to matters of which human persons are competent to judge. However, human beings are not competent to judge "interior movements, which are hidden," – that is mental judgments, motivations, purposes, etc. "Consequently, human law could not sufficiently curb and direct interior acts; and it was necessary for this purpose that a Divine law should supervene."[66]

3. As a practical matter, "human law cannot punish or forbid all evil deeds: since while aiming at doing away with all evils, it would do away with many good things, and would hinder the advance of the common good, which is necessary for human intercourse. In order, therefore, that no evil might remain unforbidden and unpunished, it was necessary for the Divine law to supervene, whereby all sins are forbidden."[67]

My purpose in rehearsing these reasons in some detail is to emphasize what they imply about human law and the political order that is the source of human law. Human law is properly concerned with the external behavior of people. There is an important sense in which the regulation of thoughts is beyond the competence of secular political authority. Moreover, Aquinas recognizes the inherent practical limitations of an attempt to 'legislate morality'. As we shall soon see, Aquinas holds that there are fundamental moral constraints on human law, as well as a fundamental moral rationale for it. However, the essential moral character of human law does not entail that it is practicable to attempt to use the secular state and its human law to enforce *all* moral principles, even some very important ones.

In order to consider Aquinas' conception of the relation of human law (which is now often referred to as 'positive law', a term also used by Aquinas himself) to natural law – and, hence, the sense in which human law is properly a matter of morality – it is necessary first to consider Aquinas' account of law in general. Although his conception of law is complex, Aquinas begins with a formulaic definition: "law is a rule and measure of acts, whereby man is induced to act or is restrained from acting. ... Now the rule and measure of human acts is the reason, which is the first principle of human acts, as is evident from what has been stated above; since it belongs to the reason to direct to the end, which is the first principle in all matters of action."[68] So, it is essential to law to be a principle of practical rationality, that is, a principle directed toward the achieving of some end. The end in question must be the common good, according to Aquinas, who quotes with approval Aristotle's claim (from the *Nicomachean Ethics*, book 5, chapter 1) that "we call those legal matters just, which are adapted to produce and preserve happiness and its parts for the body politic."[69] It thus appears that, for Aquinas, distributive justice essentially involves the promotion of the common good.

Two more conditions apply to law. The first pertains to the author or source of (human) law: "the making of a law belongs either to the whole people or to a public personage who has care of the whole people: since in all other matters the directing of anything to the end concerns him to whom the end belongs."[70] In the same place, Aquinas describes this "public personage" as a "vicegerent for the whole people" (*"aliquis gerens vicem totius multitudinis,"* "someone standing surrogate for the whole multitude"). Aquinas adds that the reason for locating the authority to make law fundamentally in the "whole people" (*totum multitudinis*), and only derivatively in some "vicegerent," is that the law is directed to the common good of the whole people and "in all other matters the directing of anything to the end concerns him to whom the end belongs."[71] Of course, Aquinas holds that, as a *practical* matter, few persons actually have the requisite aptitude for making proper human law. The final remaining condition of some dictate's being a law is the requirement that law be promulgated, since "in order that a law obtain the binding force which is proper to a law, it must needs be applied to the men who have to be ruled by it."[72]

A traditional topic in jurisprudence or the philosophy of law, and hence a topic of some importance in political philosophy as well, is the 'essence of law' – what makes law law. There has perhaps been an historical tendency towards the formulation of a straightforward or simple account of the essential nature of law as, for example, we shall see in Thomas Hobbes' account of the essence of law in 'command', the will of an authoritative law giver. Aquinas, however, begins with his account of the aspects of law that we have considered and proceeds to derive a complex, although rather radical, account of the essence of law – an account that he fully specifies in question 96 of the *Summa Theologica*'s "Treatise on Law." He claims that if human laws "be just, they have the power of binding in conscience, from the eternal law [God's providential design and rule of the entire universe] whence they are derived."[73] But, in order for a human law to be just, it must satisfy three conditions.

1. It must be just "with respect to its end": that is, it should be conducive to the common good of the relevant community (and not, for example, to the "cupidity or vainglory" of the ruler or author of the law).
2. It must be just "with respect to its author": that is, it must be properly promulgated by a person or group of persons who have the authority to do so (and who do not exceed their authority in doing so).
3. It must be just "with respect to form": that is, any burdens that it imposes must be imposed upon those to whom it applies "according to an equality of proportion."

Aquinas goes so far as to assert that orders or pronouncements that fail to satisfy any of these conditions are "acts of violence rather than laws" and "do not oblige in conscience." However, with his characteristic recognition of the importance of particular, practical considerations and of the exercise of prudence in political (and moral) matters, Aquinas immediately adds a qualification: a pronouncement that fails to satisfy one of the conditions of being a just law does not oblige in conscience "except perhaps in order to avoid scandal or disturbance, for which cause a man should even yield his right, according to Matth. 5 v. 40, 41: *If a man ... take away thy coat, let go thy cloak also unto him; and whosoever will force thee one mile, go with him other two.*"[74]

The moral and political thought of St. Thomas Aquinas, as well as the moral and political thought of the scholastic tradition that traces its origins to him, is sometimes charged with being excessively rigid and legalistic. From the contemporary perspective, Aquinas' terse and rather dry scholastic form of exposition as well as his frequent use of terms such as 'law' and 'rule' in his discussion of moral and political matters lend some credence to this charge. But, as we have seen, Aquinas has a very broad conception of law, one that can accommodate the contingencies of particular situations and that is not at all at odds with the recognition of the importance of the exercise of prudential judgment in such situations. Consequently, there is nothing 'mechanical' or particularly rigid about Aquinas' conception of the way in which human, positive law should instantiate natural law.

The natural law certainly serves, in Aquinas' view, as an independent and objective moral pattern for making, and as a moral standard for assessing human law. "Consequently every human law has just so much of the nature of law, as it is derived from the law of nature. But if in any point it deflects from the law of nature, it is no longer a law but a perversion of law."[75] However, Aquinas proceeds to distinguish two ways in which human law is 'derived': "first, as a conclusion from premises, secondly by way of determination of certain generalities."[76] The first sort of derivation yields what one might call fundamental moral principles (for example, "murder is not to be done") which should be reflected in human law if it is to count as law. Having divided positive law into *ius gentium* (the law of nations or of people) and *ius civile* (civil law), Aquinas identifies the former with those fundamental but general moral principles derived "as premises" from the natural law: "*e.g.*, just buyings and sellings, and the like, without which men cannot live together, which is the point of the law of nature, since man is by nature a social animal."[77] It is, then, no accident that one finds certain moral principles built into the legal and political practices of a wide variety of peoples. Aquinas perhaps holds a more sanguine view than many contemporary thinkers concerning the breadth and depth of 'cross-cultural' agreement about fundamental moral principles. But he readily admits that, just as in the case of some persons, in some cultures and some peoples knowledge of the more specific but still universally binding moral principles derived as conclusions from the natural law may be blotted out "by evil persuasions ...; or by vicious customs and corrupt habits, as among some men, theft, and even unnatural vices, as the Apostle states (*Rom.* i.), were not esteemed sinful."[78]

The second manner of derivation of human law from natural law, by 'determination', is really more a matter of supplementing and concretizing natural law than deriving something from it. It includes a variety of ways that human law can contribute to promoting the common good of persons in a community – *specific* means about which the natural law is silent, so to speak. Thus, to take one of Aquinas' examples, it contributes to the common good (and, in that broad sense, pertains to the law of nature) "that the evildoer should be punished; but that he be punished in this or that way, is a determination of the law of nature."[79] To consider another (anachronistic) example, it no doubt contributes to the common good that persons traveling in one direction on a highway should generally keep to one side, persons traveling in the opposite direction generally on the other. But it is obvious that natural law is silent about the details, which need to be worked out 'by determination' of human law. It is particularly with respect to *ius civile* in this sense that Aquinas emphasizes the importance of custom, which "has the force of law, abolishes law, and is the interpreter of law."[80]

Thus far, I have said little about the specifics of the common good to which human law must be directed if it is to be law. Of course, it is virtually a matter of definition that the common good is interpreted by Aquinas in terms of what promotes the natural aspect of the objective human function or good – i.e., imperfect happiness. It is also to be noted that satisfaction of individual persons' preferences or desires is not to be equated with the promotion of the human function or imperfect happiness in this sense. The degree to which a person's preferences and desires correspond with what promotes natural but imperfect happiness depends on the degree of that person's virtuousness or viciousness. However, when we turn to the more specific content of Aquinas' conception of the common good that it is the business of human law and the state to secure, I believe that we find a 'thicker', more inclusive notion of this common good and a 'thinner', less inclusive notion.

The thicker notion is the more theoretical conception of the common good: "But law, as stated above, is ordained to the common good. Wherefore there is no virtue whose acts cannot be prescribed by the law."[81] And, in contrast to Augustine, Aquinas maintains that the purpose of human law is not just to restrain those who are "depraved, and prone to vice" in order that they might "leave others in peace," but also:

> that they themselves, by being habituated in this way [i.e., by being restrained from evil by force and fear], might be brought to do willingly what hitherto they did from fear, and thus become virtuous. Now this kind of training, which compels through fear of punishment, is the discipline of laws. Therefore, in order that man might have peace and virtue, it was necessary for laws to be framed.[82]

Note that Aquinas says not just "that man might have peace", as Augustine did, but "that man might have peace *and virtue.*" So, from a theoretical perspective, nothing that involves the inculcation of virtue in citizens (where, of course, virtue is what is necessary for the attainment of the natural aspect of the common good of 'excellent human functioning' and, thus, imperfect happiness) is off limits – an inappropriate subject for legislation or inappropriate activity of the state. The natural *acquired* moral virtues are, Aquinas claims, caused by practice or habit (*assuetudo*), which is something to which human law and political authority can certainly contribute. But such training, according to Aquinas' theology, can favorably *dispose* an agent to the reception of even the infused virtues (whose immediate cause, of course, is God's grace).[83] So, it is theoretically possible that political authority and human law might have a rôle in 'preparing the seed bed', so to speak – that is, in providing the sort of social climate most conducive to the acquisition of the infused moral virtues.

On the other hand, Aquinas' thinner conception of the common good is much more pragmatic, prudential, and concrete – and also, one might add, more Augustinian. While, *in theory*, nothing is off limits to human law, from a prudential perspective, it is proper that "human law does not prescribe concerning all the acts of every virtue." Since it is concerned with the *common* good of its citizens, it should be framed with a view to the capacities of all citizens, the more vicious as well as the more virtuous. Consequently, it is appropriate that it be especially directed to "certain things pertaining to good order (*ad bonam disciplinam*), whereby the citizens are directed in the upholding of the common good of justice and peace."[84] In a similar vein, Aquinas quotes with approval a comment of Isidore[85] that "law should be possible both according to nature, and according to the customs of the country," adding that "many things are permissible to men not perfect in virtue, which would be intolerable in a virtuous man."[86] The conclusion concerning human law that he draws is the following:

> Now human law is framed for a number of human beings, the majority of whom are not perfect in virtue. Wherefore human laws do not forbid all vices, from which the virtuous abstain, but only the more grievous vices, from which it is possible for the majority to abstain; and chiefly those that are to the hurt of others, without the prohibition of which human society could not be maintained: thus human law prohibits murder, theft and suchlike.[87]

So, Aquinas' thin conception of the common good provides some basis for a limitation of the legitimate concerns of the state and legitimate matters of legislation. And in the preceding passage's emphasis on legal concern with vices "that are to the hurt of others," a contemporary reader may see an anticipation of what is often referred to as the 'harm principle'. This principle is invoked by some contemporary political theories in an attempt to distinguish between what such a theory takes to be the illegitimate paternalistic enterprise of promoting the 'private' virtues of its citizens and the legitimate political task of protecting citizens from harmful behavior of other citizens. However, insofar as Aquinas is attracted to such a principle – or to similar limitations on the concerns of human law and the state – his rationale is not a theoretical one (developed, for example, in terms of rights that citizens might invoke against the state). Rather, it is a corollary of his recognition of the practical limitations of politics. This pragmatic cast to Aquinas' political theory is perhaps even more manifest in his writings about procedures and forms of government.

Political forms, procedures, and other particulars

With respect to procedures and forms of government, the fundamental theoretical principle of Aquinas is that the actions of any legitimate government should be directed toward the common good. His notion of a common good comprises those various means, which are especially achievable through cooperative behavior, that contribute to individual citizens' fulfilling the common human function – that is, achieving the ultimate human end. From what we have already learned about Aquinas' conception of the human end or function, it might be inferred that *secular* political structures should be directed toward fulfilling the *natural* aspect of the human function, and thereby promoting the imperfect happiness of its citizens. In a sense, this is so. But Aquinas also does not hesitate to maintain that, with respect to whatever pertains to the *praeternatural* end of its citizens, a king or other secular ruler "ought to be subject to the divine government administered by the office of [Christian] priesthood."[88] Now, the secular state cannot provide *direct* aid to citizens in attaining their praeternatural end. But it can aid them in attaining their natural end by helping to provide favorable and reasonably just material conditions of life, by suppressing at least the worst vices, and by inculcating, at least to some degree, the moral virtues. While such aids may not be strictly necessary for the attainment of our praeternatural end, they provide what may at least be *some* instrumental assistance in doing so:

Therefore, since the beatitude of heaven is the end of that virtuous life which we live at present, it pertains to the king's office to pro-mote the good life of the multitude in such a way as to make it suitable for the attainment of heavenly happiness, that is to say, he should command those things which lead to the happiness of heaven and, as far as possible, forbid the contrary.[89]

Aquinas proceeds to elaborate on this theme. In order for an individual person "to lead a good life," he says, the first and most important thing "is to act in a virtuous manner (for virtue is that by which one lives well); the second, which is secondary and instrumental, is a sufficiency of those bodily goods whose use is necessary for virtuous life."[90] He adds that,

therefore, to establish virtuous living in a multitude three things are necessary. First of all, that the multitude be established in the unity of peace. Second that the multitude thus united in the bond of peace be directed to acting well [i.e., acting virtuously]. ... In the third place, it is necessary that there be at hand a sufficient supply of things required for proper living, procured by the ruler's efforts.[91]

Thus, the material welfare of its citizens is certainly a legitimate concern of the secular state. However, a more important concern of the state is inculcating the natural virtues in the citizens. Recollect that, according to Aquinas' version of the functionalistic conception of the virtues, they are those traits of character that allow their possessor to fulfill the nat-ural human function and thereby achieve imperfect happiness. However, since Aquinas believes that there is considerable continuity between the natural and praeternatural human functions or ends, the secular state also has a legitimate concern in promoting a moral and social climate that may prove of instrumental value in its citizens' attaining their praeternatural end.

Nonetheless, political authority or 'dominion' (*dominium*) does not ordinarily devolve upon those who possess it directly from the hands of God or through the mediation of the Church. Rather, Aquinas main-tains, it is a matter of *ius gentium*, that part of virtually universally shared human law and custom that reflects general (and often rather indeterminate) principles of natural law.[92] In other words, it is a princi-ple of common law reflected in the customary practice of all peoples that "there exist among men some means by which the group may be governed. For where there are many men together and each one is looking after his own interest, the multitude would be broken up and scattered unless there were also an agency to take care of what appertains to the commonweal."[93] That agency, he adds, must be "something which impels toward the common good of the many, over and above that which impels toward the particular good of each individual."[94]

While the existence of a government with authority sufficient to accomplish or fulfill its rôle is enjoined by natural law, the particular forms and procedures in which this is accomplished is a matter of *determination* by human law and custom – that is, is a matter of the supplementation of natural law. Here, Aquinas is sensitive to the influence of contingencies. His several discussions are also influenced by a variety of motivations. One of his enterprises in the *De Regno* is the common ancient and medieval one of discussing the various 'regimes' or forms of government, assessing their respective merits and faults, and providing an account of what causes one such regime to transform into another. Following the tradition, Aquinas' discussion is partly descriptive and empirical and partly normative and hortatory. Also, in certain places, he is obviously engaged in justifying the legitimacy of the Church's – especially the Pope's – exercise of temporal or secular authority, as well as of spiritual authority.

Following Aristotle rather closely, Aquinas distinguishes regimes in terms of the number of persons who actively participate in governing: a single person, a minority, or a majority (or 'whole people'). He also distinguishes between regimes that promote the common good and those that promote only what the rulers regard as their private good. Those that promote the common good (monarchy or kingship, aristocracy, and what, following Aristotle, Aquinas calls *politia*) are just; those that promote the perceived private good of the ruler or rulers (tyranny, oligarchy, and democracy) are unjust. At a general, theoretical level, Aquinas endorses monarchy as the best regime. Because of the concentration of authority in one person, that person can most effectively maintain unity and direct society toward the common good. "Therefore, the rule of one man is more useful (*utilius*) than the rule of many."[95] In the optimal (theoretical) case, the king must be a person of preeminent virtue possessing, in particular, the fundamental political virtue of prudence or practical wisdom to an extraordinary degree. However, Aquinas readily admits that rule by one person that is directed by that person's conception, which is usually a misconception, of his or her own private good (as opposed to the common good) is tyranny, which is the theoretically worst form of regime.

Aquinas recognizes just forms of rule by a minority (aristocracy) and of rule by the majority – that is, rule by the 'people' or 'multitude' (*politia*). However, he believes that what we might call the motivating rationale of rule by a minority is usually class-based economic egoism rather than the promotion of the common good. Similarly, he believes that the motivating rationale of rule 'by the people' (multitude) is typically a desire for individual freedom of some sort rather than the promotion of the common good. In the state, the politically most important form of liberty is self-government. Such a form of government can be just – that is, directed toward the common good – and can even work at the practical level if the whole body of citizens is sufficiently virtuous; but this is a very rare occurrence. "There are more," Aquinas says, "who follow the inclinations of the sensuous nature than who follow the order of reason."[96] Quoting Augustine, he comments that,

> if the people have a sense of moderation and responsibility, and are most careful guardians of the common weal, it is right to enact a law allowing such a people to choose their own magistrates for the government of the commonwealth. But if, as time goes on, the same people become so corrupt as to sell their votes, and entrust the government to scoundrels and criminals, the power of appointing their public officials is rightly forfeit to such a people, and the choice devolves to a few good men.[97]

The liberty involved in self-government introduces a form of political equality that, Aquinas thinks, is easily transformed into belief in the desirability of 'absolute' equality, or at least the desirability of equality in many other respects.[98] Aquinas believes that this is an error but, as we shall see, certain later political theories thought otherwise.

Aquinas is certainly aware of practical considerations that affect even his theoretically favored regime of monarchy. For example, he suggests that "it frequently happens that men living under a king strive more sluggishly for the common good, inasmuch as they consider [albeit *wrongly* consider, in a just monarchy] that what they devote to the common good, they do not confer upon themselves but upon another, under whose power they see the common goods to be."[99] Also, as a psychological matter, it not infrequently happens that "small services exacted by kings weigh more heavily than great burdens imposed by the community of citizens."[100] And the resentment on the part of the many who do not share in political decision-making in a monarchy, however just and efficient that monarchy may be, can be cause of resentment and dissension.[101] With Aquinas' emphasis on the proper influence of contingent circumstances on prudential judgments concerning concrete political matters, such consideration might weigh decisively against monarchical rule in some circumstances.

While it is certainly true, as D. Bigongiari claims, that Aquinas holds that "no state can possess absolute power" and that "there is no room in [his] theory of government for a lay world emperor,"[102] Aquinas readily admits various sorts of prudential qualification and pragmatic compromise to his more abstract theory of the limitations of political authority. The abstract theory is particularly apparent in his account of the virtue of obedience. Obedience to God, "whereby we contemn our own will for God's sake, is more praiseworthy than the other moral virtues, which contemn other [lesser] goods for the sake of God."[103]

However, with respect to obedience to other persons, Aquinas maintains the principle that a person is not bound to obey a superior (i) if that superior should command something contrary to the command of a *higher* authority or (ii) if the command pertains to a matter with respect to which one is not bound to obey the authority in question. In particular, he concludes that "in matters touching the internal movement of the will man is not bound to obey his fellow-man, but God alone."[104] He then proceeds to draw some further distinctions:

> nevertheless man is bound to obey his fellow-man [who has the appropriate authority over him] in things that have to be done externally by means of the body: and yet, since by nature all men are equal, he is not bound to obey another man in matters touching the nature of the body, for instance in those relating to the support of his body or the begetting of children. Wherefore servants are not bound to obey their masters, nor children their parents, in the question of contracting marriage or remaining in the state of virginity or the like. But in matters concerning the disposal of actions and human affairs, a subject is bound to obey his superior within the sphere of his authority.[105]

This passage obviously could serve as the basis for arguments (which in fact have been made in Thomistic circles) that the state has no competence to regulate matters such as marrying or begetting children. What appears to be the most important premise used to derive this conclusion, that of the natural equality of human persons, is invoked almost in passing; and its relevance to legitimate restrictions of obedience is not all that clear. So far as I can determine, the nature of the relation between equality and illicit restrictions on autonomy – a relation that was to become so important in later political theory – is here explicated in the following way. The natural equality of human beings yields significant obligations concerning the respect that should be accorded to the autonomy of the person's soul (particularly, the will and 'interior life') and 'essential bodily nature and functions'. However, it yields significantly fewer (or less important) obligations concerning the respect that should be accorded to the autonomy of a person's actions – those "things that have to be done externally by means of the body."

The distinction between such actions and the 'essential bodily nature and functions' is not a clear-cut one. Some of what Aquinas takes to be the consequences of the distinction seem clear enough. For example, state restrictions on the number of children parents are permitted to bear would certainly be illicit. But other issues are far from clear. For example, would political intervention (of the sort envisioned in Plato's *Republic*, for example) in the choice of occupations or professions of citizens constitute a theoretically legitimate regulation of external actions or a theoretically illicit interference with the means by which one 'supports' one's body?

Aquinas' conception of the source of political authority in *ius gentium* also has theoretical consequences about the limitation of religious authority with respect to political issues. In answer to the question of whether unbelievers may have legitimate political authority over the faithful (that is, Christians), Aquinas maintains that since "dominion and authority are institutions of human law, while the distinction between faithful and unbelievers arises from the Divine law" and since the "Divine law, which is the law of grace, does not do away with the human law, which is the law of reason," it follows that the "distinction between faithful and unbelievers, considered in itself, does not do away with the dominion and authority of unbelievers over the faithful."[106]

However, Aquinas introduces significant qualifications to this 'purely theoretical' proposition. First of all, he makes a distinction between political authority of unbelievers over Christians that is "already in force," which he is generally willing to accept on the foregoing theoretical basis. But he is not willing to allow such authority to be established anew "for the first time" because of what seems to be a pragmatic reason: doing so "would provoke scandal and endanger the faith."[107]

Moreover (evidently appealing to the idea of a hierarchy of authority found, for example, in his discussion of obedience), he argues that the "right of dominion or authority can be justly done away with by the sentence or ordination of the Church who has the authority of God."[108] In this discussion, he approves the general practice of the Church in exercising authority over unbelievers only in those locations where the

Church possesses temporal authority over them but not in the case of "unbelievers who are not subject to her or her members in temporal matters." Yet, he claims that the Church has the *right* to exercise such authority over nonbelievers who do not happen to be her temporal dependents. Following a similar line of thought, Aquinas argues that the Church (in particular, the Pope) has the authority to absolve citizens from their duty of allegiance to a ruler who becomes a heretic or an apostate from the faith.[109] But, in this instance, he maintains that "it is not within the competency of the Church to punish unbelief in those who have never received the faith."[110] To most contemporary readers, all of this will seem quite anachronistic – and perhaps either disturbing or quaintly charming. From a theoretical perspective, it may also seem rather messy. I reflect on the messiness of Aquinas' political thought in the next and concluding section of this chapter.

Aquinas' political philosophy: some concluding observations

Particularly if one is committed to doing so, it is possible to find in Aquinas' discussion of political matters many doctrines that were to assume positions of fundamental importance in later secular political theories. I have commented on some of these in the preceding discussion. Here is a partial list: (a) a doctrine of natural equality; (b) the fundamental political importance of something like the harm principle; (c) a theoretical doctrine that carves out separate spheres of authority for church (divine law) and state (human law); (d) a conception of limited political authority and a conception of law that entails that law – in order to *be* law – must be directed toward the common good with just distribution of the burdens it imposes; (e) the idea that the source of human law is fundamentally the "whole people" – and only derivatively any "vicegerent" acting for them (since the law is directed to the common good of the whole people and "the directing of anything to the end concerns him to whom the end belongs").[111]

But a contemporary reader may see several problems in Aquinas' invocation of these contemporary-seeming principles. One such supposed problem is that Aquinas often does not seem to accord these principles the emphasis that more contemporary political theory has come to believe that they deserve. He often does not draw what many of us now might regard as the obvious concrete political corollaries of the principles. And he sometimes seems to forget or ignore them altogether (as in his assertion of the Church's right to interfere, in various ways, in affairs of the secular state). A second problem is that Aquinas frequently seems to lack any very clear and systematic way of co-ordinating the application of his principles. The result is that many of his discussions of political issues have an *ad hoc* appearance. They seem to rely on arguments and considerations garnered in a rather unsystematic way from a variety of principles and authorities without any clear indication of why *those* principles and sources should be applicable in that context – rather than some others that might have different consequences.

Do these complaints have force? The answer, I think, depends upon what one expects from a political theory. There has been (perhaps beginning in about the seventeenth century) an increasing tendency to expect a great deal from a political theory. According to such expectations, a political theory should be a theory that is fundamental, in the sense of not dependent upon any particular religious tradition or social or historical contingencies. It should either be freestanding or, at most, a consequence of some secular moral theory, which itself is independent of any particular religious, social, or historical context. And the theory should provide some general account and justification both of political authority, in general, and of some general principle or principles of distributive justice (often formulated in terms of 'rights'). A further assumption is often made that, in providing its account and justification of political authority and of distributive justice, the theory will yield some corollaries about a range of morally acceptable and unacceptable political institutions and procedures.

It seems evident that Aquinas had a much less ambitious conception of 'political theory' and, consequently, few such expectations. As a thirteenth-century Aristotelian intellectual, he certainly was prepared to take to heart Aristotle's warning about not expecting more precision in a particular branch of knowledge than its subject matter permits. He fully recognizes the central importance of the particular and the contingent – that is, of special circumstances often not easily assimilated into a simple and elegant theoretical framework – not only in politics but in our study of politics. This naturally leads to less of a concern on Aquinas' part than that found in many later political theorists in constructing a political theory consisting of systematically ordered definitive doctrinal principles. As a thirteenth-century Christian intellectual – one willing to accord a more positive significance to the secular political realm than was Augustine – Aquinas nonetheless agrees with Augustine in his conviction that the place to look for ultimate answers is not in *any* sort of secular theory but in the Christian faith.

When we turn, in the next chapter, to contractarian political theory of the seventeenth century, we find a conception of political theory that has not entirely jettisoned the conceptual mechanism of Plato and Aristotle, of Augustine and Aquinas. Yet, seventeenth-century contractarianism fits much more closely common contemporary ideas of what political theory ought to be and ought to do – and how it should do it.

7

Hobbes and Locke: Seventeenth-Century Contractarianism

By the seventeenth century, the thirteenth-century European world of St. Thomas Aquinas was long gone. Medieval feudalism, with its complicated and often uneasy relations among local princelings (owing limited allegiance to regional monarchs), trans-European religious orders, and the catholic or 'universal' Roman Church, had begun to give way to the rise of powerful nation-states with more centralized, autocratic governments. Exploration of the 'new world' of the western hemisphere and exploitation of its natural resources combined with increasing trade and mercantilism to form the foundation of a European bourgeoisie that impinged on the social and political domain of old, landed aristocracies. The formal 'catholic' unity of Western Christianity had been fragmented by the Protestant reformation of the sixteenth century. The heliocentric cosmology, which was introduced in the sixteenth century by Copernicus, and which was championed and developed in the early seventeenth century by Galileo and Kepler, achieved a position of intellectual dominance by the middle of the century. More generally, the seventeenth century (which is often characterized as the century of the scientific revolution) saw the development of a new natural philosophy (which we would now call natural science) that tended to be mechanistic and typically involved the repudiation of what was taken to be the outmoded Aristotelian idea of an orderly hierarchy of natural kinds or species of things, each characterized by its distinctive essence. Natural philosophy came to be regarded as fundamentally a matter of physics, which is concerned with the behavior of matter (*any* kind of matter) in motion. And, depending upon the particular natural philosopher consulted, there either is or is not a separate realm of 'thinking' (immaterial or spiritual) substances. If such a self-contained realm of thinking or spiritual substances exists, then it apparently somehow, rather mysteriously interacts with the realm of intrinsically inert matter.

It was virtually inevitable that new forms of political theory – new ways of conceptualizing the nature of political authority and of its relation to human beings – would develop in such an altered world. And it was not unusual for such new forms of political theorizing to present themselves as radically new – without significant pedigree in the older, classical tradition of political philosophy that we have thus far considered. Such characterizations were exaggerated: the new forms of political theory of the seventeenth century quite clearly have their roots in the classical tradition of political philosophy. But they do develop that tradition in novel ways; and in so doing they produce a very different kind of political theory. Before I turn to details of the political thought of two preeminent proponents of the contractarian tradition of the seventeenth century, Thomas Hobbes and John Locke, I wish to consider in a more general way some of the more significant changes in political philosophy that were introduced by that contractarian tradition.

Contractarianism itself is not a seventeenth-century novelty, of course. We saw, in Chapter 2 of this book, the character Glaucon in Plato's *Republic* setting forth a contractarian political theory: the foundation of the *polis* – or, more broadly, of political organization and positive law – lies in some form of *contract*, mutual agreement, or promise that certain human persons explicitly or implicitly make with one another. This sort of general theoretical approach to politics brings with it a number of fundamental presuppositions and consequences.

Perhaps the most fundamental of these is that political organization is a matter of *nomos* rather than *physis*, to use the classical Greek terminology that we have been employing. That is, political organization is regarded as a matter of convention or agreement and, in that sense, as something that is a result of human artifice rather than a straightforward consequence of human biology (or of human nature, more broadly). Unlike the instinctual patterns of association of the so-called social animals, patterns of political association of human beings are a matter of choice. According to this perspective, it then makes sense to conceive of human existence as it would be *without* any political organization – that is, as it would have been had human beings 'opted out' altogether with respect to political organization. It is significant that such a conceptual possibility came to be designated, within the contractarian tradition, as the 'state of nature'.

Of course, the picture of a state of nature in which a social contract of some sort brings about the political organization of previously apolitical human beings lends itself easily to a sort of armchair, historical interpretation: the contractarian theorist may be interpreted as giving an *a priori* account of a process of human social evolution. Seventeenth- and eighteenth-century proponents of contractarianism do sometimes make their theories sound historical in this way. This factual, historical appearance very much fits the spirit of the seventeenth century. Is it not more scientific to talk about empirical biology and psychology and about historical epochs and events than to speculate about abstractions such as the classical human function or end, which, as we saw, has a normative element that prevents its identification with such facts? This largely specious appearance of 'confining oneself to the facts', important as it may have been to the contractarian tradition from a rhetorical point of view, was not essential to that tradition. Even its early adherents by and large realized that issues concerning the actual historical existence of a state of nature or of the 'event' of a social contract were not essentially important issues. In its essence, contractarianism is an *analytic* conceptual device. What, for example, would human existence be like in the absence of political organization (irrespective of whether such a state has ever been historically instantiated)? And what would constitute legitimate political authority other than the rational endorsement of all citizens (irrespective of whether such endorsement ever explicitly occurs)?

A second important characteristic of contractarianism is that it shifts the emphasis of political theory from the faculty of practical rationality to that of the will. In the classical tradition of political philosophy represented, for example, by Aristotle and Aquinas, law is first and foremost a dictate of practical reason. The job, so to speak, of positive law – and of those political structures that determine and implement it – is to direct human beings toward the common good, the content of which is determined by the objective human function or end. So, from this perspective, it is essential to positive law that it be a rationally determined means for furthering the (objective) good or end of human persons. Although seventeenth-century contractarians such as Hobbes and Locke do not entirely dispense with the connection between law and practical rationality, they focus on the idea that command and consent (which are functions of the will or volitional faculty) are essential to the *legitimacy* of law and the political order. In other words, it is either command or consent (or both) that distinguish what has the moral authority of law from what is merely 'good advice' or prudential counsel.

The shift in emphasis from practical reason to the will seems to be related to a distinctive feature of much modern and contemporary political theory that originates in the contractarian tradition: the privileging in political philosophy of the idea of *agreement* (in a broad sense that can include promises, contracts, and even tacit consent). In at least some varieties of contractarianism, a corollary is the political employment of a paradigm of commutative justice, rather than the paradigm of distributive justice. Recall that these concepts, introduced earlier in this book, are the following: commutative justice is a matter of the fairness of private transactions among citizens; distributive justice is a matter of the fairness of the distribution of the benefits and burdens of social cooperation. The classical assumption, as we saw, was that the fairness of distributive justice is not necessarily a matter of *equal* distribution, but rather a matter of distribution *in proportion* to criteria of desert (or merit or worth) of some sort. So achieving distributive justice will certainly involve the exercise of practical rationality. However, in many (although not necessarily all) cases, it seems quite plausible to identify the instantiation of commutative justice with that to which the parties involved freely consent. It may thus seem that issues of commutative justice (determined by that to which persons are willing to assent) are relatively more straightforward and less controversial than issues of distributive justice (determined by criteria that may well be both difficult to ascertain and controversial). This, as we shall see, is essentially the line of Thomas Hobbes. He is more explicit than later theorists; but the tendency to interpret fairness, in the political sense, essentially in terms of commutative justice remains an important element of much later political thought.

Finally, it is with contractarianism that the idea of human or natural rights begins to achieve the prominence that it still enjoys in much contemporary political theory (as well as in virtually all contemporary popular political rhetoric). Rights in this sense are *not* thought to belong to persons as a result of positive legislation or the largesse of any concrete political organization. Rather, they belong to human persons in some deeper and more fundamental sense. According to the older classical tradition of political philosophy, the rôle of political structures was to implement the natural *law* – that is, to promote the common good of its citizens. The promotion of the common good was understood as the promotion of social means (in accord with the dictates of prudence) that are conducive to those citizens' fulfilling the objective human function or achieving the objective human good. In other words, promotion of the citizens' good was conceived in terms of the promotion of their human goodness, where 'human goodness' is cashed out in terms of the functionalistic idea of 'fulfilling the human function well' or 'living the best sort of human life'.

It is arguable that the notion of natural or human *rights*, insofar as that notion had any place at all in the classical tradition of political philosophy, was intimately tied to the notion of natural law: a person possesses natural rights only as a necessary means of fulfilling the obligations imposed by natural law, obligations that are directed toward the perfection of his or her nature (i.e., the fulfilling of the human *ergon* or function). Eventually, natural rights came to be seen as detached from this source and as constituting a 'freestanding' and fundamental moral constraint on political organization. The fundamental rôle of the state, in other words, came to be regarded as the securing of the natural rights of its citizens – as opposed to the implementing of the natural law so as to further the citizens' fulfilling an objective human function. The seventeenth-century contractarian tradition constitutes an important chapter in the transition from the one paradigm to the other.

Thomas Hobbes: natural law simplified and modernized

The English philosopher Thomas Hobbes (1588–1679) lived through a turbulent period of social and political change. As a young man, he saw the first Stuart monarch of England James I (who had been James VI of Scotland) succeed the last Tudor, the aged Elizabeth I. In his late middle age, the English civil war resulted in the death of the second Stuart king, Charles I, and the temporary displacement of the Stuart monarchy by the Commonwealth, which was eventually headed (until his death in 1658) by the 'Lord Protector', Oliver Cromwell. Hobbes accompanied many royalists into exile and even served for a time as the mathematics tutor to the future Stuart monarch, Charles II. But, because he was anxious concerning the enmity of various exiled royalists and members of the English and French clergy, he returned to England in 1651 (at the age of sixty-three) and made his peace with the Commonwealth government by taking an oath of loyalty, the

Engagement Oath. It is somewhat surprising (though fortunate for Hobbes) that when the Stuart dynasty was restored under Charles II in 1660, Hobbes was welcomed at court by his former pupil, who took a characteristically perverse delight in the displeasure that Hobbes' presence caused to a significant number of courtiers, clerical and lay. At Hobbes' appearance he would announce, "Here comes the bear to be baited."

In the last decade of Hobbes' life, he published translations of Homer's epic poems the *Odyssey* and the *Iliad* because, he said, he had nothing better to do. He also composed a Latin autobiography, in verse, in which appears his famous quip about his birth. He had been born in 1588, the year of the threatened invasion of England by the Spanish Armada; and his mother, Hobbes claimed, was so frightened by the rumors that she gave birth prematurely, "to twins, myself and fear."[1] As Hobbes was no doubt well aware, this story nicely encapsulates what was to become the dominant and most famous theme of his political philosophy: the preeminent danger of social turmoil and anarchy, with political absolutism – the creation out of disparate human persons of a single, artificial political person (the commonwealth or "Leviathan"), whose will is embodied in a supremely powerful governmental authority (the 'sovereign') – as the only workable remedy for this danger. As simple and straightforward as this theme is, Hobbes develops an extremely powerful and elegant theory to support it.

Natural law, natural rights, and the human function

Like earlier theorists belonging to the classical tradition of political philosophy, Hobbes rests his political philosophy squarely on his conception of an objective human nature or function. However, he viewed his conception of human nature as being grounded not in the old Aristotelian metaphysical concept of an ideal human essence (which was only loosely connected to the observable properties and actions of actual human beings) but in readily observable empirical 'facts' about human beings and their behavior. The metaphysics underlying this empirical attitude was a thoroughgoing materialism: the only things that exist, in the true and proper sense of 'exist', are bodies; and the only changes that they undergo, in the true and proper sense of 'change', are changes in position ('local motion'). Moreover, the only true causes are efficient causes, which Hobbes conceives mechanically – in terms of collisions, pushings, and pullings. While Hobbes does not count as a scientist in the contemporary sense of that term, he was certainly plugged into the largely mechanistic natural philosophy or science of the seventeenth century; and his unified system of metaphysics, epistemology (philosophy of knowledge), and rational psychology may be regarded as one of the more radical attempts to undergird and apply that tradition.[2]

It is his rational psychology that is of particular interest to us since it is this part of Hobbes' philosophical system that gives him his conception of a distinctively human nature. As it was for the ancient Sophist Protagoras, so it was for Hobbes that "man is the measure" of good and evil. As he puts it in his *Leviathan*, "whatsoever is the object of any man's appetite or desire, that is it which he for his part calls *good*; and the object of hate and aversion, *evil*; and of his contempt, *vile* and *inconsiderable*. For these words of good, evil, and contemptible are ever used with relation to the person that uses them, there being nothing simply and absolutely so, nor any common rule of good and evil to be taken from the nature of the objects themselves."[3] Hobbes here inverts the classical tradition of Plato, Aristotle, Augustine, and Aquinas, according to which an objective human function (*ergon*), end or good supplies a "common rule of good and evil" for human persons, against which the *actual* appetites and desires of *actual* human beings can be measured. For Hobbes, however, the actual desires (appetites of an attractive variety) of an actual person determine what is *good for that person*, and the actual aversions (appetites of a repulsive variety) determine what is *evil for that person*.

With his typical penchant for systematization and simplification, Hobbes develops a hedonistic interpretation of this doctrine in the *De Cive*: "Now whatsoever seems good, is pleasant, and related either to the senses, or the mind. But all the mind's pleasure is either glory, (or to have a good opinion of oneself), or refers to glory in the end; the rest are sensual, or conducing to sensuality, which may be all comprehended under the word *conveniences*."[4] A bit later in the *De Cive* Hobbes adds that "all pleasure and jollity of mind consists in this, even to get some, with whom comparing, it may find somewhat wherein to triumph and vaunt itself."[5] Whether Hobbes was a psychological egoist in a very strong sense of the term (that is, maintaining that "men *never* act in order to benefit others, or because they believe a certain course of action to be morally right"[6]) is a matter of contemporary scholarly disagreement. However, he clearly asserts that the *ultimate* 'springs of human action' (whatever the force of 'ultimate' might here be)[7] are the passions – the aversion to physical and mental pain and the desire for physical and mental pleasure.

In keeping with his materialism, his analysis of desire is not subtle. What many have regarded as his pessimistic attitude toward human motivation may perhaps partly be understood as reflecting the experience of someone who spent his life as a courtier and retainer in the households of the nobility. And, if Hobbes' professions of Christian belief were sincere (which many have doubted), his rather grim view of human nature can be interpreted as a description of fallen human nature that is not that different from the conceptions of many Protestant reformers.[8] With respect to the desire for physical or sensual pleasures (for "gain" or "conveniences", in his terminology), Hobbes' picture of human nature is essentially the same as that presupposed in Glaucon's contractarian doctrine as found in Plato's *Republic*: the human function or *ergon* is that of unlimitedly acquisitive consumption of satisfactions; the natural human good, goal (*telos*) or *ergon*, is to acquire as many satisfactions as one can. But humans also are motivated by the desire for mental pleasures, which are all ultimately reducible to or are subordinated to what he calls "glory" or "vainglory." In its unvarnished form, this is the claim that all 'mental' pleasures – which were traditionally held to be the 'higher' and more distinctively human pleasures – ultimately derive from thinking ourselves to be better than other persons (and detecting the signs that other persons, too, recognize that we are better than them). Although as we shall see, the idea of human rationality continues to play a key rôle in Hobbes' political thought, gone is the classical idea that (a part of) the human function is to understand or know the truth, with the corollary that the pursuit of knowledge is undertaken by human beings for its own sake and brings with it its own rich and distinctive pleasure. According to Hobbes, we are interested in acquiring knowledge only because (a) it supplies us with the means for increasing our stock of physical pleasures (and decreasing pains) or (b) it affords us the pleasure of thinking ourselves superior to those who lack whatever knowledge we believe that we possess.

The basic consequences of this conception of human nature for human social and political interaction are not too difficult to guess, and Hobbes makes those consequences quite clear, particularly in the *De Cive*. Human beings are *not* creatures "born fit for society": in explicit opposition to Aristotle, Hobbes denies that man is a *zôon politikon* (political animal), "which axiom, though received by most, is yet certainly false."[9] It is obvious that, with respect to pleasures of sense, the unlimitedly acquisitive human nature together with at least some degree of scarcity of those things that produce pleasures of sense lead to conflict among human persons. And, with respect to pleasures of the mind, it is obvious that their pursuit constitutes what contemporary game theorists call a zero-sum game. My having more 'glory' (that is, the pleasure of considering myself superior to other people and of seeing that they recognize that superiority) must depend upon others' having less. "We do not," Hobbes says, "seek society for its own sake, but that we may have some honour or profit from it."[10] But, as Hobbes adds, such benefits would naturally be better achieved by the domination of other persons (for example, making slaves or vassals of them) than by establishing 'society', in the sense of a system of cooperation yielding reciprocal benefits.

A consequence of Hobbes' conception of human nature is his famous conception of the 'state of nature', that actual or imagined condition in which human persons exist without the benefit of any political structures or other artificial social arrangements. This state of nature is a "war of all men against all men,"[11] and life in it is famously characterized by Hobbes as "solitary, poor, nasty, brutish, and short."[12] All human beings are motivated by the desire for pleasures of body and pleasures of mind; but Hobbes recognizes individual differences with respect to the degree individual personalities manifest anti-social egoism. Consequently, while "all men in the state of nature have a desire and will to hurt," the reasons for this willingness differ: in the case of the more aggressive, it derives from greed and "vainglory"; in the case of the more "temperate", it is simply a matter of reasonable defense of oneself as a pursuer of pleasures and avoider of pains.[13] "But," Hobbes concludes, "the most frequent reason why men desire to hurt each other, ariseth hence, that many men at the same time have an appetite to the same thing; which yet very often they can neither enjoy in common, nor yet divide it; whence it follows that the strongest must have it."[14]

Since life in the state of nature is insupportable, it is singularly important to us human beings to escape from it, if we are so unfortunate as to find ourselves actually in it, and to prevent it from becoming an actuality if we do not in fact exist in it. How are we to do this? It is arguable that Hobbes provides two answers to this question. The first answer, one that derives from the tradition of classical political philosophy, proves to be inadequate in Hobbes' estimation. The second answer, to which we will turn in the next section, leads to Hobbes' political absolutism.

The former answer begins with Hobbes' conceptions of natural law (*lex naturalis*) and of natural right (*ius naturale*). In the *Leviathan* Hobbes gives succinct definitions of the two notions. A right of nature or natural right "is the liberty each man has [in the state of nature] to use his own power, as he will himself, for the preservation of his own nature – that is to say, of his own life – and consequently of doing anything which, in his own judgment and reason, he shall conceive to be the aptest means thereunto."[15] A law of nature or natural law, however, is "a precept or general rule, found out by reason, by which a man is forbidden to do that which is destructive of his life or takes away the means of preserving the same and to omit that by which he thinks it may best be preserved."[16] Hobbes proceeds to complain that the classical tradition frequently confuses the two notions of (natural) right and law, which should be distinguished and are, in fact, contrary concepts: "because RIGHT consists in liberty to do or forbear, whereas LAW determines and binds to one of them."[17] In particular, the liberty essential to a right is understood by Hobbes in terms of "absence of external impediments."[18]

A feature common to Hobbes' concept of natural right and his concept of natural law is that they are both ultimately directed toward individual self-preservation and physical security, the "constant preservation of life and members," as he puts it in the *De Cive.*[19] Hobbes initially appears to adopt the quite classical (Aristotelian and Thomistic) doctrine that natural law is somehow to be identified with practical rationality. In that tradition, the ultimate end of natural law is fulfillment of the objective human function or, in the scholastic terminology of Aquinas, the "proper act and end" of human beings.[20] Aquinas (and the scholastic tradition in general) allow that biological self-preservation is *part* of the human function – or at least a necessary condition, in most instances, of fulfilling that function: "every substance seeks the preservation of its own being, according to its nature: and by reason of this inclination, whatever is a means of preserving human life, and of warding off its obstacles, belongs to the natural law."[21] But, as we saw in the preceding chapter, self-preservation is only part of what is involved in the human function and, consequently, only one aspect of the natural law according to Aquinas. He (and Aristotle) have a rich, complex, hierarchically structured conception of the human function, end, or good. And, in some instances, the higher aspects of that function may trump the natural law's injunctions concerning the biological preservation of life. According to Aquinas, it is not always irrational to sacrifice one's life, if one must, in pursuit of some higher good or aspect of the human function.

Of course, it is precisely claims about these supposed 'higher' aspects of the human function, and about the moral significance of their interrelations, that have become – and perhaps always were – controversial. Hobbes sees himself as doing away with this problem by adopting a streamlined and stripped-down doctrine of the end of natural law. The exclusive end of natural law is biological preservation and security; and natural *laws* (in the plural) are those principles, discovered by practical reason, that are seen as the necessary means for attaining this exclusive end. Hobbes no doubt regarded his stripped-down version of natural-law theory as more factual and empirical than its scholastic antecedents. Indeed, the part of Aquinas' doctrine of natural law pertaining to a thing's "preservation of its own being, according to its nature" applies to *all* kinds of substance indifferently and became the foundation of various principles of conservation in the new science of the seventeenth century. Thus, for Descartes, the "first law of nature" is "that each thing as far as in it lies, continues always in the same state."[22] Hobbes thus has the authority of contemporary precedent for streamlining the doctrine of natural law in the way that he does.

It is worth noting that if one attributes to Hobbes – as it is quite plausible to do – the hedonistic doctrine that the human function, end, or good is the acquisition of pleasures of sense and of mind, then he departs from the classical tradition in not regarding this 'complete' human function as the end of natural law. That is, according to Hobbes natural law is *not* directed toward the end of individual pleasure acquisition, to securing the most pleasurable life for oneself. Why not? A possible answer is that Hobbes sees the securing of biological life and security as an essential necessary condition for pleasure acquisition *and* also as a *shared* end of all human persons. My pleasure acquisition often comes in conflict with yours. So it seems unlikely that there could be any *general* or *universal* principles (which are, in that limited but important sense, 'laws') the observance of which would be conducive to everyone's acquisition of pleasure. But Hobbes believes that there are such general principles, which reason can discover and which are conducive to everyone's preservation – because they are conducive to the state of social peace (the absence of the "war of each against all"), which he holds to be a necessary condition of *individual* self-preservation.

We shall return to the particular laws of nature that Hobbes deduces from his stripped-down conception of the human function. First, however, let us consider his conception of natural rights and the relation between that conception and that of natural law. Recollect that natural right is defined in the *Leviathan* by Hobbes as that "liberty each man has to use his own power, as he will himself, for the preservation of his own nature – that is to say, of his own life – and consequently of doing anything which, in his own judgment and reason, he shall conceive to be the aptest means thereunto." The virtually identical definition in *De Cive* is "that liberty which every man hath to make use of his natural faculties according to right reason" in order "to protect his life and members."[23] The idea seems to be essentially that of the classical tradition of political philosophy. That is, practical reason manifests the objective human function of good and discovers the means to attain it, which means constitute natural law. Practical reason, in this capacity, imposes certain obligations on us. Natural *rights*, then, provide us with the necessary liberty to discharge the obligations imposed by natural law. Hence the sort of liberty involved in this concept of natural rights is 'positive' liberty, in the sense discussed by the contemporary political theorist Isaiah Berlin: they are rights 'with a purpose', namely, the fulfillment of the objective human function.[24] In one passage in *De Cive* Hobbes sketches exactly this doctrine:

> But since all do grant, that is done by *right*, which is not done against reason, we ought to judge those actions only *wrong*, which are repugnant to right reason, that is, which contradict some certain truth collected by right reasoning from true principles. But that *wrong* which is done, we say it is done against some law. Therefore, *true reason* is a certain *law*; which, since it is not less a part of human nature than any other faculty or affection of the mind, is also termed natural.[25]

It seems clear, however, that Hobbes doesn't mean it. In other words, he ultimately repudiates these classical doctrines of the connection between natural law and natural right and of reason as constituting the essence of natural law (considered as law, and not simply as good advice). While natural rights may be introduced by him as positive rights to do what is necessary to satisfy the ultimate aim (self-preservation) of natural law, he famously concludes that each person in the state of nature has a right to everything: "That is, it was lawful for every man, in the bare state of nature, or before such time as men had engaged themselves by covenants or bonds, to do what he would, and against whom he thought fit, and to possess, use, and enjoy all what he would, or could get."[26] Hobbes' principal argument for this conclusion is that since each person in the state of nature is the sole judge as to what is necessary for securing his or her preservation, there is nothing that a person could not, *with right*, claim as being necessary for self preservation. Now if the sense of 'right' here is that of a positive right – a right I possess to something or a right I have to perform some action in virtue of that thing's or that action's *actually* being necessary to my preservation – Hobbes' conclusion is obviously fallacious. My claiming (or even sincerely believing) that something is necessary to my self-preservation does not make it so. However, it transpires that what he *really* intends by the phrase 'right of nature' is 'negative liberty' in Berlin's sense: the absence of impediment to do what one wishes, whatever that might be and for whatever reason (or none) one might wish it. In the state of nature, according to Hobbes, "the notions of right and wrong, justice and injustice, have there no place. Where there is no common power, there is no law; where no law, no justice."[27] Since (so Hobbes here claims) there is an absence of law in the state of nature (because of the absence of a "common power" regulating the interrelations of persons) and since, by definition, persons in the state of nature have not obligated themselves by "covenants or bonds" or other promises, there is no impediment to my doing whatever I wish. The sense of 'impediment' here seems to be that of a moral or legal impediment, something that could be the source of an obligation on my part to act or refrain from acting. In the state of nature there are, of course, plenty of physical impediments in the form of other persons pursuing their own self-interest in ways that conflict with my pursuit of my self-interest; and these impediments prove to be disastrous from a practical viewpoint. But Hobbes does not seem to think of them as in any way limiting my natural right to everything in the state of nature – or the corresponding right of everyone else to everything. What they limit is the effectiveness of our exercise of those all-encompassing natural rights.

The observant reader will now ask, "What about natural law?" If, as Hobbes claims in the passage quoted earlier, "true reason is a certain law" (that is, *natural* law), and if true reason directed toward individual self-preservation is a faculty of the mind operative in the state of nature, does not natural law impose certain obligations, at least of enlightened self-interest, that would limit our natural right to everything in the state of nature? Hobbes' answer is a most equivocal "yes and no." It is for this reason that the appeal to natural law constitutes what I referred to, some time ago, as the first, inadequate answer to the question of how human persons are to avoid the state of war that Hobbes identifies with the state of nature. Let us briefly consider the content of Hobbes' natural laws. We will then return to their 'form'.

I have already characterized the natural laws as general principles directed toward securing social peace and stability. Hobbes does not believe that each person has an *ultimate* interest in securing such peace. What he does believe is that every person has as an ultimate end which is to "shun" the "chiefest of natural evils, which is death; and this he doth by a certain impulsion of nature, no less than that whereby a stone moves downward."[28] This avoidance of death (and serious injury) becomes, as we have seen, the exclusive end of the natural law. Although we may be directed toward the ultimate end of natural law "by a certain impulsion," we may pursue this end more or less rationally, which is to say more or less efficiently and, thus, more or less successfully. It is possible to interpret Hobbes' concrete natural laws as principles of 'rule egoism'. That is, these are the most rational (most efficient) general principles of behavior for securing my preservation. They are egoistic in the sense that Hobbes need only assume an interest on the part of each person in his or her own preservation, not necessarily an interest in the preservation of anyone else. They are 'rules' in the sense that they are supposed to work 'indirectly' – that is, by securing the social peace and stability that Hobbes holds to be a necessary condition of my self-preservation. Thus, they are supposed to secure my preservation by securing the preservation of *all* persons. That fact gives them their 'universal' or 'rule-like' character: They are principles of behavior applicable to everyone, not tailor-made for any individual.

What are these natural laws? Not surprisingly the fundamental natural law is that "peace is to be sought after, where it may be found."[29] An immediate corollary is that "a man be willing, when others are too ... to lay down his right to all things, and be contented with so much liberty against other men as he would allow other men against himself."[30] This is obviously the heart of Hobbes' interpretation of the natural law: the natural law essentially appeals to a principle of reciprocity (like the 'Golden Rule')[31] according to which I limit those 'natural' actions in pursuit of my pleasures of body and of mind that may be detrimental to other persons' pursuit of their pleasures – on the condition that they impose a like limitation on their actions. Hobbes argues that such a principle of reciprocity is instantiated through 'agreements' – promises, contracts, covenants – explicit or implicit. Hence, the next natural law is "that men perform their covenants made" and that they "keep trust."[32] The remaining particular laws of nature consist of much of traditional Western morality. They prescribe gratitude, impartiality, forgiveness, and accommodation to one's fellows and forbid hatred (or "contumely"), pride, and arrogance. Of course, the 'rational derivations' that Hobbes gives to justify these laws are egoistic: the traditional virtues they enjoin are enjoined because they contribute to social peace and security and, thus, to one's own preservation. The traditional vices that they forbid are forbidden because they have the opposite effect.

Hobbes explicitly identifies the natural law, understood as a principle of rule egoism, with the moral law:

> The laws of nature, therefore, are the sum of *moral* philosophy; whereof I have only delivered such precepts in this place, as appertain to the preservation of ourselves against those dangers which arise from discord. But there are other precepts of *rational* nature, from whence spring other virtues; for temperance, also, is a precept of reason, because intemperance tends to sickness and death. And so fortitude too, that is, that same faculty of resisting stoutly in present dangers, and which are more hardly declined than overcome; because it is a means tending to the preservation of him that resists.[33]

Moreover, Hobbes identifies natural law not only with the moral law but with the divine law, that is, with the commandments of God. As at least a nominal Protestant, he appeals to holy scripture as the source of information concerning God's commandments and spends considerable space in *De Cive* quoting scriptural passages that support his claim that the natural laws that he has deduced as principles of rule egoism can also be found in the Bible.

But, then, is it not the case that Hobbes' identification of the natural law with both the moral and divine law all the more suggests that the natural law imposes obligations in the state of nature, obligations that would limit the right of each person to everything? Although I believe that there are tensions in Hobbes' doctrine, his most considered view seems to be the following. Insofar as the laws of nature are dictates of reason, in the sense of counsels of prudential egoism, they embody extremely good advice – but they are not laws, in a true and strict sense of law. Hobbes draws a quite clear and sharp distinction between *counsel* and *command*. Counsel is a precept "in which the reason of my obeying is taken from *the thing itself advised*; but *command* is a *precept*, in which the cause of my obedience depends on *the will of the commander*."[34] In other words, my compliance with counsel or a piece of advice depends on its content, whether I deem it good or bad advice. But my compliance with a command depends on the authority of the person or persons issuing the command. Law, Hobbes concludes, is fundamentally a matter of command, not counsel: "law is the command of that person, whether man or court, whose precept contains in it the reason of obedience: as the precepts of God in regard to men, of magistrates in respect of their subjects, and universally of all the powerful in respect of them who cannot resist, may be termed their laws."[35] As Hobbes explicitly claims, the laws of nature are only laws, as opposed to counsel, *insofar as they are the commandments of God.*[36] It thus appears that they impose obligations only in this sense as well.

There is a certain irony is this consequence since, both in his time and thereafter, Hobbes has been suspected of atheism, despite all his talk of God in both the *Leviathan* and *De Cive.* Whether Hobbes believed in the existence of God and, if so, what the nature of that belief was are still controverted issues that need not detain us here. However, if we take his doctrine at face value, it would appear that the natural law does impose obligations in the state of nature only insofar as the natural law is equivalent to divine commandment. What obligation does it oppose? A brief answer to this question is the following: only a conditional obligation, and one in which the antecedent of the conditional is never satisfied in the state of nature; consequently, there are no obligations *with respect to actual behavior* imposed by the natural law in the state of nature.

Since the ultimate end of natural law is self-preservation, acting in conformity with those laws in the absence of a guarantee that other persons are also going to observe them is counterproductive. That is, in the absence of such a guarantee, moral behavior would decrease one's security and make one's violent demise all the more likely, thus frustrating the very purpose of the natural law (= the moral law = the divine law). But in the state of nature, Hobbes believes, we never have such a guarantee. We human beings are naturally motivated by the pursuit of pleasure and the avoidance of pain. But we are not typically very efficient at fulfilling this natural function. In a calm and recollected moment, we can understand that observing the natural laws as principles of rule egoism is a necessary condition for social peace and security, which is itself a necessary condition of self-preservation, which obviously is a necessary condition of my obtaining any pleasure whatsoever. But, as Hobbes puts it, tempted by our "perverse desire of present profit, [we] are very unapt to observe these laws."[37] In other words, we are tempted to behave as 'act egoists', choosing the particular action that, in the present circumstances, maximizes pleasure or reduces pain. In so behaving, we act irrationally in suppressing, ignoring, or rationalizing away our awareness that this behavior undermines social peace and security, and thus undermines the prospects of our long-term success as acquirers of pleasure and avoiders of pain. This tendency to violate "right reason" exists to some degree in all of us and is sufficiently strong in enough of us to eliminate any assurance of general conformity to the laws of nature in the state of nature.

Consequently, Hobbes claims that, in the state of nature, the laws of nature do not oblige "*in foro externo*" – "in the external court" of actual behavior. However, he does maintain that they oblige "*in foro interno*" – "in the internal court" of conscience.[38] As it turns out, fulfilling the latter sort of obligation requires of a person only that he or she should have a "desire that [the natural laws] should take place"[39] or a "readiness of mind to observe them, whensoever their observation shall seem to conduce to the end for which they were ordained."[40] Since such a state of affairs never actually occurs in the state of nature, Hobbes remarks, perhaps with some intentional irony, that the laws of nature "are easy to be observed."[41] Not even when considered as divine commandments, then, do the natural laws constitute an adequate means for removing ourselves from, or keeping ourselves out of, the state of war of each against all that is the state of nature. We turn now to what Hobbes regards as the only satisfactory means for achieving this fundamental political goal.

Law, contracts, and the 'Leviathan'

The state of nature is constituted by autonomous persons, each a potentially unlimitedly acquisitive consumer of pleasures and avoider of pains and each possessing unlimited natural rights. No agreements, bonds of cooperation, or other social structures mitigate the autonomy of these individuals; and, as we have seen, the laws of nature "are silent" in the state of nature.[42] Morever, such persons are equal in the only sense of equality that really matters in the state of nature – they are equally able to kill and equally susceptible to being killed.[43]

As I have said, the resulting state of war of each against all is considered by Hobbes to be unsupportable. How, then, are we to escape and avoid it? Hobbes' 'effective' solution is the social contract, by means of which all the natural rights (and the powers) of the signatories (as I shall call the persons that are thought of as entering into the contract)[44] are invested in an artificial person created by the contract. In the contract, each signatory makes the following agreement with every other signatory: "I authorize and give up my right of governing myself to this man, or to this assembly of men [the artificial person], on this condition, that you give up your right to him and authorize all his actions in a like manner."[45] As Hobbes conceives the contract, from the individual, warring persons in the state of nature it creates "one person [which] is called a COMMONWEALTH, in the Latin CIVITAS. This is the generation of that great LEVIATHAN (or rather, to speak more reverently, of that *mortal god*) to which we owe, under the *immortal God,* our peace and defense."[46] As a result of the contract, all the signatories

> have made themselves every one the author, to the end he [the artificial person, mortal god, or Leviathan] may use the strength and means of them all as he shall think expedient for their peace and common defense. And he that carries this person is called SOVEREIGN and said to have *sovereign power*; and every one besides, his SUBJECT.[47]

The unlimited but quite useless natural rights (originally directed toward self-defense, it will be remembered) of a collection of 'natural' human persons in the state of nature have been exchanged for the unlimited political authority and power of a single, artificial person. Human beings thus exchange the state of nature for the 'civil state' of existence. I do not believe that Hobbes is simply appealing to an exaggerated metaphor in depicting this exchange in terms of the loss of the separate *political* identities of individual subjects in the civil state and the forging of a single political person in their stead. The price of avoidance of the war of each against all is the relinquishing of our individual political identities. This is Hobbes' 'effective' solution to what might be regarded as the problem of political cooperation. It is a simple and elegant solution despite the fact that Hobbes' working out of its details has generally been regarded as unpalatable. In the next section, I shall return to the question of what remains of 'natural persons' in the civil state, as well as to the status of the political person, the mortal god or Leviathan, created by the social contract. In the remainder of this section, however, I wish to consider Hobbes' concepts of law and of contracts and their relation to his notion of obligation.

Does Hobbes recognize a distinction between power and authority, where 'authority' signifies 'rightful power' or 'power that carries with it some moral obligation of respect'? The short answer to this question is "Yes." However, perhaps not surprisingly, Hobbes bears great respect for power. Consequently and perhaps somewhat paradoxically – he seems to accord it *moral* weight. In fact, he distinguishes two sources for *natural* obligation (that is, obligation not derived from agreement): (a) one occurs "when liberty is taken away by corporal impediments"; the other "when it is taken away by hope or fear."[48] However, Hobbes more often considers 'non-natural obligation', which is based upon an agreement of some sort – a promise, a contract, a covenant, or some sort of reciprocal social arrangement. "All obligation," he says in *De Cive,* "derives from contract."[49] The concept of law, as well as that of political authority in general, has the added element of coercive power. As Hobbes puts it (also in *De Cive*), "contracts oblige us; laws tie us fast, being obliged. A *contract* obligeth of *itself*; the *law* holds the party obliged by virtue of the universal *contract* of yielding obedience."[50] In a note added in response to critics who doubted that there is any real distinction between "obliges us" and "ties us fast, being obliged," Hobbes responds that a "man is obliged by his contracts, that is, that he ought to perform for his promise sake"; but what it means to say that "the law ties him being obliged" is that the "law compels him to make good his promise for fear of the punishment appointed by the law."[51]

Hobbes' doctrine concerning the rôles of power and contract in generating obligation is not altogether clear, and may perhaps not be consistent. However, several elements of it are clear. For one thing, we have seen that he usually holds that an agreement or 'covenant', at least in the sense of tacit consent, is necessary to generate an obligation. Despite his doctrine of natural obligation mentioned above, it does not seem that Hobbes unequivocally holds that "might makes right" – that is, generates obligations – in itself. But it may do so indirectly. Thus he maintains that when political sovereignty arises by "acquisition" (for instance, by force of conquest), the vanquished in effect contract with the sovereign power by submitting to him or it. Hobbes denies that what we might characterize as an agreement or contract coerced through fear – when such an agreement is not inconsistent with existing civil law – is 'invalid', in the sense of not imposing the same kind of obligation that any agreement imposes. His rationale for this doctrine is clear. As he points out, it is fear (of one another) that impels persons in the state of nature to make the social contract, just as it is fear (of the conquering power) that impels the vanquished to submit to the victor. If Hobbes were to maintain that fear of the consequences of not 'making an agreement' eliminate any obligations deriving from the agreement, he would undermine his central doctrine of political authority.[52] In Hobbes' words, "It is not, therefore, the victory that gives the right of dominion over the vanquished but his own covenant. Nor is he obliged because he is conquered – that is to say, beaten and taken, or put to flight – but because he comes in and submits to the victor."[53]

Hobbes draws some consequences from this doctrine that many of us would find counterintuitive. A captive (say, a slave or a prisoner of war) is under no obligation not to resist his or her captor or master if "kept in prison or bonds." But if such a captive is given some bodily freedom in return for an agreement not to flee (or an agreement to return with a ransom payment, etc.), obligation on the part of the captive is generated by that agreement.[54] It seems clear that Hobbes is motivated by the desire for theoretical consistency here. That is, since in the case of the 'big agreement' – that is, the social contract – he cannot maintain that fear or intimidation invalidates the agreement or dispenses with obligations deriving from it, he decides that he is bound to maintain this doctrine as a general principle with respect to all agreements.

However, Hobbes' quest for consistency in this particular matter conflicts with his general tendency to be dismissive of claims to find obligations where coercive power to enforce those obligations is lacking. For example, he criticizes Aristotle's definition of law ("a speech, limited according to the common consent of the city, declaring everything that we ought to do") with the following argument: if the relevant 'consent' is understood to be the consent of one person, the idea of its being a *common* consent makes no sense. But if the consent is that of a "multitude of men," those consents

> are nothing else but some mutual contracts, which oblige not any man (and therefore are no laws) before a supreme power being constituted, which can compel, having sufficient remedy against the rest who otherwise are not likely to keep them. Laws, therefore, according to this definition of Aristotle, are nothing but naked and weak contracts.[55]

Hobbes here comes close to suggesting that a "naked and weak" agreement (that is, one that is not enforceable by a "supreme power") is one that does not impose obligations. As peculiar as this doctrine may seem, it does make some sense within Hobbes' theory: the ultimate end of any obligation is self-preservation, and it is Hobbes' view that the institution of making and keeping agreements is only conducive to that end in a context where those agreements are enforceable.

In the introduction to this chapter, I alluded to one significant consequence of Hobbes' emphasis on agreement or contract as the source of obligation: the privileging of the paradigm of commutative justice over distributive justice. It is arguable that in the preceding, classical tradition of political philosophy, the most fundamental political idea is that of distributive justice: the fair distribution of the benefits and burdens that result from political cooperation. Hobbes is quite dismissive concerning the supposed foundational political rôle of distributive justice, which, he says, is busied about the dignity and merits of men; so as if there be rendered to every man *kata tên aksian* [according to desert], more to him who is more worthy, and less to him that deserves less, and that proportionably; hence they say arises distributive justice. ... But what is all this to justice? For neither if I sell my goods for as much as I can get for them, do I injure the buyer, who sought and desired of me; neither if I divide more of what is mine to him who deserves less, so long as I give the other what I have agreed for, do I wrong to either. ... Yet perhaps it cannot be denied but that justice is a certain equality, as consisting in this only; that since we are all equal by nature, one should not arrogate more right to himself than he grants to another, unless he have fairly gotten it by compact.[56]

Hobbes' contention is that the only consequence, with respect to distributive justice, of the 'natural' equality of persons in the state of nature should be a willingness to observe the golden rule, that is, a principle of reciprocity. But, of course, persons are under no obligation to act in conformity with this principle in the state of nature, where there is no "supreme power" to enforce agreements. So the last clause in the preceding quotation is of fundamental importance: fair agreements or 'compacts' always serve as the basis of justice and always trump any other possible considerations of justice. The force of the qualifying adjective 'fair' is not obvious. As we have seen, Hobbes seems to want to deny that fear or intimidation vitiates an agreement; and, in terms of his theory, such duress would seem not to affect its 'fairness' either. In the civil state, 'fair compacts' can be nothing other than those allowed by the sovereign power, as we shall soon see.

The civil state: sovereign and subjects

For Hobbes, all (non-natural) obligations derive from agreements or contracts; and all issues of justice ultimately reduce to issues of agreements as well. The 'big agreement', of course, is the social contract, which I described at the beginning of the previous section. In the social contract, the signatories relinquish their political identities. Each signatory agrees to form a *single* artificial person and to identify the political will of that entity with his or her own political will. In Hobbes' civil state, there are only *subjects*, not *citizens*, in the sense of human persons retaining distinct and separate political wills. Because of his conception of human nature, Hobbes believes that the politically 'centrifugal' tendencies of groups of human persons, in their natural state, is so great that the only way to deal with it is to eliminate the plurality of political wills in favor of a single political will of the commonwealth or 'Leviathan'. Artificial though that person is, it is embodied in a quite concrete sovereign – either a single person, in the case of monarchy, or a council of persons, as in other forms of government.

Hobbes quite intentionally designs the social contract in such a way as to insure the political and moral supremacy of the sovereign power. The signatories who become subjects in the civil state are obliged by it, and virtually irrevocably obliged – only the destruction of the sovereign power (by external conquest or desertion on the part of the man or council bearing the sovereign power, for example) removes their obligation. The sovereign, however, is *created* by the contract and is not a signatory to it. Since, as we have seen, Hobbes holds that all obligation derives from agreement, the sovereign bears no obligations to the subjects in the civil state created by the social contract. Consequently, while the sovereign obviously can physically damage its subjects, it is conceptually impossible for it to injure them, in Hobbes' special (and etymologically correct) sense of 'injure': to do an injustice to some particular person.[57] Hobbes spells out the consequences of his conception of the absolute political authority vested in the sovereign with unflinching consistency. These consequences can be summarized under the heads of a positivistic conception of what is legal, a positivistic conception of what is moral, and a positivistic conception of religion.[58] I shall now briefly elaborate on these notions.

A positivistic conception of what is legal

With this phrase, I refer to Hobbes' doctrine that, for the subject or individual person in the civil state, what is legal is to be equated with what is permitted by the sovereign, what is illegal is to be equated with what is forbidden by the sovereign. Since the sovereign power is embodied in a person or group of persons, one can substitute 'government' for 'sovereign' here. The political slogan of the desirability of "a government of laws, not of men" Hobbes regards as incoherent nonsense. Although he is quite willing to admit that there may be practical benefits to be gained from the sovereign's acting in a regular, predictable, and non-capricious manner, the obligation of respect owed to any law derives from the will of the authoritative law giver. In the case of the civil law, this is the sovereign. Individual subjects, then, have no legal recourse against the independent will of that sovereign. Obvious corollaries are (a) that the acts of the sovereign are not legally punishable and (b) that the "laws of the city" do not oblige the sovereign (since Hobbes maintains that one cannot contract with oneself, in the true and proper sense of 'contract' and the "laws of the city" are nothing other than the expressions of the will of the sovereign).

A positivistic conception of what is moral

I here mean that, for the subject in the civil state, what is moral is to be equated with what is permitted by the sovereign, what is immoral is to be equated with what is forbidden by the sovereign. A consequence of the elimination of the political identity of subjects in the civil state is that subjects possess no independent right to judge what is and what is not in conformity with the natural law. The identity of the natural law with the moral law means that they have no independent right to judge what is moral and immoral. This right falls to the sovereign as the one remaining political will in the civil state. Hobbes does not shrink from drawing out the consequences of this doctrine. "It very much concerns the interest of peace, that no opinions or doctrines be delivered to citizens, by which they imagine that either by right they may not obey the laws of the city, that is, the commands of that man or council to whom the supreme power is committed, or that it is lawful to resist him."[59] Moreover, "since therefore it belongs to kings to discern good and evil, wicked are those, though usual, sayings, that he only is King who does righteously, and that kings must not be obeyed unless they command us just things."[60] On the contrary, "Legitimate kings therefore make the things they command just, by commanding them, and which they forbid, unjust, by forbidding them. But private men, while they assume to themselves the knowledge of good and evil, desire to be even as kings; which cannot be with the safety of the commonweal."[61]

A positivistic conception of religion (as far as subjects in the civil state are concerned; as we shall see, the sovereign is an exception)

Hobbes is a particularly clear exponent of what has come to be called Erastianism: the doctrine that the church, in particular, and religious matters, in general, should be completely controlled by the secular authority.[62] Hobbes is no more willing to give subjects religiously based recourse against the sovereign than he is to give them legally or morally based recourse. He argues that "their opinion therefore who teach, that subjects sin when they obey their prince's commands which to them seem unjust, is both erroneous, and to be reckoned among those which are contrary to civil obedience."[63] And he goes so far as to *identify* the 'city' or civil state and the church: "It follows what hath been already said by a necessary connexion, that a city of Christian men and a Church is altogether the same thing, of the same men, termed by two names, for two causes."[64] Therefore, religious matters (from the interpretation of sacred scripture to the regulation of public worship) should ultimately be dictated by the sovereign power of the civil state. It is only the sovereign who needs to 'worry' about religion and who is an exception to Hobbes' religious positivism, according to which piety is a matter of adhering to the religious dictates of the commonwealth. As Hobbes no doubt believed, and the experience of seventeenth-century England confirmed, to allow religious diversity or pluralism is to permit dissension that is dangerous in that it leads to the division of the one political and social will formed by the social contract and hence to the weakening of the commonwealth. It is thus a step back in the direction of the state of nature or war of each against all. As Hobbes puts the point in the *Leviathan*, "seeing that a commonwealth is but one person, it ought also to exhibit to God but one worship; which then it does when it commands it to be exhibited by private men publicly."[65]

Thus far, we have seen that subjects give up their political identities in the civil state and that the sovereign owes no obligations *to* its subjects. Two rather obvious questions remain to be addressed in this section. What sort of identity remains for human persons as subjects in the civil state? Does the sovereign have any duties or responsibilities at all? The answers to these questions turn out to be related.

To consider the second question first, Hobbes devotes a chapter of the *De Cive* to the duties of the sovereign. It is obvious that the "man or council of men" that embodies the sovereign in a given civil state owes no obligations *to* its subjects, individually or collectively, since it stands in no contractual relation with those subjects. However, Hobbes says, "all the duties of rulers are contained in this one sentence, *the safety of the people is the supreme law*."[66] He proceeds to comment that it is the rulers' "*duty* in all things, as much as possibly they can, to yield obedience unto right reason, which is the natural, moral, and divine law."[67] Of course, for Hobbes, this means acting in such a way as to secure the social peace necessary for individual self-preservation. But "by *safety* must be understood, not the sole preservation of life in what condition soever, but in order to its happiness."[68] In terms of Hobbes' hedonism, this means that rulers should "study, as much as by good laws could be effected, to furnish their subjects abundantly, not only with the good things belonging to life, but also with those which advance to delectation."[69] So, with respect to the benefits "respecting this [mortal] life only," Hobbes summarizes the duties of the sovereign under four heads: (a) the defense of subjects from foreign enemies; (b) the preservation of internal peace and security; (c) the 'enrichment' of the subjects, "as much as consist with public security"; (d) the granting of "harmless liberty" to the subjects, where "harmless liberty" is liberty that does not in any way undermine peace and security.[70] According to Hobbes' own principles, the recipient, so to speak, of these obligations can only be God. The sovereign should adhere to the natural law, which is also the moral law and the divine law. But as the sovereign is not morally obliged by the civil laws (which are nothing but an expression of the sovereign will) or by any other contractual obligations to human persons, any moral obligation to act in conformity with natural law in discharging the sovereign's duties is due to the fact that, from the perspective of that sovereign, the law of nature (= the moral law) is the divine law.

Hobbes' discussion of the duties of the sovereign suggests the answer to our first question above, "What sort of identity remains for human persons as subjects in the civil state?" As we have seen, human persons entering into the civil state give up their political identities. By the social contract, their individual political wills are yielded to the man or council embodying the sovereign power, as are their moral and religious wills. What remains in the subject is the 'natural man' as a pursuer of pleasures and avoider of pains. In other words, *homo politicus* is gone but *homo economicus* remains. Hobbes envisions economic activity on the part of the subjects (producing, distributing, buying, selling, etc.) as the source of the "delectation" that the laws of the wise sovereign will permit its subjects and as the principal sphere of the "harmless liberty" allotted to them. The combination of 'economic freedom' and 'property rights' with the lack of *political* liberty is a salient feature of Hobbes' particular version of contractarianism. As we shall soon see, John Locke develops a rather different account of the relation between economic entrepreneurship and contractarianism. And later, liberal versions of contractarianism go even further in questioning the possibility (and moral propriety) of restricting individual liberty to the economic domain. But the centrality of the idea of *homo economicus* turns out to be a feature of even the early, Hobbesian version of contractarianism.

Concluding thoughts on God and sovereigns

As I mentioned earlier in passing, it is something of an irony that God appears to be such a crucial element in the political theory of Hobbes, the sincerity of whose professions of Christian belief has often been doubted. Apparently, it is only God who makes the laws of nature to be laws, in the sense of imposing moral obligations; and it is only God to whom the sovereign power in any civil state owes any obligations. However, it transpires that, from a political perspective, "the problem of God" is really only an issue for the conscience of the individual ruler. For human beings in general – that is, everyone in the state of nature and subjects in the civil state – God (should he exist) is not politically useful: he is too distant, does not express his will with sufficient clarity and lack of ambiguity, and has not established a consistent, predictable pattern of interaction with human beings. What Hobbes has done is to establish the "mortal god" or Leviathan in the place of the immortal one as far as the individual subject in the civil state is concerned. In political, moral, and religious matters, the subject can deal with this more accessible god, whose will is not in doubt.

It falls to the rulers, those embodying the sovereign in an individual civil state, to deal with scruples about the will of the immortal God (if he exists). Hobbes provides strong theoretical support for the common political principle of the Renaissance and Reformation: *Cuius regnum, eius religio* (literally, "Whoever's rule, his religion": that is, the state will adopt the religion of its ruler). But can Hobbes really expect the individual piety of rulers to serve as a sufficient constraint on their behavior and a sufficient incentive for them to fulfill their duties concerning their subjects? Human nature is what it is – acquisitive, self-interested, and quarrelsome – and not even sincere piety is likely to turn a sow's ear into a silk purse – as Hobbes should have been fully aware from the example of his sometime pupil Charles II, an evidently pious man who lived out his strong conviction that God will not damn a man for allowing himself 'a little pleasure'.

To put the point in a different way: later forms of contractarianism tended to adopt progressively more abstract conceptions of the 'political will' or sovereign authority created by the social contract. However, for Hobbes, the sovereign is always identified with a "man or council of men" wielding that authority (and he preferred the former, monarchy, because of the efficiency of its centralization of power). Yet, as many of Hobbes' critics have pointed out, it is the same concrete human beings that, as subjects, are assumed to need the authority of external, absolute authority but, as instantiating the sovereign power, are assumed to be able to fulfill their duties without it (or on the basis of mere religious piety alone). Is there a serious conceptual (or even sentimental) chink in Hobbes' 'cynical' armor here?

Hobbes is never sentimental, and he seldom fails to see the demands of his theory. In this particular case, I believe that his view is that what makes the lack of an absolute political authority most dangerous is the *number* of persons existing in this state (as in the 'state of nature'). Concentrating political power in the hand of one or a few persons in the civil state will not substantially change the nature of that person or persons. He, she, or they will pursue his, her, or their self-interest as one would expect – in a relatively untrammeled way. However, a situation in which there is *one* or a *few* persons behaving in this way is much less dangerous than a situation in which everyone is similarly unfettered. And, if the subjects of a commonwealth are reasonably fortunate, that person or persons exercising sovereign power may find the pursuit of 'a little pleasure' quite consistent with the exercise of a sufficient care for the safety of the commonwealth.

John Locke: divinely mandated autonomy, natural rights, and property

John Locke (1632–1704), a much younger seventeenth-century contemporary of Hobbes, came from a moderately wealthy Puritan family which had strong Parliamentary sympathies in the English civil war of the 1640s. He attended one of the best schools in England, Westminster School, and then Christ Church at Oxford, where he in due course became a scholar, which was normally a lifetime position. He took a medical degree (rather than holy orders in the Church of England, the more normal course for scholars) and, in 1667, became the personal physician to Anthony Ashley Cooper, Baron Ashley, who had been created Lord Shaftesbury by the restored Charles II in 1666. Locke soon became his trusted confidential secretary and advisor. During this period Locke became increasingly interested in natural science, formed a close relationship with the scientist Robert Boyle, and was elected a Fellow of the Royal Society in 1668. He also became both increasingly attached to the tenets of the Whig party[71] (whose mercantile and commercial interests made him a wealthy man) and increasingly enmeshed in the conspiracies of Shaftesbury and other Whigs to prevent the accession to the throne of Charles' Catholic brother (who nonetheless became James II at Charles' death in 1685). After acquittal on a treason charge, Shaftesbury fled England to Holland in 1683, and Locke followed him into exile later in the same year. The exile was temporary. The so-called Glorious Revolution of 1688 bolstered Whig fortunes, replacing James II on the English throne by his Protestant eldest daughter Mary and her Dutch husband William of Orange. Locke returned to England in 1689 escorting the soon-to-be Queen Mary. Although he had done substantial work on them years before, Locke's two principal works were published only after the revolution: the *Two Treatises of Government* (1689–1690) and *An Essay Concerning Human Understanding* (1689). Locke lived on, in high esteem but increasingly fragile health, until 1704.

Locke was a 'party man' and his party was the Whig party. The *First Treatise of Government* is a rebuttal of Sir Robert Filmer's version of the divine-right-of-kings theory, dear to the hearts of many Stuart royalists. It is really only of historical interest and, consequently, is now seldom read. The perennially popular *Second Treatise of Government* is Locke's positive contribution to political theory, a defense of the concept of limited government the *raison d'être* of which should be to protect the property rights of its citizens. Many contemporary scholars believe that a draft of the *Treatises* was written in the early 1680s as a theoretical support for the political machinations of Shaftesbury and his Whig compatriots. Then, after the success of the Glorious Revolution, a version was presented as an explicit defense of that Whig venture: as Locke puts it in the Preface to the *Second Treatise*, he intends to present a discourse "sufficient to establish the throne of our great restorer, our present King William; to make good his title, in the consent of the people, which being the only one of all lawful governments, he has more fully and clearly, than any prince in Christendom; and to justify to the world the people of England, whose love of their just and natural rights, with their resolution to preserve them, saved the nation when it was on the very brink of slavery and ruin."[72]

The *Second Treatise* also saw service on behalf of the American revolutionary cause in the late eighteenth century and has acquired the status of a canonical theoretical support for the liberal-democratic, constitutional form of polity. In Locke's political philosophy, three themes central to many versions of the liberal-democratic political tradition are theoretically intertwined: limited government, individual liberties, and property rights. The twentieth-century scholar and political philosopher C.B. Macpherson (who, while an eminent editor and scholar of Locke's political philosophy, was no supporter of it) has maintained that one reason for the continuing popularity of Locke's political thought is that it is an "acceptable theoretical fall-back for publicists who accept the modern liberal state and society uncritically."[73] Whether this claim is true or not, it does appear that Locke's political theory is intended to secure limited government, individual liberties, and property rights as inseparable constituents of a sort of 'package'. Consequently, Locke's theory has proved less useful to later theorists who wished to de-emphasize some or one of these elements (say, property rights). Before examining the doctrine of Locke's *Second Treatise of Government*, it is necessary to discuss briefly Locke's theory of moral knowledge and of human motivation.

Moral knowledge and human motivation

In *An Essay Concerning Human Understanding* Locke develops a doctrine according to which there is a noticeable lack of relation between moral knowledge, on the one hand, and the motivation of humans to conform their behavior to that knowledge, on the other. I shall later suggest that this fact is manifested in what some commentators have taken to be a certain ambivalence in Locke's attitude toward the state of nature.

Locke holds that the requirements of morality can, in principle, be exhibited as a deductive system of relations among ideas:

> The *Idea* of a supreme Being, infinite in Power, Goodness, and Wisdom, whose Workmanship we are, and on whom we depend; and the *Idea* of our selves, as understanding, rational Beings, being such as are clear in us, would, I suppose, if duly considered, and pursued, afford such Foundations of our Duty and Rules of Action, as might place *Morality amongst the Sciences capable of Demonstration*: wherein I doubt not, but from self-evident Propositions, by necessary Consequences, as incontestable as those in Mathematicks, the measures of right and wrong might be made out, to any one that will apply himself with the same Indifferency and Attention to the one, as he does to the other of these Sciences.[74]

Locke is quite skeptical about the human capacity to develop a deductive science of nature (as opposed to a 'useful' natural history or collection of facts about nature). As he puts it, "our natural Faculties are not fitted to penetrate into the internal Fabrick and real Essences of Bodies."[75] But, in his estimation, those same faculties are sufficient "to lead us into a full and clear discovery of our Duty. ... Hence, I think I may conclude, that *Morality is the proper Science, and Business of Mankind in general* (who are both concerned, and fitted to search out their *Summum Bonum*), as several Arts, conversant about several parts of Nature, are the Lot and private Talent of particular Men."[76]

It is not surprising that Locke uses the traditional terminology of 'law of nature' and 'right rule of reason'[77] for those parts of rational morality that particularly pertain to interpersonal relations and to the relation between human beings and God, their Lord and Creator. Locke also refers to the law of nature as a rule of "common equity,"[78] a description that is singularly appropriate in view of his characterization of the foundation of the law of nature:

> The *state of nature* has a law of nature to govern it, which obliges every one: and reason, which is that law, teaches all mankind, who but consult it, that being all *equal and independent*, no one ought to harm another in his life, health, liberty, or possessions: for men being all the workmanship of one omnipotent, and infinitely wise maker; all the servants of one sovereign master, sent into the world by his order, and about his business; they are his property, whose workmanship they are, made to last during his, not one another's pleasure: and being furnished with like faculties, sharing all in one community of nature, there cannot be supposed any such *subordination* among us, that may authorize us to destroy one another, as if we were made for one another's uses, as the inferior ranks of creatures are for our's. Every one, as he is *bound to preserve himself*, and not to quit his station wilfully, so by the like reason, when his own preservation comes not in competition, ought he, as much as he can, *to preserve the rest of mankind*, and may not, unless it be to do justice on an offender, take away, or impair the life, or what tends to the preservation of the life, the liberty, health, limb, or goods of another.[79]

According to Locke, the foundation of natural law lies in the application of a principle of distributive justice within a distinctively Protestant theodicy.[80]

What does this claim mean? First, Locke (quoting the sixteenth-century Anglican theologian Richard Hooker), maintains that "things which are equal, must needs have one measure."[81] That is, distributive justice requires that benefits (or burdens) be distributed 'in proportion' to recipients' possession of some relevant sort of merit, worth, or desert. So, if the recipients are 'equal' in the relevant respect, distributive justice entails an equal distribution.

Second, according to Locke's Protestant theodicy, human beings are equal in a fundamental sense. All of us are equally the chattel or property of God, all of us are equally servants of God our "sovereign master," and all of us are, as Locke says, equally "sent into the world by his order, and about his business." This 'business' represents a Protestant, individualized and privatized version of the classical concept of a distinctively human function (*telos*), end, purpose, or 'good'. It is, in other words, a Protestant normative anthropology. In Locke's thought, the notion of a shared, common human *telos* has become a private vocation, in the sense of an assignment from God, individually given to each one of us. Each of us should be regarded as on his or her own individual 'mission from God'; and at least so far as we humans know, all of these missions, and the agents to which they are individually entrusted, are equally important to God. It is, then, the basic business of each of us to determine what our vocation or mission is and to be about it. But, it is also important to allow other people the liberty and means to be about *their* missions, which, insofar as we know, are equally important to God.

With Locke's conception of equally important but individualized and privatized human functions, two related political ideas become fundamentally important. One is the idea of allowing human persons equal and maximal liberty to work out their 'designer', tailor-made individual functions or missions. It seems fairly obvious that if this human function is essentially a private matter, if it is the business only of the individual person and God, undue interference in people's business (whether from other persons individually, or from altar or throne – state or church) is to be deprecated and resisted. The second political idea that becomes especially important is that of property in a broad sense. That is, it is "life, health, liberty, or possessions" – in short, the means necessary for carrying out one's individual mission. This is property in an etymological sense of the term, deriving from the Latin '*proprium*': what is 'one's own' or 'proper' to oneself, about which I, following Locke, shall have more to say later.

Locke holds that reason is entirely capable of discovering moral principles, in general, and the principles of natural law, in particular. He also seems to hold that reason is the source of the obligatory character of such principles. However, the actual psychological motivation to conform to these principles and to respect the obligations they impose is a quite separate matter. Locke's view of human motivation or the 'springs of action' is a hedonistic one very similar to that of Hobbes: as he puts it in *An Essay Concerning Human Understanding*, "*That which is properly good or bad, is nothing but barely Pleasure or Pain.*"[82] But with respect to 'natural' pleasures and pains attendant upon various objects and kinds of behavior in this mortal life, human beings notoriously disagree with respect to what gives them pleasure and pain: "The Mind has a different relish, as well as the Palate: and you will as fruitlessly endeavor to delight all Men with Riches or Glory, (which yet some Men place their Happiness in,) as you would to satisfy all men's Hunger with Cheese or Lobsters, which though very agreeable and delicious fare to some, are to others extremely nauseous and offensive."[83] Locke concludes that, were we to consider only such subjective and varying 'natural' pleasures and pains, if, in other words, "there be no Prospect beyond the Grave, the inference is certainly right, *Let us eat and drink,* let us enjoy what we delight in, *for tomorrow we shall die.*"[84] Locke also appears to believe that there would be no motivation to conform our behavior to the natural law or other demonstrable moral truths – unless we are so constituted that doing so happens to give us pleasure, a state of affairs that he evidently thinks is rare.

As a source of pleasures and pains that both have a uniform effect on all humans and support behavior in conformity to the rational dictates of morality, Locke must appeal to God, who has a very big carrot and very big stick at his disposal. That is, there is the promise of reward (after biological death), in the form of pleasure so great that it is incommensurable with any natural pleasures or pains of this mortal life, for moral compliance. And there is the threat of punishment after biological death, in the form of pain that is similarly incommensurable, for noncompliance. In Locke's estimation these are the singularly important means by which human behavior can be led into the paths of morality. The promise of such exquisite pleasures and threat of such exquisite pains will motivate in a similar way all who take those promises and threats seriously:

> Change but a Man's view of these things; let him see, that Virtue and Religion are necessary to his Happiness; let him look into the future State of Bliss or Misery, and see there God the righteous Judge, ready to *render to every Man according to his Deeds*; ... To him, I say, who hath a prospect of the different State of perfect Happiness or Misery, that attends all men after this Life, depending on their Behaviour here, the measures of Good and Evil, that govern his choice, are mightily changed.[85]

This doctrine had consequences in Locke's thought. One consequence is his exclusion of atheists (along with Romans Catholics, but not Muslims or Jews) from the umbrella of religious toleration that he proposes in his *A Letter on Toleration.* "Those who deny that Deity exists are in no manner to be tolerated," he insists, because "neither trust nor contract nor oath, which are the bonds of human society, can be anything stable or sacred to the atheist."[86] In keeping with his doctrine of *An Essay Concerning Human Understanding*, Locke believes that, in the case of the convinced atheist, there is an absence of the prospect of the sorts of pleasure and pain that is necessary to motivate a human agent to act morally.

We see, then, that God plays at least two quite important but distinct rôles in Locke's thought. (a) It is our obligation to be about God's business, in terms of carrying out the individual mission or function that he has assigned to each of us, that serves as the ultimate foundation of Locke's doctrine of the moral importance of equal maximal liberty and of property rights. (b) It is only God in his rôle as righteous, omnipotent, and omniscient judge, promising eternal pleasure and threatening eternal pain, that can provide sufficient motivation to obtain human compliance with the rationally demonstrable demands of morality.

The state of nature and the social contract

For Locke, as for Hobbes, the state of nature is that real or imagined state in which a group of human beings exist in the absence of political organization. It is conceived by Locke as a state in which individual human persons are free from any obligations deriving from the 'will' of any other person: it is "a *state of perfect freedom* to order their actions, and dispose of their possessions and persons, as they think fit, within the bounds of the law of nature, without asking leave, or depending upon the will of any other man."[87] And, says Locke, "where-ever any persons are, who have not such an authority to appeal to, for the decision of any difference between them, there those persons are still *in the state of nature*."[88]

As a number of commentators have noted, Locke needs the state of nature to be pretty bad but not as bad as Hobbes had thought. It must be bad enough that human beings have adequate motivation to enter into a social contract by means of which the civil state is formed. However, it must not be so bad that the only alternative to it is for human beings to relinquish their political and moral wills to an absolute sovereign. Among contemporary commentators, C.B. Macpherson has claimed that there is an ambiguity, or even indecisiveness, on Locke's part concerning the state of nature that reflects his ambiguity concerning human nature: "In the first picture men generally are naturally reasonable enough to impose on themselves individually the moral rules needed to curb their contentious appetites. In the second picture they are not."[89]

Such 'indecisiveness' as Locke may manifest in this matter is largely due, I believe, to the separation in his thought between the source and content of moral obligation, on the one hand, and the motivation for action in conformity with moral obligation, on the other. For Hobbes, in contrast to Locke, whatever obligation that may exist in the state of nature to observe the laws of nature derives from individual self interest, and more particularly, from the preeminent interest in self-preservation that all persons naturally exhibit. It is this same egoistic foundation of the Hobbesian laws of nature that render them morally 'silent' in the state of nature – because of the lack of guarantee of their effectiveness, in that state, in procuring self-preservation. In the case of Locke, however, the foundation of the laws of nature is not egoistic. The Lockean laws of nature equally enjoin the preservation of the life, liberty, and property of all humans and are never silent in the state of nature. In the state of nature, because there is a law of nature "common to them all, [a person] and all the rest of *mankind are one community*, make up one society, distinct from all other creatures. And were it not for the corruption and vitiousness of degenerate men, there would be no need of any other; no necessity that men should separate from this great and natural community, and by positive agreements combine into smaller and divided associations."[90]

Appealing to a doctrine of corrupted human motivation, which is quite consistent with orthodox Christianity, Locke argues that while the moral force of the laws of nature is fully present in the state of nature, their motivational force is not adequate to insure more-or-less general compliance with them. Nor, it seems, is the motivation supplied by belief in a righteous God with his big carrot and his big stick. Hence, the need for the compacts, contracts, or "positive agreements" that produce the political structures of society. Since a definitional characteristic of the state of nature is the lack of subordination of any person to any other person, it follows that it is the business of each person to determine, in a given situation, what the law of nature requires and to apply and to enforce it.

This situation leads to three 'inconveniences' of the state of nature discussed by Locke. (a) "*First*, there wants an *established*, settled, known *law*, received and allowed by common consent to be the standard of right and wrong, and common measure to decide all controversies."[91] Any problems with respect to the determination of the content of the law of nature in the state of nature are not intellectual, but motivational problems due to the 'corrupt' human tendencies toward egoism and laziness: "For though the law of nature be plain and intelligible to all rational creatures; yet men being biassed by their interest, as well as ignorant for want of study of it, are not apt to allow of it as a law binding to them in the application of it to their particular cases."[92] (b) "*Secondly, In the state of nature there wants a known and indifferent judge*, with authority to determine all differences according to the established law."[93] While the moral obligation exists in the state of nature to preserve the life, liberty, and property of everyone 'indifferently', the motivational fact of partiality to one's own interest impairs the effectiveness of a key feature of the state of nature: the fact that everyone is a judge and enforcer of the natural law. "Passion and revenge is very apt to carry them too far, and with too much heat, in their own cases; as well as negligence and unconcernedness, to make them too remiss in other men's."[94] (c) "*Thirdly*, in the state of nature there often wants *power* to back and support the sentence when right, and to *give* it due *execution*."[95]

In the state of nature, according to Locke, in addition to "the liberty he has of innocent delights," each person has two powers that are either given up entirely or mitigated when he enters into civil or political society. One such power is to punish infractions against the natural law, and this power is entirely relinquished in the civil state. The other is "to do whatsoever he thinks fit for the preservation of himself and others within the permission of the *law of nature*."[96] This power each person "*gives up* to be regulated by laws made by society, so far forth as the preservation of himself, and the rest of that society shall require."[97]

The qualifying clause, "so far forth as the preservation of himself, and the rest of that society shall require," is of fundamental importance: it encapsulates Locke's principle of limited government. For Hobbes, it is essential that the social contract yield an all-powerful Leviathan to escape from the intolerable anarchy, the state of war of each against all, of the state of nature. Locke turns this argument on its head. The state of nature is a state in which "men live together according to reason, without a common superior on earth, with authority to judge between them."[98] A person in such a state "who attempts to get another man into his absolute power, does thereby *put himself into a state of war* with him."[99] A government or sovereign that claims absolute power over its subjects (as in the case of Hobbes' doctrine of absolute monarchy) exists in a state of nature (and state of war) with respect to those who are under its dominion: for there is no "common superior on earth, with authority to judge" between the absolute monarch and any one of its subjects.[100] Consequently, Locke concludes that a government with only limited authority is necessary to transform the state of nature into the state of civil society.

As a contractarian, Locke holds that it is only the social contract, the "consent of any number of freemen capable of a majority to unite and incorporate into such a [civil] society" that "did, or could give beginning to any *lawful government* in the world."[101] The civil or political state is the result of each person's divesting himself of his natural liberty and the putting on of "the *bonds of civil society*" by an agreement of each signatory "with other men to join and unite into a community for their comfortable, safe, and peaceable living one amongst another, in a secure enjoyment of their properties."[102] When any number of persons have made such an agreement,

> they have thereby made that *community* one body, with a power to act as one body, which is only by the will and determination of the *majority*: for that which acts any community, being only the consent of the individuals of it, and it being necessary to that which is one body to move one way; it is necessary the body should move that way whither the greater force carries it, which is the *consent of the majority*.[103]

Locke, like Hobbes, conceives of the social contract as creating an artificial person or body. In Locke's case, it is not clear whether he intends his characterization of the community or commonwealth so created as a 'body' to be understood literally or metaphorically. But it is quite clear that he intends to identify the 'will' of the commonwealth with the majority of wills of the 'signatories' to the contract. The primary and first recipient of the natural liberties given up by the signatories to the social contract is the majority of citizens – as opposed to the 'government', that person or group of persons embodying the sovereign power, in Hobbes' version of the social contract. There are several other distinctive features of Locke's version of the social contract.

The first, to which I have already alluded, is that the signatories do not endow the commonwealth, or any representative of it, with absolute or arbitrary power. The power vested in the commonwealth is not arbitrary. It "can *never be supposed to extend farther, than the common good*; but is obliged to secure every one's property, by providing against those three defects mentioned above, that made the state of nature so unsafe and uneasy."[104] The legislative power created by majority decision of the signatories to the social contract is

> only a fiduciary power to act for certain ends, [and] there remains *still in the people a supreme power to remove or alter the legislative*, when they find the *legislative* act contrary to the trust reposed in

them: for all *power given with trust* for the attaining an *end*, being limited by that end, whenever that *end* is manifestly neglected, or opposed, the *trust* must necessarily be *forfeited*, and the power devolve into the hands of those that gave it.[105]

Nor is the power vested in the commonwealth by the social contract absolute. It is not absolute because the power of none of the signatories, being limited by the natural law, is absolute – either with respect to the signatory himself or with respect to other persons: "For no body can transfer to another more power than he has in himself; and no body has an absolute arbitrary power over himself, or over any other, to destroy his own life, or take away the life or property of another."[106]

Second, many of the more concrete political provisions and claims of the *Second Treatise* were a matter of Whig party politics – even though these provisions have generally become a part of the heritage of Western constitutional democracies. A majority of signatories to the social contract construct a 'legislative' or law-making political structure for the civil society, which Locke obviously tends to think of as some form of parliament. In practical terms, it has supreme (but not arbitrary or absolute) authority in the civil state or political community. But "the *community* may be said to be *always the supreme power*, but not as considered under any form of government, because this power of the people can never take place till the government be dissolved."[107] Locke allows that "in some common-wealths, where the *legislative* is not always in being [e.g., parliament not always in session]," there is good reason to have the executive power of the civil society vested in a single person (e.g., a constitutional monarch). But (in opposition to Stuart divine-right-of-kings theorists) any such executive power is subordinate to the legislative – and has no source independent from the legislative.

Locke's discussion of the proper limitations of executive power derives, in large part, from a list of Whig complaints against what they considered to be the abuse of power by the Stuart monarchs. But the legislative authority is also limited. It "cannot assume to itself a power to rule by extemporary arbitrary decrees [as had the Stuart kings in improperly assuming legislative as well as executive power], but *is bound to dispense justice, and decide the rights of subjects by promulgated standing laws, and known authorized judges*."[108] It "*cannot take from any man any part of his property* without his own consent: for the preservation of property [is] the end of government."[109] And the constituted legislative authority "*cannot transfer making laws* to any other hands: for it being but a delegated power from the people, they who have it cannot pass it over to others."[110]

Finally, Locke holds that the natural law gives to each person in the state of nature a right to property, in a broad sense of the term, as a necessary means for accomplishing his or her divinely assigned mission. The primary purpose of the civil society created by the social contract is the protection of that property, as Locke repeatedly asserts: "Government has no other end but the preservation of property";[111] "the great end of men's entering into society [is] the enjoyment of their properties in peace and safety."[112] In the following section, we consider Locke's doctrine of property, a doctrine which he certainly regards as fundamental to his political philosophy.

Property and liberal political theory: Lockean origins

There has typically been a close connection between property and the liberal-democratic tradition of which Locke was an early exponent. Eighteenth- and nineteenth-century critics of this tradition – both sympathetic critics such as Rousseau, and unsympathetic ones such as Marx – believed that the Lockean doctrines of the social contract and of liberal representative government as a protector of private property easily become rhetorical tools serving the interests of the propertied class within society. From the contrary perspective, some defenders of the connection between property and liberal-democratic forms of polity have argued that the various liberties dear to the heart of the liberal-democratic tradition cannot be sustained without economic liberty, which in turn can be protected only by a strong political commitment to property rights. Locke's emphasis on the centrality of the notion of property to the liberal-democratic tradition was surely an important historical factor in forging the connection between property and liberal representative government, a connection still very pertinent to practical politics within contemporary liberal democracies. However, his conception of the connection between property and politics is ambiguous: as we shall see, his doctrine of the foundation of property rights, although it seems to preclude unequal property distribution, is trumped by his doctrine of the moral centrality of agreements or contracts in such a way as to permit quite unequal distribution of property.

Locke's doctrine of property begins with the broad and etymological sense to which I have previously alluded: one's property is what is *proprium* to oneself – what is one's own. The property of persons is, Locke says, a "general name" designating "their lives, liberties, and estates."[113] One's right, in the state of nature, to property is a positive right, in Isaiah Berlin's sense. It is a right that one possesses in virtue of one's individual divinely assigned function or mission: the preservation of one's life, liberty, and estate is to be thought of not as an ultimate end but as a means for carrying out the mission of God, whose chattel we are. Locke holds that a person in the state of nature can acquire a right to property in the narrower (and now more common) sense – one's "estate," possessions, or material goods – *without* any agreement or "express compact of all the commoners."[114]

According to Locke, God has given the "world," that is, the natural resources from which humans can derive sustenance, "to men in common."[115] But, in order for these resources to be so used, they must be appropriated by the individual. Locke maintains that a person gains rights to such resources, transforming them into his or her property, by investing his or her labor in them:

> Though the earth, and all inferior creatures, be common to all men, yet every man has a *property* in his own *person*: this no body has any right to but himself. The *labour* of his body, and the *work* of his hands, we may say, are properly his. Whatsoever then he removes out of the state that nature hath provided, and left it in, hath mixed his *labour* with, and joined to it something that is his own, and thereby makes it his *property* ...: for this *labour* being the unquestionable property of the labourer, no man but he can have a right to what that is once joined to, at least where there is enough, and as good, left in common for others.[116]

This labor theory of property yields, for all persons in the state of nature, limited and roughly equal rights to property, as Locke well realizes: "The same law of nature, that does by this means give us property, does also *bound* that *property* too."[117] The law of nature gives everyone a right to property for the same reason. In terms of moral considerations, if not actual human motivation, my right to property in no way trumps yours. As a factual matter, it would seem that the amount of resources with which we are capable of mixing our labor is limited and at least roughly equal for all healthy, non-deformed adult persons. A further limitation, Locke claims, is that I must be able to use whatever I mix my labor with without those resources spoiling: "As much as any one can make use of to any advantage of life before it spoils, so much he may by his labour fix a property in: whatever is beyond this, is more than his share, and belongs to others."[118]

If the foregoing had constituted the sum of Locke's doctrine of property, it would not have been a doctrine having much appeal to Locke's Whig patrons, who enjoyed the benefits of a very unequal distribution of property. But it is not the sum of Locke's doctrine. To shorten the story a bit, Locke maintains that the introduction of money, as a conventional standard of value and exchange, morally legitimizes quite unequal distribution of property. Money has only conventional value and does not spoil. Locke really has two arguments that these obvious facts entail the moral permissibility of the unequal distribution of property. One of these arguments concludes that, because of the conventional worth and durability of money, a person can accumulate it without limit without trespassing on the property rights of others:

> But since gold and silver, being little useful to the life of man in proportion to food, raiment, and carriage, has its *value* only from the consent of men, whereof *labour* yet *makes*, in great part, *the measure*, it is plain, that men have agreed to a disproportionate and unequal *possession of the earth*, they having, by a tacit and voluntary consent, found a way how a man may fairly possess more land than he himself can use the product of, by receiving in exchange for the overplus gold and silver, which may be hoarded up without injury to any one; these metals not spoiling or decaying in the hands of the possessor.[119]

Locke's argument, which is so weak as to seem ridiculous, appears to be that since gold and silver (or some other conventional standard of value) does not spoil, I can accumulate as much as possible without infringement on the property rights of other persons: since money is not something that is directly consumable by other persons in the sense of being usable as food, clothing, shelter, transportation, etc. (and does not spoil), I can accumulate a disproportional amount of it without depriving anyone else of something usable for that person's sustenance. This argument rather wilfully neglects the fact that money, having been introduced as a standard of exchange and value, is 'fungible' – that is, exchangeable for what directly contributes to human sustenance. Therefore, on the assumption of a limited supply of money (which is necessary if it is to have value), my possession of a disproportionate amount of it may well deprive someone else of what he or she needs.

One reason that Locke invokes against accumulating such excessive property that it spoils is that doing so deprives other people of potential property, which may be necessary for their sustaining themselves in such a manner that they are able to carry out their divinely assigned function. But another reason seems to be, simply, a deep Protestant aversion to waste: "Nothing was made by God for man to spoil or destroy."[120] The two reasons are still frequently confused: many American and English children of my generation were admonished, when leaving uneaten food on the plate, to think of the "poor, starving children in China (or Africa or . . .)." There is little doubt that more than one of those children found some difficulty in understanding the potential benefits to be derived by Chinese children from his not wasting his overcooked vegetables. Locke seems to be suffering from a form of the confusion detected by such sapient children. The fact that the use of some conventional standard of exchange can enable me to be disproportionately wealthy without wasting any of my goods from spoilage does not entail that my disproportionate wealth does not deprive someone else of property that he or she may need to pursue his or her own ends (in God's service, of course, according to Locke).

However, there is in Locke's discussion a deeper and less silly rationale for departing from the *natural* limited and roughly equal right to property. It is simply that people have explicitly or tacitly agreed to do so. Locke may be read as claiming that if one endorses the social and political structures, including the monetary ones, that facilitate the acquisition of capital, one is also implicitly endorsing the possibility that some persons will be more successful than others in taking advantage of those structures. Such arrangements (which are a matter of *nomos* rather than *physis*, to use our venerable Greek terms) can even be made consistent with Locke's labor theory of property. Although it was Marx rather than Locke who explicitly made the point, the economic structures that permit labor to become a commodity, upon which monetary value can be set and which can then be bought and sold, enable the capitalist to use his wealth to hire labor and to treat that hired labor as his own – 'mixing' it with resources to obtain much more property than would be possible were he to employ only the labor of his own body.

The fundamental fiduciary responsibility of the civil state to protect the property rights of its citizens apparently is the responsibility to protect the right to unequal distribution of property. It is perhaps not surprising, however, that Locke does not stress this point, preferring to take by way of illustrations of the sacrosanctness of property rights persons of modest means. A noteworthy example is that of a soldier who, for the sake of the "preservation of the army, and in it of the whole common-wealth," owes "an *absolute obedience* to the command of every superior officer, and it is justly death to disobey or dispute the most dangerous or unreasonable" such command.[121] Yet, Locke says, neither the sarjeant, that could command a soldier to march up to the mouth of a cannon, or stand in a breach, where he is almost sure to perish, can command that soldier to give him one penny of his money; nor the *general*, that can condemn him to death for deserting his post, or for not obeying the most desperate orders, can yet, with all his *absolute power* of life and death, dispose of one farthing of that soldier's estate, or seize one jot of his goods.[122]

In a passage of much irony, C.B. Macpherson pays Locke's doctrine of property an equivocal compliment:

Locke makes a unique and ingenious case for a natural right of unlimited private property, with which society and government are not entitled to interfere: no-one, before or after, has come near his skill in moving from a limited and equal to an unlimited and unequal property right by invoking rationality and consent.[123]

What seems to me to be mistaken in this passage is Macpherson's characterization of Locke's doctrine of the "right of unlimited private property" as a *natural* right. On the contrary, it is a right deriving – as Macpherson himself notes – from "consent," from agreement or contract that is either explicit or tacit. Locke's quite nonclassical assumption seems to be that such consent or agreement can override considerations of natural law and the natural rights that are derived from it. As a seminal figure in the contractarian tradition, Locke tends to see political (and often moral) obligations as deriving from consent or agreement.

Macpherson concludes that Locke may "well be said to have written the title-deeds of the liberal bourgeois state. Those who wish to question that title, or to reinforce it, may well begin by narrowly examining the *Second Treatise*."[124] A fundamental feature of Lockean (and, more generally, contractarian) political theory is the doctrine of consent and agreement as constituting the fountainhead of political morality. This feature of Locke's thought is certainly deserving of narrow examination. As we shall see in the following chapter, it received that examination, in quite different ways, from Rousseau and Marx.

8

Rousseau and Marx: Reaction to Bourgeois-Liberalism

A strong connection was established in seventeenth-century contract-arianism, particularly that of John Locke, between individual liberty and the protection of property. By the term 'bourgeois-liberalism' used in the title to this chapter, I mean to comprehend those varieties of political thought that are committed to maintaining this connection.[1] More particularly, the term usually connotes one (or both) of two sorts of doctrine. (a) The first is a political theory that emphasizes government's function as a preserver of some list of individual liberties or free-doms (usually conceptualized in terms of rights) and includes the rights of property ownership and, usually, more-or-less unlimited property acquisition as prominent items on that list. (b) The second is a political theory that emphasizes government's function as a preserver of some list of individual liberties and that conceptualizes these liberties as belonging to persons whose essential nature is that of autonomous, self-interested agents motivated by considerations that might be termed 'economic', in a broad sense of the term. That is, the human agent is conceived as a *homo economicus*, who is motivated exclusively or principally by considerations of material and social self-aggrandizement (the concrete manifestation of which includes, prominently, property or wealth and the status that accompanies wealth). In short, the human agent is conceived as a '*bourgeois*', in one (often somewhat pejorative) sense of the French noun.

Rousseau and Marx criticize bourgeois-liberal political theory in both senses. With respect to the first sense (a), they maintain that political theory of this sort is generally simply a device employed by representatives of the wealthier classes to supply a moral justification for the unequal distribution of wealth and to protect the social and economic *status quo*. However, their deeper critique of the tradition pertains to the second sense (b). Both repudiate the idea of an essential human nature, invariant and 'natural' to the human kind. Consequently, they repudiate the idea that the essential or 'given' human nature is the 'bourgeois' nature of the *homo economicus*. Although we shall see that neither Rousseau nor Marx entirely dispenses with the very idea of a human nature, function, good, or end, both philosophers hold that human nature has undergone historical change and is socially malleable. That is, human nature is wholly or in large part determined by the nexus of social and economic relationships in which individual persons, at different historical periods, find themselves. This sort of historicism exemplifies the *Gemeinschaft* paradigm of social organization described by Ferdinand Tônnies and discussed in Chapter 1 of this book. According to that paradigm, the 'nature' of us human beings – which includes our conception of our interests and our systems of preferences – is in large part if not wholly defined by the political context within which we find ourselves. It might thus be doubtful whether there would be any *independent* plausible criteria that could serve to justify or legitimate one form of polity over another in any way that would not be historically relative. It would seem that the classical criterion for the discussion of and assessment of the purpose and function of political organization has been completely lost. In other words, lost is the idea of an objective function (*ergon*) or end (*telos*), which is held to be proper to humankind as such and to have normative implications about how human beings *should* live their lives. Thus, the assumption that some sort of normative anthropology is a key component of political theory would appear to be eliminated.

In fact, neither Rousseau nor Marx wishes to embrace a thoroughgoing political relativism, according to which any sort of political organization that may historically manifest itself is immune to criticism. Moreover, it is arguable that both of them *do* make normative use of the concept of a human nature or a human *ergon* and, in that sense, that they both appeal to a normative anthropology. But their assumption of the historical mutability of human nature means that, in order to avoid incoherence in their use of this concept, some very particular assumptions about which 'human nature' has positive normative significance (and why it is *that* nature which has such significance) must be made.

Jean-Jacques Rousseau: autonomous citizens for the true republic

Jean-Jacques Rousseau (1712–1778) was born in Geneva, the son of a sentimental and rather irresponsible watchmaker father and a mother who died within days of his birth. He lacked all but the most rudimentary formal education, having learned to read from his father's library of novels and Plutarch's *Lives*. He was apprenticed early to an engraver, suffered brutal treatment from the engraver and his wife, and deserted his master and Geneva at the age of sixteen. Rousseau ended up as a convert to Catholicism[2] in the household of another recent convert, a Baroness de Warens (only twelve years his senior), one of whose lovers he in due course became. While a member of Mme. de Warens' household, he undertook an intensive course of self-education.

Thereafter, Rousseau lived an irregular and troubled existence. He did manage to obtain entrance into the most advanced French intellectual circle. This was the circle of the so-called *philosophes*, such as Denis Diderot and Jean le Rond d'Alembert, who were the relentlessly 'progressively minded' moving force behind the great French eighteenth-century intellectual project, the *Encylopédie*, to which Rousseau (who had invented a system of musical notation) contributed articles on musical topics. As a group, *les philosophes* were intellectually committed to the development of the new science of the seventeenth century (usually with a materialist metaphysical underpinning), steadfastly opposed to the established political and social order of the French *ancien régime*, and dismissive of all forms of revealed religion (usually professing deism,[3] either sincerely or as a socially convenient cover for atheism). Rousseau began to establish his intellectual and literary reputation with the publication of the *Discourse on the Sciences and Arts* in 1750. This was the first of three *Discourses* published by Rousseau (the *Discourse on the Origin of Inequality* [1755] and the *Discourse on Political Economy* [1755 and 1758] are the second and third, respectively) and won the prize offered by the Academy of Dijon for the best essay addressing the question, "Has the reestablishment of the sciences and arts served to purify or corrupt manners and morals?" In opposition to the generally progressively minded outlook of the *philosophes*, Rousseau argued for the corrupting effect of the sciences and arts – a fact that no doubt did much to establish the widespread but erroneous view of Rousseau as a romantic primitivist, a champion of the ideal of the 'noble savage' (a phrase that does not appear in his writings).

The works of Rousseau's full intellectual maturity appeared in the early 1760s: *Julie, ou la Nouvelle Héloïse* (dealing with sex and marriage, in the form of an epistolary novel), *Émile* (dealing with education, also partly in novelistic form), and *On the Social Contract, or Principles of Political Right* (Rousseau's principal work on political theory). Following the official condemnation of his works both in France and in his native Geneva, Rousseau settled briefly in Neuchâtel and then accepted an invitation to seek refuge in England, an invitation that had been extended by the Scots philosopher and historian David Hume. By this time Rousseau was certainly suffering from mental illness, and it became almost impossible for him to maintain normal social intercourse. He quarreled with Hume, a man with whom it was very difficult to quarrel, and fled to France where he lived the remainder of his life, for the most part under an assumed name and in an increasingly deep state of paranoid despair.

It is easy to read crucial elements of Rousseau's sad biography into his political thought: the yearning for the 'lost Eden' of the idealized republic of Geneva and also of the idealized Roman republic to which the young Rousseau was introduced in his father's classical but sentimental library. Until official opposition to his work by Genevan officials provoked his polemical *Letters Written from the Mountain* in 1764, Rousseau regularly identified himself, in his published writings, as "a citizen of Geneva," despite the fact that he had not really lived in Geneva subsequent to his early adolescence. In the words of the critic P. Gay, for Rousseau, "the best of good societies would always be a republic unfettered by a hereditary aristocracy."[4] The phrase "unfettered by a hereditary aristocracy" is of the utmost importance. Perhaps the principal theme informing all of Rousseau's writings on political and social topics is the vice of what might be termed 'personal dependency', the dependence of the will of one human being on that of another. Again, one may readily trace Rousseau's aversion to personal dependency to his frustrating experiences of the rigid social hierarchies he encountered in the French *ancien régime*. But Rousseau develops a political theory of great brilliance, subtlety, and complexity that far transcends whatever unhappy biographical details may have underlaid it.

In the second *Discourse* (the *Discourse on the Origin of Inequality*) Rousseau provides an *a priori*, armchair prehistory of humankind, tracing the development of personal dependency and of the inequalities that such dependency inevitably entails. But along with this corruption there arise morality and those social virtues that Rousseau associates with his normative conception of what a human being should be. The *Émile* investigates the education of a person toward this normative ideal, in which an attempt is made to reconcile autonomy (absence of personal dependency) and the demands of social life. The *Social Contract*, on the other hand, considers the sort of political structure ('city', 'republic', or 'body politic'[5]) in which it is possible to reconcile autonomy with social life. We turn first to Rousseau's history of human corruption and civilization – he believes that the two are quite inseparable – in the second *Discourse*.

The intertwined development of civilization, corruption, and morality

The armchair prehistory of humankind described by Rousseau in his *Discourse on the Origin of Inequality*, the second *Discourse*, appears to depict the species as going to hell in a handbasket. From a state of nature in which humans lived solitary, animal-like, but generally peaceful lives, there have developed civilized civil states (such as France), which are characterized by an "excess of corruption": "From the extreme inequality of conditions and fortunes, from the diversity of passions and talents, from useless arts, from pernicious arts, from frivolous sciences there would come a pack of prejudices equally contrary to reason, happiness and virtue."[6] Rousseau's reputation as a romantic primitivist, yearning for a pre-political, Edenic, natural state of humankind, is perhaps most due to the second *Discourse*. But a careful reading of its text discloses a more ambiguous, subtle, and interesting view.

In the second *Discourse* Rousseau appropriates the conceptual mechanism of seventeenth-century contractarianism, in particular, the concepts of the state of nature and the social contract. But he puts this mechanism to a use quite different from Hobbes' and Locke's employment of it. To begin with, Rousseau conceives of the pre-political state of nature not as a static condition but as a developmental sequence of states of human existence. There is, perhaps, some historical necessity to this sequence; but, if so, it is a necessity that "required the chance coming together of several unconnected causes that might never have come into being and without which [man] would have remained eternally in his primitive constitution."[7] For human existence in the initial and "pure" stage of the state of nature, Rousseau chooses the model of the solitary, as opposed to social or 'herding', animal:

> I see an animal less strong than some, less agile than others, but all in all, the most advantageously organized of all. I see him satisfying his hunger under an oak tree, quenching his thirst at the first

stream, finding his bed at the foot of the same tree that supplied his meal; and thus all his needs are satisfied.[8]

Human beings in this most primitive of states exist without language and with only the most instinctual intellectual capacities. They are motivated exclusively by self-love (*amour de soi-même*) and a 'natural' pity having as its principal object the sufferings of others of the same species. Rousseau regards *amour de soi-même* as a 'natural and good' sort of self-love and, in a note to the second *Discourse*, distinguishes it from an 'artificial and bad' sort of self-love, *amour-propre* or egocentrism:

> *L'amour de soi-même* is a natural sentiment which moves every animal to be vigilant in its own preservation and which, directed in man by reason and modified by pity, produced humanity and virtue. *L'amour-propre* is merely a sentiment that is relative, artificial and born in society, which moves each individual to value himself more than anyone else, which inspires in men all the evils they cause one another, and which is the true source of honor.
>
> With this well understood, I say that in our primitive state, in the veritable state of nature, *amour-propre* does not exist.[9]

According to Rousseau, *amour-propre* always has an essential other-regarding component: it always involves comparative judgments pertaining to one's own welfare, ease, comfort, etc. relative to the status of others; it always involves explicit or implicit appeal to the attitudes, opinions, and status of other persons in the assessment of one's own condition. The growth of *amour-propre* is one of the developmental features of Rousseau's conception of the state of nature, and its growth goes hand in glove with the development of the sort of personal dependency that Rousseau so deprecates. One of the paradoxes characteristic of Rousseau's thought is that the development of egocentrism (*amour-propre*) necessarily involves a diminution of autonomy – in the form of the development of an attitude requiring one to assess one's own welfare in comparison to the welfare of others and from the viewpoint of others.

However, as the preceding quotation makes clear, mankind in the *most primitive* stage of the state of nature is not afflicted with *amour-propre*. At that state, a human's natural *amour de soi-même* is balanced by his natural sentiment of pity. Since, at this stage, "the concern for our self-preservation is least prejudicial to that of others, that state was consequently the most appropriate for peace and the best suited for the human race."[10] Rousseau explicitly criticizes Hobbes for mistakenly attributing to man in the state of nature the character of man corrupted by the development of *amour-propre* and beset by "the need to satisfy a multitude of passions which are the product of society and which have made laws necessary."[11]

Then, is not this initial state of nature an altogether idyllic state of human existence? And is it not then the case that the 'caricature' of Rousseau as romantic primitivist is accurate? No – and for the simple reason that *human persons* do not really exist at this stage; there exist only animals that are potentially human. Reason is so little developed that it would be quite false to categorize humans at this stage as rational animals. And Rousseau is quite clear that "men in that state, having among themselves no type of moral relations or acknowledged duties, could be neither good nor evil, and had neither vices or virtues, unless, if we take these words in a physical sense, we call those qualities that can harm an individual's preservation 'vices' in him, and those that can contribute to it 'virtues'."[12] But, Rousseau proceeds to claim, such a use of the terminology of virtues and vices would depart "from the standard meaning of these words." Rousseau here adopts the common contractarian assumption that morality is fundamentally a matter of conventional or artificial, as opposed to natural, relations among persons. In other words, he adopts the assumption that morality is ultimately founded in rational agreement or assent of some sort. It is a matter of *nomos* rather than *physis*, to use our venerable Greek terminology.

Rousseau is also sufficiently imbued with classical ideals to attach positive normative value both to rationality and to the traditional moral virtues. Consequently, it is really a later, transitional stage of the state of nature, in which these distinctively human characteristics manifest themselves, that Rousseau takes to be the "happiest epoch" of human existence. But this second stage also witnesses increasing human corruption. One source of corruption is the development of the idea of property, an idea that is treated by Rousseau in a way quite different from Locke's treatment:

> The first person who, having enclosed a plot of land, took it into his head to say *this is mine* and found people simple enough to believe him, was the true founder of civil society. What crimes, wars, murders, what miseries and horrors would the human race have been spared, had someone pulled up the stakes or filled in the ditch and cried out to his fellow men: "Do not listen to this imposter. You are lost if you forget that the fruits of the earth

belong to all and earth to no one!" But it is quite likely that by then things had already reached the point where they could no longer continue as they were.[13]

Rousseau expands on this last point: the development of language and human rational capacities, of "industry and enlightenment", and of human familial and social bonds – in short many of the distinctively human intellectual and moral characteristics – is a prelude that seemingly inevitably leads to the institution of private property. "As the mind and heart are trained, the human race continues to be tamed, relationships spread and bonds are tightened."[14] One result is that "each one began to look at the others and to want to be looked at himself, and public esteem had a value"; and "as soon as men had begun mutually to value one another, and the idea of esteem (*la considération*) was formed in their minds, each one claimed to have a right to it, and it was no longer possible for anyone to be lacking it with impunity."[15] What this all amounts to, according to Rousseau, is that "morality [began] to be introduced into human actions."[16]

In the initial state of human beings, the instinctual sentiments of *amour de soi-même* and pity made possible an animal-like state of human coexistence, in which humans for the most part left one another alone and in which there were no stable social relations. As people become more human, as rationality increases and social bonds are formed, morality must replace instinct in regulating human relations. Morality is grounded, first of all, in reason. It involves coming to understand that other persons have needs and desires, including a desire for esteem, similar to mine; it involves seeing that considerations of reciprocity can lead to general moral principles in which the needs and wants of other persons are accorded consideration neither more nor less weighty than that accorded to my own needs and wants. Why, however, should we *care* about such moral principles? Rousseau's answer is that it is not just healthy, instinctual self-regard (*amour de soi-même*) but *amour-propre*, and our consequent concern with esteem and precedence, that provide the motivation to make us care about issues of equity and justice and morality in general. So, another of Rousseau's paradoxes is that the development of morality depends on the development of the egocentrism, the *amour-propre*, which is also the wellspring of vice and social corruption.

There is, to say the least, a delicate balance here, and Rousseau believes that it was achieved at the second, transitional stage of the state of nature, in which reason and *amour-propre* have manifested themselves with the consequent establishment of morality, but in which humans have not been completely corrupted by personal dependency. At this stage,

> although men had become less forbearing, and although natural pity had already undergone some alteration, this period of the development of human faculties, maintaining a middle position between the indolence of our primitive state and the petulant activity of our egocentrism (*de notre amour-propre*), must have been the happiest and most durable epoch. The more one reflects on it, the more one finds that this state was the least subject to upheavals and the best for man, and that he must have left it only by virtue of some fatal chance happening that, for the common good, ought never have happened.[17]

But Rousseau believes that it is clear that there did indeed occur such a "fatal chance happening," which led to the third and final stage of the state of nature which, in turn, led to the formation of civil society by means of the social contract.

In the third and final stage of the state of nature, there is good news and bad, but the bad far outweighs the good. Here "we find all our faculties developed, memory and imagination in play, *amour-propre* looking out for its interests, reason rendered active, and mind having nearly reached the limit of the perfection of which it is capable."[18] But personal dependency has dramatically increased. We find man,

> so to speak, subject, by virtue of a multitude of fresh needs, to all of nature and particularly to his fellowmen, whose slave in a sense he becomes even in becoming their master; rich, he needs their services; poor, he needs their help; and being midway in between wealth and poverty does not put him in a position to get along without them. It is therefore necessary for him to seek incessantly to interest them in his fate and to make them find their own profit, in fact or in appearance, in working for his. This makes him two-faced and crooked with some, imperious and harsh with others, and puts him in the position of having to abuse everyone whom he needs when he cannot make them fear him and he does not find it in his interest to be of useful service to them.[19]

In such circumstances, without the benefit of civil society (formal political structures), something quite similar to Hobbes' war of each against all develops. And (as in the case of Hobbes' political thought) Rousseau presents the social contract as the solution to what had become an intolerable situation.

However, in clear opposition to both Hobbes and Locke, Rousseau regards the social contract at this stage of the state of nature as in large part a confidence trick, a ruse devised by the more clever among the class of those with the most to lose (by way of property) from the continuation of such anarchy. Such a person makes a proposal:

> "Let us unite," he says to them, "in order to protect the weak from oppression, restrain the ambitious, and assure everyone of possessing what belongs to him. Let us institute rules of justice and peace to which all will be obliged to conform, which will make special exceptions for no one, and which in some way compensate for the caprices of fortune by subjecting the strong and weak to mutual obligations. In short, turning our forces against ourselves, let us gather them into one supreme power that governs us according to wise laws, that protects and defends the members of the association, repulses common enemies, and maintains us in an eternal concord."[20]

Rousseau comments that "considerably less" than such an appeal "was needed to convince crude, easily seduced men."[21] "They all ran to chain themselves," he adds, "in the belief that they secured their liberty, for although they had enough sense to realize the advantages of a political establishment, they did not have enough experience to foresee its dangers. Those most capable of anticipating the abuses were precisely those who counted on profiting from them."[22] For Hobbes and Locke, the analytic device of the social contract is supposed to account for the *legitimacy* of political organization, which will always have a coercive aspect. For Rousseau in the second *Discourse*, the social contract accounts for the legitimacy of nothing. Rather, it "gave new fetters to the weak and new forces to the rich, irretrievably destroyed natural liberty, established forever the law of property and of inequality, changed adroit usurpation into an irrevocable right, and for the profit of a few ambitious men henceforth subjected the entire human race to labor, servitude and misery."[23] The ultimate result of the formation of civil society is – another of Rousseau's paradoxes – an *artificial* state of nature much worse than the natural one: despite the rhetoric of the social contract, the *real* civil state produced by that contract is a state in which the "law of the strongest" prevails and in which political power can be maintained only by force: "The uprising that ends in the strangulation and dethronement of a sultan is as lawful an act as those by which he disposed of the lives and goods of his subjects the day before."[24]

In other words, the *dénouement* of the social contract is the France of the *ancien régime*. (Rousseau did not live to see the French revolution, but it is not surprising that he was appropriated as a proto-hero of that momentous event.) In the next section, we shall turn to Rousseau's work *On the Social Contract*, where he begins by stating the fundamental question of the work: "Whether there can be some legitimate and sure rule of administration of the civil order, taking men as they are and laws as they might be."[25] In view of the doctrine of the second *Discourse* that we have been discussing, it is scarcely less than astounding that Rousseau's answer to this question is the social contract!

The *Social Contract* and the *Émile*: republics and republican citizens

Unless we are to regard the two works as blatantly inconsistent with one another, the social contract of the second *Discourse* must be a different social contract from that of the *Social Contract*. The former is what we may term a Lockean social contract. It presupposes preexistent rights and preexistent property and attempts to legitimate, morally, an inegalitarian structure of social relations in terms of the fundamental contractarian notion of agreement or assent. Rousseau, I believe, has made it abundantly clear in the second *Discourse* his conviction that a Lockean social contract cannot be the basis of political legitimacy. In the *Social Contract* he notes that even the fundamental Lockean principle of "the law of majority rule is itself an established convention."[26] In the *Social Contract*, Rousseau also maintains that "force does not bring about right, and that one is obliged to obey only legitimate powers,"[27] and such legitimacy must rest upon a "*première convention*," an "act whereby a people is a people."[28] This *première convention* is the second sort of social contract, the one discussed in the *Social Contract* that is the only possible source of political legitimacy.

It should be noted, to begin with, that Rousseau's conception of this second, legitimacy-conferring sort of social contract is extraordinarily abstract. For Hobbes, the sovereign power created by the social contract is vested in the government (whatever form it may assume), and for Locke, it is vested in the majority of the signatories. For Rousseau, however, the sovereign created by the social contract is identified with the general will (*la volonté générale*). One anticipates that Rousseau must conceive of the social contract and this sovereign power created by it (i.e., the general will) in quite abstract terms from his description of what he expects from it: to provide "a form of association which defends and protects with all common forces the person and goods of each associate, and by means of which each one, while uniting with all, nevertheless obeys only himself and remains as free as before."[29] Rousseau would seem to expect a great deal of the social contract, which he characterizes as follows: it is an agreement that each signatory makes with every other signatory that "each of us places his person and all his power in common under the supreme direction of the general will; and as one we receive each member as an indivisible part of the whole."[30]

In view of the results that he expects from the social contract and the sovereign power created by it (that each person in entering into civil society "obeys only himself and remains as free as before"), Rousseau makes some surprising claims about the social contract and the sovereign that it creates. (1) The alienation (of person and power) by each signatory "is made without reservation." This could not be the case "if some rights remained with private individuals."[31] (2) The sovereign or general will "neither has nor could have an interest contrary to" that "of the private individuals who make it up (*des particuliers qui le composent*)." Consequently, it cannot "harm any one of them in particular. The sovereign, by the mere fact that it exists, is always all that it should be."[32] (3) "Since sovereignty is merely the exercise of the general will, it can never be alienated, and ... the sovereign, which is only a collective being, cannot be represented by anything but itself. Power can perfectly well be transmitted, but not the will."[33] (4) The general will cannot err: "The general will is always right and always tends toward the public utility." (5) But there is a difference between the "sum of private wills" or "the will of all (*la volonté de tous*)," on the one hand, and the general will, on the other. "The latter considers only the general interest, whereas the former considers private interest."[34] (6) So, "each individual can, as a man, have a private will contrary to or different from the general will that he has as a citizen. His private interest can speak to him in an entirely different manner than the common interest."[35] (7) The preceding consideration leads Rousseau to make a famous (or infamous) claim about the social contract's tacitly entailing the "commitment – which alone can give force to the others – that whoever refuses to obey the general will will be forced to do so by the entire body. This means merely that he will be forced to be free."[36]

Central to Rousseau's abstract and difficult conception of the general will is the distinction that it entails between the interest that each of us has as a citizen, which is the object of the general will, and the interest each of us has as a private, self-interested person or *bourgeois*, which is the object of our private wills. Rousseau's claim is that the former common interest is the same for all persons and, hence, entirely interchangeable. It is what constitutes our common self (*moi commun*) and serves as the rational basis of the state. It is the common interest of this common self that, by definition, constitutes the object of the general will. Therefore, in obeying the general will, we are obeying only the will of *this* self; and, by definition, the general will cannot have any interest different from the will of this self. "Why is the general will always right ..." Rousseau asks,

> if not because everyone applies this word *each* to himself and thinks of himself as he votes for all? This proves that the quality of right and the notion of justice it produces are derived from the preference each person gives himself, and thus from the nature of man; that the general will, to be really such, must be general in its object as well as in its essence; that it must derive from all in order to be applied to all; and that it loses its natural rectitude when it tends toward any individual, determinate object. For then, judging what is foreign to us, we have no true principle of equity to guide us.[37]

We may think of individual public decisions as either being or not being expressions of the abstract notion of the Rousseauian general will. In order to be such, a decision must satisfy the two conditions of generality of essence and generality of object.

Generality of essence evidently pertains to *how* such a public decision gets made. Rousseau clearly follows the contractarian tradition in holding that the agreement or consent of those individuals affected by a decision is necessary for its legitimacy. One might term such agreement/consent the 'democratic condition of political legitimacy'. However, Rousseau also maintains that *actual* unanimous agreement is not necessary for a decision to count as an expression of the general will. It is only one's *common* interest (which is identical to the interest of each other person) that should be represented in determining the general will. If one 'votes' in such a way as to express one's private interest – one's interest as a *bourgeois* – and that interest conflicts with the common interest, then one's vote can be properly ignored and one can be "forced to be free." This is a matter of being forced to act in conformity with one's will as a citizen, which Rousseau seems to regard as one's 'truer' will.

In sum, Rousseau's generality of essence condition seems to amount to no more than a sort of conditional version of the democratic condition of political legitimacy: for a decision to count as a decision of the general will, it must be a decision that each citizen *would* agree to if he or she were sufficiently rational, duly informed, not corrupted by excessive *amour-propre*, etc. However, even if each person is prepared to act only on his or her common interest in making public decisions, it is not the case that, with respect to all public decisions, there *is* a common interest or expression of the general will to be ascertained. In order for a decision to be an expression of the general will, it must also be general in its object.

The generality of object condition with respect to what constitutes an expression of the general will seems to be of more fundamental importance than the generality of essence condition. It is also more difficult to understand. To begin with, Rousseau clearly believes that there are certain questions that might be termed 'public' which cannot be answered by appeal to the general will because there is no expression of the general will to be ascertained in such cases. For example, suppose the question is whether to seize the property of some immensely wealthy citizen C and to distribute it equally among all the citizens. This question is 'particular' in the sense that no answer to it will affect all citizens in a similar way. It would not be rational for citizen C to identify himself with any other randomly selected citizen in determining his 'real' interest in such a case because there does not exist, in Rousseau's sense, a *common* interest.

An analytical device from contemporary decision theory may be of some use in gaining a clearer understanding of how Rousseau's conceptions of generality of object and of common interest might be interpreted. The device, which is termed 'the prisoners' dilemma', begins with the assumption that two prisoners have been arrested for committing a serious crime as well as a less serious crime. There is sufficient evidence to convict them of the less serious crime, but conviction of both of them for the more serious crime will occur if and only if one or both of them confesses. The prosecutor makes identical offers to them, as follows:

> If you confess to the more serious crime and agree to become a witness for the prosecution but your accomplice refuses to confess, we will give you a special deal: two years' prison sentence, and your accomplice will receive the full sentence of ten years.
>
> If both you and your accomplice confess, your confessions will not, individually, be so important. But we shall give you some consideration for sparing the state the trouble and expense of a trial: so you will each receive eight years.
>
> If neither of you confesses, you can both expect to be convicted of the lesser crime and to receive the maximum sentence of five years. (See matrix diagram, p. 174.)

What should each prisoner do? (Since their situations are entirely symmetrical, we can speak of 'each' prisoner here.) The assumption is that each is self-interested, or motivated exclusively by *amour de soi-même*, which in this case is a desire to minimize his or her sentence; neither is concerned with the fate of the other prisoner except to the extent that the other's fate is linked to his own.

The classical decision procedure would begin with a prisoner, say prisoner A, considering his two options (to confess, not to confess) relative to the same two options of another prisoner, B. Suppose that B confesses; then if A does not confess, A receives ten years as opposed to the eight that he would receive if he too confessed. So it seems that, in that situation, A should confess. Suppose, on the other hand, that B does not confess. If A confesses, A receives two years as opposed to the ten he would receive if he did not. Then in this situation, too, it seems that A should confess. So, it appears that, whatever B does, A should confess. Because of the symmetry of the situation, B will reason to the same effect, they will both confess, and will both receive eight years.

The rather obvious fact is that there is another outcome which is *equally* better for both prisoners: if they agree not to confess and both adhere to the agreement, both will receive sentences of five rather than eight years. So, in such circumstances there is, in Rousseauian terminology, a genuine *common* interest and, hence, an expression of the general will. In these circumstances, it is *rational* for "everyone to think of each (*chacun*)" in making a decision what to do. In other words, in deciding what is best for 'them' (*each* person) to do, every person is deciding what is best for 'him', in the circumstances, to do. This is so because of the symmetry of the situation, because each person is assumed to have the same sort of motivation and the same rational capacities as other persons and each person stands to benefit in the same way and to the same degree by social cooperation.

For the 'Hobbesian person', the person corrupted by *amour-propre*, the temptation to renege on one's agreement will be overwhelming: by

	Prisoner B confesses	Prisoner B does not confess
Prisoner A confesses	(8 years for A; 8 years for B)	(2 years for A; 10 years for B)
Prisoner A does not confess	(10 years for A; 2 years for B)	(5 years for A; 5 years for B)

reneging and confessing, I can take advantage of the other prisoner's adherence to his agreement and obtain a two year sentence, while saddling my fellow prisoner with a full ten years – on the assumption, of course, that he sticks to his agreement not to confess. My recognition that he will be similarly motivated encourages me all the more to renege because if *he* reneges and I do not, the worst possible outcome, a sentence of ten years, awaits me.

However, for a group of persons in the 'right' sort of social circumstances who are not unduly corrupted by *amour-propre*, their true common interest can be pursued. Such a person will see the advantages of social cooperation; and he will *not* see the limitations on the pursuit of his self-interest that are imposed by cooperation with other similarly constituted and similarly motivated citizens as a matter of intolerable personal dependency on their wills, individually or collectively. Rather, he will see them as 'natural' limitations which it is rational to accept without the rancor attendant on a belief that he is being *personally* thwarted – just as it is rational to accept any other such natural fact. Thus he will be able to internalize the interchangeable, common interest (not to confess, in our illustration) as his own.

It should be noted that the generality of object condition assumed in our illustration of the prisoners' dilemma is very strong. The situation of the prisoners is *exactly* symmetrical; in particular, they stand to be affected in exactly the same way by the decision that is to be made. In 'real-world' situations of social cooperation, it would seem to be rarely (if ever) the case that all participants stand to benefit or to suffer to exactly the same degree from a public decision. If such an exacting symmetry were to be required for the generality of object condition to be satisfied, it might well turn out that there is virtually never an expression of the general will to be discerned and that the concept would be without theoretical value.

However, if the symmetry condition is weakened, do considerations of rational *amour de soi-même* dictate to what degree there remains a genuine common interest that should be identified with the 'true' interest of the self? If, perhaps, a decision stands to benefit everyone to *some* (but not necessarily the same) degree? Or if it stands to harm no one? The situation can be modeled by versions of the prisoners' dilemma in which the 'deals' offered to the prisoners differ. Suppose the prosecuting attorney has the authority to increase the sentence for the lesser crime and tells both the prisoners that, if neither of them confesses, then A will receive a five-year sentence, but B six years. Or that, if neither of them confesses, A will receive a five-year sentence but B eight years. In the former case B will do better by social cooperation than he would do if each prisoner were to go his own way, adhering to his own 'private will' (six years rather than eight), but not as well as A (five years rather than eight). In the latter case, B will not benefit at all by cooperation but neither will he be harmed (eight years versus eight). Is there, then, still a common interest to cooperate – that is, an expression of the general will – in these cases? If B were to refuse to cooperate (or perhaps to renege on his agreement to cooperate) in these cases, could that refusal plausibly be explained by his 'concern for justice', based on self-respect or rational *amour de soi-même*? Or must it be an expression of peevish resentment deriving from vicious *amour-propre*?

Rousseau neither addresses nor answers such questions. Nor, in the *Social Contract*, does he directly address the issue of the condition of the 'ambient' social conditions in which expressions of the general will are being sought. Let me attempt to explain this rather obscure claim. It may seem that, as a matter of fact, persons are more willing to engage in social cooperation, in the sense of searching for a common interest and proceeding to regard it as their own, in more egalitarian social contexts. In the context of great preexistent inequalities, it is reasonable to expect that the disadvantaged may not be inclined to cooperate in ventures that stand to benefit *all* to the same degree. And I think that it is not obvious, in terms of Rousseau's principles, that such a refusal to co-operate would be 'immoral', a violation of the dictates of rational *amour de soi-même*.

These considerations raise a central problem concerning the *Social Contract*. In the preface to the first book of the *Social Contract*, Rousseau proposes to inquire "whether there can be some legitimate and sure rule of administration in the civil order, taking men as they are and laws as they might be."[38] I see no way that the condition "taking men as they are" can be consistently maintained by Rousseau. Even in the *Social Contract* itself, the rôle of the 'legislator' seems to violate this condition. The legislator is essentially a benevolent 'social genius' whose function is to establish the 'laws' and basic political institutions for a people in such a way that those laws and institutions will best instantiate the general will. The historical models for the concept are the quasi-mythical lawgivers of Greek and Roman antiquity (such as Lycurgus and Solon), Moses (regarded as the author of the Jewish law), and the theologian and Reformer Jean Calvin (the lawgiver for Geneva). Rousseau emphasizes the enormous task of the lawgiver: "an undertaking that transcends human force, and to execute it, authority that is nil."[39]

The lawgiver cannot use force to accomplish his ends and does not incorporate himself or his position as a part of the political machinery of the state. He does his work and disappears. He must rely on the art of persuasion; and Rousseau suggests that an important rhetorical tool – much more important than rational argument – will be appropriate religious mythology. "Fathers of nations," says Rousseau, have always been forced

> to credit the gods with their own wisdom, so that the peoples, subject to the laws of the state as to those of nature and recognizing the same power in the formation of man and of the city, might obey with liberty and bear the yoke of public felicity.
>
> It is this sublime reason, which transcends the grasp of ordinary men, whose decisions the legislator puts in the mouth of the immortals in order to compel by divine authority those whom human prudence could not move.[40]

Particularly significant is Rousseau's claim that the legislator "should feel that he is, so to speak, in a position to change human nature, to transform each individual (who by himself is a perfect and solitary whole), into a part of a larger whole from which this individual receives, in a sense, his life and his being; to alter man's constitution in order to strengthen it; to substitute a partial and moral existence for the physical and independent existence we all received from nature."[41] So, in fact, Rousseau does *not* in the *Social Contract* entirely take "men as they are." A system of "laws as they might be" – that is, a republic whose one and only sovereign power is the general will – is workable only if its citizens are educated for and socialized into it. Part of the rôle of the legislator is to represent (figuratively?) the *public* aspect of this education and socialization, which includes the inculcation of 'old-fashioned' republican virtues and old-fashioned civic religiosity.[42]

In the *Émile*, however, Rousseau expresses reservations concerning the possibility of a 'public' education in the civilized modern world (of the eighteenth century): "Public instruction no longer exists and no longer can exist, because where there is no longer fatherland, there can no longer be citizens."[43] Education, Rousseau claims, "comes to us from nature or from men or from things. ... He alone in whom they all [three] coincide at the same points and tend to the same ends reaches his goal and lives consistently. He alone is well raised."[44] Of the three sources, we have no direct control over nature and only limited control, in certain respects, over things. So education needs to be primarily directed to what, in Rousseau's estimation, we can most readily control, the part of human education that derives from one's relation to other persons. He proceeds to claim that there is, or appears to be, a fundamental incompatibility between educating a person to become a 'man' (*homme*) and educating him or her to become a 'citizen' (*citoyen*): "Forced to combat nature or the social institutions, one must choose between making a man and making a citizen, for one cannot make both at the same time."[45]

However, it is just this dubitable possibility that Rousseau sets out to consider in the *Émile*. Contemporary social institutions are so corrupted that the possibility of a true public education, one that equips a person to be at once a man and a citizen of a true republic, has been lost. This leaves only the possibility of a "domestic education or the education of nature":

> But what will a man raised uniquely for himself become for others? If perchance the double object we set for ourselves [i.e, the education of an individual to become a man and to become a citizen] could be joined in a single one by removing the contradictions of man, a great obstacle to his happiness would be removed. ... I believe that one will have made a few steps in these researches when one has read this writing.[46]

P. Gay perceptively notes that "the liberals of Rousseau's time, and those both before [such as John Locke] and after him, had sought to delimit the respective boundaries of freedom and constraint, giving freedom as much scope as seemed reasonable. And Rousseau, like them, attempts to establish the respective rights of the sovereign and citizen. But he goes further. He sees this tension not as a relation to be mapped, but as a paradox to be solved."[47] Fundamental to the resolution of this 'paradox' is the sort of education that Rousseau envisions in the *Émile*. This is an education that enables a person to be *un homme*, a man who is governed by rational self-interest and self-respect (*amour de soi-même*): he or she does not measure self-value in terms of the opinions of other persons and will possess an autonomy that is quite inconsistent with the sort of personal dependency or 'subjection of wills' characteristic of hierarchical French (or English, or – in general – European) society of the eighteenth century. On the other hand, such a person will be able to accept the social rôle of a *citoyen*, a citizen of a true republic that is governed only by the general will. For the sort of social integration implied by the concept of *citoyen* does not imply a personal dependency. And the education sketched by Rousseau in the *Émile* is intended to prevent the development of the egocentrism (*amour-propre*) that causes a person to confuse the two.

A fundamental tenet of that education is that children should be reared in such a way that any opposition to their desires or will deemed necessary for their own welfare (as that imposed by Émile's tutor Jean-Jacques) should be made to seem not the arbitrary expression of the wills of their superiors but as a fact of nature: "As long as children find resistance only in things and never in wills, they will become neither rebellious nor irascible and will preserve their health better."[48] It is therefore necessary that Émile be brought up, initially, in a virtually solitary condition and only gradually and carefully be made aware of other persons. As the commentator A. Bloom notes, "Émile's first observations of men are directed to the poor, the sick, the oppressed, and the unfortunate. This is flattering to him, and his first sentiments towards others are gentle. He becomes a kind of social worker." Bloom adds that "Rousseau singlehandedly invented the category of the disadvantaged."[49] Since Rousseau believes that the good fortune of others has a strong tendency to put "a chill on our heart,"[50] Émile is led to regard the rich, the powerful, the titled, and the 'successful' in terms of the fragility of their status and the elements of vanity, pretense, and self-deceit that inevitably are a part of the 'lifestyles of the rich and famous'. So Émile's upbringing produces a kind of "contempt for the great of this world, not a slave's contempt founded in envy, indignation, and resentment, but the contempt stemming from a conviction of superiority which admits of honest fellow feeling and is the precondition of compassion."[51] In summary and very theoretical terms, Émile is raised in such a way that he is governed by healthy *amour de soi-même*, directed by very practical rationality and mitigated by carefully inculcated compassion. Moreover, the influence of *amour-propre* and the dependency of the will that accompanies it are minimized by Émile's education.

Many critics have commented on the impracticality of the scheme of education proposed in the *Émile*. With respect to this issue, the comments of Bloom seem to me to be on target:

> This is to misunderstand the book. It is not an educational manual, any more than Plato's *Republic* is advice to rulers. Each adopts a convention – the founding of a city or the rearing of a boy – in order to survey the entire human condition. They are books for philosophers and are meant to influence practice only in the sense that those who read them well cannot help but change their general perspective.[52]

A fundamental conclusion of the book seems to me to be the following: a person reared as Émile has been reared is, by and large, more able than other persons to live the life of a true man, an *homme*, in corrupt societies as we find them. But it is *only* a person reared as Émile has been reared that is fit to be a *citoyen*, a citizen of the true republic.

Politics and the human function

To what extent does Rousseau follow what we have called the classical tradition of political theory, according to which there is an objective human function (*ergon*), good, or end which it is the business of political organization to promote in the persons of its citizens? This question is, I believe, not easy to answer. Although Rousseau believes in the malleability of human nature, he certainly has a normative ideal of what that nature should be and, in that sense, he possesses a normative anthropology. Perhaps, not surprisingly, this normative anthropology is recognizable as an eighteenth-century Enlightenment ideal – a person like Émile, in fact. Such a person will be guided by 'enlightened self-interest' and moderate passions: his or her concrete, empirical (and not-too-speculative) rationality will seek to satisfy the desires associated with those passions in ways minimally detrimental to other human beings. Such a person will entertain a tolerant skepticism toward religious conceptions of human life and destiny and, indeed, will be concerned with religion only to the extent that it can be used to support an essentially secular morality. Such a person will be willing to cooperate on an equal basis with others within an egalitarian, republican setting and will exhibit in a restrained, rational form the traditional republican virtues. But he or she will remain, in an important sense, a *private person*, a person who is principally interested in the private pursuit of his or her own preferences (whatever they may be) and who always returns to those private pursuits when not wearing the hat of a *citoyen* – in the way that the 'noble Roman' Cincinnatus returned to his farming having 'done his bit' by serving the Roman republic as dictator.

This last point suggests the second of two political doctrines that seem to be especially fundamental in Rousseau's political thought. The first is the axiom that political legitimacy must rest in some form of consent or agreement – a doctrine which, as we have seen, is basic to the contractarian traditions but which is particularly emphasized by Rousseau. The function of political organization is to 'do the will' of the citizens, to accomplish what they *want*. A fact that is certainly recognized by Rousseau – that people can be corrupted in various ways and, consequently, want the wrong things – does not seem to diminish his commitment to this axiom although it certainly creates many political problems.

Which 'will' of the individual is the political order to serve? This question leads back to the second fundamental Rousseauian political doctrine: the distinction between private person (*homme*, or in some contexts, *bourgeois*) and citizen. According to Rousseau, if we wish to speak of a *common* human function or *ergon*, we must speak of the artificially created rôle of a citizen, whose will is interchangeable with that of every other citizen, who sees his or her interest as indistinguishable from that of every person, and who regards himself as an integral part of the larger political whole. The great problems created by Rousseau's distinction are fairly obvious and can be comprehended in the question of how the *homme* and the *citoyen* into which each concrete person is, as it were, divided are to be related. Is the artificial rôle of *citoyen* entirely to serve the private, self-interested ends and goals of the *homme* or *bourgeois*? Does the person as *citoyen* have ends and goals – that is, an ultimate *ergon* – independent of and perhaps superior to the wants, desires, and needs of the *bourgeois/homme*? As we shall see, these are questions of central importance to the political thought of the young Karl Marx, as well as to later liberal-democratic theory.

Karl Marx: distortion of the human function within the bourgeois-liberal state

Karl Marx (1818–1883) was born in the German Rhineland (then under Prussian political control), the son of a Jewish lawyer who had converted to Lutheran Christianity in order to avoid legal anti-Jewish disabilities imposed after the defeat of Napoleon. Young Marx was a precocious student who read law and eventually took a doctorate in philosophy with a dissertation on ancient atomism. Along the way he acquired an aristocratic wife, Jenny von Westphalen, with whom he had a family, only three children of which survived to adulthood. The support of his wife and family was a continuing worry for Marx, a worry that was only partly alleviated by a legacy he received later in life (1864). Because of his political and social radicalism and his atheism, he had no hope of an academic career in Germany. Becoming a journalist and political agitator, he was forced to leave Germany for Paris in 1843 and, because of Prussian pressure on the French government, to leave Paris for Brussels in 1845.

During his time in Paris, Marx had met Frederick Engels, who came from a wealthy English mercantile family. Engels became a lifelong friend and intellectual collaborator of Marx; he also supplied Marx with various forms of support, sometimes in monetary form and sometimes in the form of journalistic tasks that Marx, for various reasons, delegated to him. Together they collaborated on *The Communist Manifesto*, the publication of which coincided with various political uprisings throughout Europe in 1848. Marx and Engels had high expectations for this ferment, and Marx returned to Germany briefly in the hope of playing an active political rôle in revolutionary events. But, as the various European revolutionary movements failed, Marx was again forced to leave Germany and settled in London in 1849, where he spent the remainder of his life. There Marx worked on his social-political and economic theory while undertaking various political activities and attempting to support himself and his family with journalism, which included considerable hack journalism as well as a stint as the London correspondent for the *New York Daily Tribune*. He lived in poverty that was, at first, grinding and never was as genteel as he wished; and, as his health deteriorated, the prickly aspect of his character became more dominant: as J. Wolff notes, he seemed to develop a particular talent for quarreling with persons "who were potential allies."[53] Although the first volume of his great work *Das Kapital* was published in 1867, the second and third volumes were edited after his death by Engels from the vast amount of manuscript material that he left (which also included what became the *Theories of Surplus Value*, edited by Karl Kautsky).

It is obvious that contemporary attitudes toward Marx are colored by the history of those twentieth-century communist political movements that find fundamental intellectual support in Marx's thought. In the following discussion I hope to abstract from such considerations as much as possible, and I intend to follow the line of J. Wolff (and many others): while Marx develops a very acute critique of bourgeois-liberal society and political theory, his 'positive' political philosophy (insofar as it exists) has less to be said for it. Consequently, I shall focus on the early Marx – the early writings in which we find the most political *philosophy*. Marx is one of those philosophers who developed a philosophical theory that calls the whole enterprise of philosophical theorizing into question. It is thus no surprise that in the mature Marx there is a turning away from political philosophy toward what Marx regarded as the 'scientific' discipline of economics.

With respect to the more 'positive' features of his social-political doctrine, Marx seems to me to be very much a child of his nineteenth-century, Victorian times. On the one hand, like many other nineteenth-century thinkers (for example, utilitarians such as Jeremy Bentham and J.S. Mill, as well as a host of slavery-abolitionists, advocates of women's suffrage, teetotalism, etc.), Marx is motivated by reforming zeal. The depredations wrought by the so-called industrial revolution and by unfettered capitalism had become apparent. There was an idealistic, even utopian element to Marx's zeal, despite the fact that he would have objected vehemently to the characterization of his thought as 'utopian'. The reason for this objection rests on the other distinctively nineteenth-century feature of his mature thought – namely, its scientism. As I use the term 'scientism' it can mean either (or both) of two things. First, it can designate the conviction that the 'methods of natural science' (whatever they may be) constitute the only possible means for acquiring *any* sort of knowledge. Second, it can mean that *any* claims about morality or value in human life (including both factual and normative social, political, and religious claims), if they are to be legitimate, must be capable of being extrapolated from the methods or content of natural science. In brief, scientism is the quite dubitable view that 'science' provides the exclusive basis for the development of a reasonable or 'justifiable' comprehensive conception of human life or, to use terminology of later, twentieth-century political philosophy, a reasonable "comprehensive doctrine" or "comprehensive conception of the good." In Marx's case, his scientism is particularly manifest in his commitment to historical or 'dialectical' materialism, a form of determinism in which economic developments in the form of production and distribution of commodities dictate corresponding developments in human social and political organization, as well as developments in higher (intellectual and cultural) 'forms of consciousness'.

It is noteworthy, however, that Marx combines his reformer's zeal and his scientism with a quite classical piece of conceptual apparatus. This is the concept of a human essential nature (which, following the German philosopher Ludwig Feuerbach, Marx refers to as the human "species-essence," "species-being," or "species-life"), which really represents the old conception of an objective human end (*telos*) or function (*ergon*), a conception that has now surfaced so often in this book. For Marx, a human being is essentially a *homo faber*, a producer, maker, or worker; and deterministic historical forces will eventually bring the human species to the (communistic) point where this human function will be fully and freely – but socially – expressed. We shall later return to a significant ambiguity in this concept: a *homo faber* can be interpreted to be a 'worker' in a narrow sense, as a producer of what is necessary for human material or biological sustenance. But a *homo faber* can also be understood as a producer in a much broader sense, a sense that includes and perhaps privileges intellectual, literary, and artistic production – that is, man may be understood as a 'producer' of high (and perhaps not-so-high) *Kultur*.[54]

Marx's fundamental criticism of the bourgeois-liberal state and of the capitalistic economic system that he believes to constitute its necessary foundation is that they inhibit and deform the essential nature of man as *homo faber*. He uses one of those Marxist catch-all phrases, "alienation," to signify that inhibition and deformation. In the following section, we shall turn to a more detailed examination of the criticism Marx develops in his early, more philosophical works of the bourgeois-liberal form of polity. In particular, we shall focus on the early "On the Jewish Question," which J. Wolff characterizes (correctly, in my view) as "possibly one of the most important and influential works of political philosophy of the last two hundred years."[55]

Political emancipation and the bourgeois-liberal state

Marx's "On the Jewish Question" is a response to several articles by the 'Young Hegelian'[56] Bruno Bauer on the issue of proposed legislation that would eliminate legal anti-Jewish discrimination in Prussia. Like other Young Hegelians, Bauer and Marx were atheists, believing that the concept of God was simply a 'projection' or fictitious concept embodying a variety of human ideals, aspirations, hopes, and fears. Perhaps somewhat surprisingly, then, Bauer argues *against* ending legal anti-Jewish discrimination. But he does so on the following grounds: it is inconsistent for Jews to demand full participation in the state while at the same time maintaining their Jewish identity as the 'chosen people', an identity that sets them apart from other citizens. So, in order to become full citizens of the state, Jews need to renounce their Judaism. Similarly, Christians need to renounce their Christianity in order to become members of the state. And the state needs to renounce any distinctive religious character that it may retain. So, in general, Bauer advocates the state's proclaiming 'religious freedom' or indifferentism: that is, it must exclude the influence of any religious tradition or traditions from public, political life. The other side of the coin is that citizens must exclude any religious influence from their public or political decisions and actions – from their actions as *citoyens*, to use Rousseau's concept. As Marx summarizes Bauer's position,

> Bauer demands on the one hand that Jews give up Judaism –
> in fact, that man give up religion in general – in order to be
> emancipated as *citizens of the State*. On the other hand he takes the

political abolition of religion to be logically equivalent to the abolition of religion *in toto*. The state which presupposes religion is not yet a true, an actual state.[57]

Marx's response to Bauer is quite theoretical. In effect, he claims that Bauer's position involves a confusion between the concept of *political emancipation* and the much more profound and far-reaching concept of *human emancipation*. Marx asks, "Does the standpoint of *political* emancipation have the right to demand of the Jews the abolition of Judaism, and of mankind in general the abolition of religion?"[58] "No," Marx answers, and proceeds to argue that that negative answer is indicative of the shortcoming of the concept of the "political emancipation from" or "political abolition" of religion – and of political emancipation, in general.

What, then, does Marx mean by "political emancipation" and the "political abolition" of something? In order to answer this question, we begin by noting that Marx identifies the "political state" – that is, political organization in its fully developed and essential form – with the bourgeois-liberal state as instantiated in the developing nineteenth-century constitutional democracies. The most developed of these, he suggests, are the United States or "North American free states."[59] Such a fully developed or 'true' political state exhibits various forms of political emancipation. In the case of religion, the state will eschew any state religion and refuse to be directed by any distinctively religious or theological considerations; and it will proclaim 'religious liberty' or 'liberty of conscience' for its citizens as a fundamental political principle. Marx regards this stance as fundamentally but indirectly 'anti-religious'. It is, in effect, the doctrine that religious or theological doctrines are (or should be) irrelevant to the public, political life of the state; and it involves the concomitant attempt to eliminate the influence of religious considerations from the lives of those persons constituting the state *insofar as they are citizens*. Marx puts the point as follows:

It follows from this that man frees himself from a barrier *politically*, via the *medium of the state*, in that, in contradiction with himself, he raises himself above it partially, in an *abstract* and *limited* fashion. Further, it follows that in freeing himself *politically* he frees himself in a round-about way, through a *medium*, even if a *necessary medium*. Finally, it follows that even if the person proclaims himself an atheist through the mediation of the state, i.e. if he proclaims the state to be atheistic, he still remains locked in a religious frame of reference, precisely because he recognises himself only in this round-about way, through a medium.[60]

Despite its title, "On the Jewish Question" is not limited to a discussion of the political emancipation from or abolition of religion. The fully developed political state, the bourgeois-liberal state, is also characterized by other forms of political emancipation or "abolition," which are just as important, in Marx's view, as the political emancipation from religion. "The state *qua* state annuls, for example, *private property*" when it removes any legal property qualification on voting or assuming office in the state. The state is thus saying that considerations of wealth are irrelevant to the public, political life of the state and that differences in wealth do not characterize the persons constituting the state *insofar as they are considered citizens*. Again, Marx regards this move as fundamentally but indirectly 'anti-private property', posing the rhetorical question, "Is not private property ideally superseded when individuals without property become legislators for those with property?"[61] A similar argument applies to still further characteristics of the bourgeois-liberal state:

> The state dissolves distinctions of *birth*, of *social rank*, of *education*, and of *occupation* if it declares birth, social rank, education, and occupation to be *non-political* distinctions; if without consideration of these distinctions it calls on every member of the nation to be an *equal* participant in the national sovereignty; it treats all elements of the actual life of the nation from the point of view of the state.[62]

But Marx proceeds at once to the limitations of the notion of political emancipation from or abolition of some 'X':

> Nonetheless, the political annulment of private property does not supersede private property, but on the contrary presupposes it. ... The state allows private property, education, occupation to *function* and affirm their *particular* nature in *their own* way, i.e. as private property, education, and occupation. Far from superseding these factual distinctions, the state's existence presupposes them: it feels itself to be a *political state* and can affirm its *universality* only in opposition to these factors.[63]

More generally, "the restricted character of political emancipation immediately appears in the fact that the *state* can free itself of a limitation without the human being *truly* being free of it, in the fact that the state can be a *free state* without the man being a *free man*."[64] Marx's point is that all these forms of political emancipation are (not always conscious?) attempts to eliminate the influence of what Marx regards as "human limitations" from the public, political sphere of the life of persons. Thus, although they are essentially 'anti-religious', 'anti-private property', 'anti-class', etc. they are also indirect, round-about, half-hearted, and contradictory attempts at removing these human limitations. Political emancipation is the fundamental characteristic of the fully actualized, bourgeois-liberal form of polity. And what that polity does is to bifurcate the individual human being into (a) his or her communal "species-life" as a *citoyen* in the political community and (b) his or her private "egoistic" life as a bourgeois in what Marx calls "civil society." Marx regards the former common, essential species-life as the normatively real, true existence of the human being. But in the politically emancipated bourgeois-liberal state, it appears in only a limited, distorted and abstract form – in a person's rôle as *citoyen*. In other words, although we are not willing to countenance differences in religion, wealth, class, occupation, etc. as affecting our status as citizens or as compromising our supposed political equality, this fact does not mean that these distinctions do not affect our *real*, concrete relations with one another.

Within the bourgeois-liberal state, the latter, private life of persons in civil society is taken by them as their 'real' existence. In Marx's view, it is an existence in which a person "acts as a *private individual*, views other people as means, debases himself to the status of means, and becomes the plaything of alien powers."[65] A person considered as *bourgeois* or *homme* is basically a *homo economicus*, motivated exclusively by the desire for individual (or family, or group) material and social aggrandizement; and the "civil society" in which he or she acts is the "sphere of egoism, of the *bellum omnium contra omnes* [Hobbesian 'war of each against all']. It is no longer the essence of *community*, but rather the essence of the *separation*. It has become the expression of the *diremption*, or bifurcation, of man from his *communal being*, from himself and other men."[66] While a necessary historical process inevitably leads to this 'diremption' of the human person and to the state of affairs in which a person identifies his private, Hobbesian, egoistic *persona* with his or her 'true self', Marx believes that this identification is, in some sense, a mistake. In civil society, "where [a person] counts for himself and others as a real individual, he is a *false* semblance. In the state, on the other hand, where man counts as a species-being, he is an imaginary member of an illusory sovereignty, he is robbed of his actual individual life, and is filled with an unreal universality."[67]

Marx regards as a failure Rousseau's attempt to formulate the conditions of bourgeois-liberal polity in which each person regards his 'real' will as the general will and in which the rôle of *citoyen* is invested with concrete, substantial reality. As a *citoyen*, I stand on equal footing with David Rockefeller: his vote counts neither more nor less than mine, and he is neither more nor less legally eligible than am I for any public office. But does anyone really think that we have equal political influence or that my interests and those of Mr. Rockefeller will receive equal consideration in the public, political sphere? We have here, I believe, a concrete illustration of what Marx calls the "sophistry of the political state." The political emancipation that results in the political or bourgeoisliberal state "is to be sure a great advance, but it is certainly not the final form of human emancipation in general. Rather it is the final form of human emancipation *within* the previous order of things."[68] This attitude grounds Marx's criticism of the notion of 'human rights' (*droits de l'homme*), which Marx recognizes as lying at the constitutional heart of bourgeois-liberal states (such as the French and North American ones) emerging in the nineteenth century.

Marx distinguishes from human rights 'political rights' or the 'rights of the citizen' (*droits du citoyen*). "*Participation* in the *community*, in the state constitute [the content of the latter]. They fall under the category of *political freedom*, under the category of the *rights of citizenship*."[69] But what of the former *human* rights? Drawing examples from various foundational documents of bourgeois-liberal states (including what he regards as the most "radical" of these, the French revolutionary *Declaration of the Rights of Man and of the Citizen* [1793]), Marx argues that, ultimately, all of these rights are directed toward securing property, the acquisition and protection of which is *the* fundamental concern of the *bourgeois*.

According to Marx, the supposed human right of freedom, which is particularly fundamental to the bourgeois-liberal state, "is the freedom of man as a monad isolated and withdrawn into himself. ... But the human right of freedom is not based on the connection of man with man, but much more on the separation of man from man. It is the *right* of the individual who is *limited*, enclosed within himself."[70] Within the bourgeois-liberal or 'perfected' political state, the practical application of the right of liberty is always the right to enjoy and dispose of one's 'private property' (in something like the broad, Lockean sense of property discussed in the last chapter): the supposed human right to property is the right of a person "to enjoy and dispose *as he pleases* of his goods, of his revenues, of the fruit of his labor and of his industry."[71]

Marx concludes that it is "thus the right to enjoy and dispose of ones' wealth arbitrarily (as one pleases), without relation to other men, independently of society, the right of personal use. ... It allows each man to find in the others not the *actualisation*, but much more the *limit*, of his freedom."[72] The right of equality (as a supposed *human* right, "in its non-political significance") is "nothing but the parity of the *liberté* described above, namely: that every human as such is equally considered to be a self-based monad."[73] Finally the supposed human right of security, which Marx denominates "the highest social concept of civil society," is "the concept of the *police*, the concept that the entire society exists only to guarantee each of its members the preservation of his person, of his rights, and of his property."[74] It is, in other words, the guarantee of the egoism (and, more fundamentally, the egoistic use and disposal of property) of each individual person-considered-as-*bourgeois* in civil society.[75]

Marx's basic criticism of the "so-called human rights" is that none "goes beyond the egoistic man, beyond man as a member of civil society, namely withdrawn into his private interests and his private will, separated from the community. Not only is man not considered in these human rights to be a species-being, but also species-life itself, society, appears to be a context external to the individuals, and a restriction of their original independence."[76] In the politically emancipated (i.e., bourgeois-liberal) state, citizenship and the "political community" are reduced "to the status of a mere *means* for the preservation of these so-called human rights, in other words ... the citizen is declared to be the servant of the egoistic man and the sphere in which man functions as a communal being is degraded and subordinated to the sphere in which he functions as a partial being; finally ... it is not man as citizen but man as bourgeois who is taken to be the *real* and *true* human being."[77]

I believe that many of us who have been reared in contemporary bourgeois-liberal constitutional democracies – at least many of us who have ended up in fairly 'comfortable' positions in those societies – are likely to respond, "Yes, by and large, that's right. But what is so wrong about the bourgeois-liberal relation between the 'political community' and 'egoistic civil society'? Hasn't it yielded unprecedentedly high levels of individual liberty – not just liberty with respect to property issues – and of education and of health and of material welfare, etc.?" As we shall see in the following chapter, an important twentieth-century strand of liberal political theory has agreed that there is nothing wrong with this outcome; or, at least, that there is not *much* wrong with this outcome that could not be rectified by a certain amount of institutional or bureaucratic 'adjustment' of the bourgeois-liberal state. However, Marx's criticism of this outcome – particularly in his earlier writings – is a quite classical, theoretical criticism. The bourgeois-liberal state, with its division of persons into 'abstract', equal *citoyens*, on the one hand, and 'concrete', independent (egoistic and unequal) *bourgeois/hommes*, on the other, distorts the true human function (*ergon*), end (*telos*), or good. This 'theoretical' distortion has very concrete manifestations – namely, the various forms of alienation brought about by capitalistic economic organization, which Marx takes to be a necessary concomitant or, rather, the necessary material foundation of the bourgeois-liberal state.

Alienation and the human function

I have already said that, for Marx, the human essence or "species-being" is that of *homo faber*, 'man the producer or worker'. Although the *expression* of this essence is dictated by historical, political, and social context, Marx does have as a normative ideal the free, creative, and social activity of human beings. I have usually in this book translated the Greek term '*ergon*', the active expression of the human essence, as 'function'. But I mentioned that the more common, literal translation is 'work'. Marx's training in classical Greek thought is perhaps not altogether irrelevant to the fact that he takes the human function (*ergon*) to be work (*ergon*)! As I mentioned earlier in this chapter, he sometimes takes human work or production in a narrower sense of producing what is necessary for human biological or material existence; and he sometimes takes work/production in a broader sense of producing all of human *nomos* (to use our now familiar Greek term) or 'culture' – including 'high' intellectual, literary, and artistic culture. Marx tends to focus on whichever sense of 'production' that best suits his argument or the point that he is making. But it is unclear that this 'equivocation' is really pernicious. And his tendency is to consider all of human production as of a piece anyway. How does work or production, as the expression of the human species-being, fare in the bourgeois-liberal state with its underlying capitalist economy? Not at all well, according to Marx – which brings us to his discussion of alienation.

An early discussion of alienation is found in Marx's *Economic and Philosophical Manuscripts* (also known as the *Paris Manuscripts*), which were written in 1844 but only posthumously published much later, in 1932. In the *Manuscripts* Marx discusses a cluster of forms of alienation that center on a central sense of 'alienation', which is virtually definitive of the capitalist economy. In a capitalist economy, work or labor itself becomes a commodity, something that is bought and sold on the open market. One result is the creation of the two principal classes of bourgeois-liberal, capitalist society: there is the *bourgeoisie* (in Marx's special sense of the term), which controls the means of production and distribution in the society and, in particular, have the wherewithal to buy labor. And there is the proletariat, composed of persons who have no share in the control of the means of production and distribution in the society and who are forced to sell their labor on the open market in order to sustain themselves and their families. Another result of this objectification of labor – that is, turning it into a commodity – are the various forms of alienation.

Objectified or purchased labor is no longer under the control of the worker who sells it. It is no longer the worker but his or her employer who determines when and how the worker works and what he or she produces. Consequently, a worker's labor and the product of that labor cannot plausibly be considered a free and natural expression of the human essence of the worker, a manifestation of what he or she *is*. (1) There results alienation from the product of labor. Particularly as a result of the economic specialization or 'division of labor' of advanced capitalistic societies, a worker may spend his time turning out many 'thingamabobs', or repetitively performing one small task involved in making a thingamabob. The thingamabobs that are the product of the worker's labor may figure not at all, or only to a negligible degree, in his or her life. And, in fact, the worker may not understand the purpose or even the workings of the thingamabobs at all. Moreover, the worker typically doesn't *care* about the thingamabobs he or she produces – often for the very good reason that they are not the sort of thing any rational human would care about.

(2) There also results the alienation of the worker from the 'working activity' as such. The activity or working or producing is seen not as a free expression of who or what one is but exclusively as a *means*, usually as a means for having things. *In itself* it is typically regarded by the worker as distasteful:

> He does not confirm himself in his work, he denies himself, feels miserable instead of happy, deploys no free physical and intellectual energy, but mortifies his body and ruins his mind. Thus the worker only feels a stranger. He is at home when he is not working and when he works he is not at home. His labour is therefore not voluntary but compulsory, forced labour. ... How alien it really is

is very evident from the fact when there is no physical or other compulsion, labour is avoided like the plague.[78]

Marx proceeds to claim that a consequence of the alienation of the activity of labor is that the worker looks elsewhere to find a true expression of himself or herself: "man (the worker) only feels himself freely active in his animal functions of eating, drinking, and procreating at most also in his dwelling and dress."[79] This displacement of one's true human self into one's 'animal' (biological) functions and into artificial and fairly trivial concerns interlocks with the sort of consumerism characteristic of capitalist economies. Capitalism inculcates a variety of artificial wants and 'needs' for its commodities. Consumers, who cannot regard the labor that they sell as an expression of their true, human selves, create such an expression in the process of acquiring and in the state of possessing 'stuff'. 'Shopping until one drops' (or a mania for possessing the very latest 'cutting-edge' computer or audio equipment etc.) can become a substitute for work or production when that production has become alienated.

(3) Finally, there results from the objectification of labor the alienation of man from man: "each man measures his relationship to other men by the relationship in which he finds himself placed as a worker."[80] The main feature of this relationship is competition. Workers must compete with one another in the sale of their labor. If you are able to sell your labor more cheaply than I am able to sell mine, you end up working and I do not. Labor or production, in Marx' view, *should* be a natural expression of our shared species-being, a social transformation of various aspects of our environment. But within a capitalist economy of bourgeois-liberal society, it becomes socially divisive to the extent that human beings *become* Hobbesian agents and something like Hobbes' war of each against all ensues.

One might conclude that the forms of alienation described by Hobbes really only affect members of the proletariat in a situation of unregulated capitalism, such as Marx was indeed familiar with in the late nineteenth-century industrialized world. But he holds that it is endemic to the capitalist system as such and that it affects all participants, *bourgeois* as well as proletariat. Members of the proletariat suffer more from its effects, but the coupon-clipping and rent-collecting (and typical 'gentlemanly' leisure activities) of the *bourgeois* no more serve as an authentic expression of his or her species-being than does the daily drudgery of the assembly-line worker. As Marx puts the point in *The Holy Family*, the propertied class and the class of proletariat present the same human self-alienation. But the former class finds in this self-alienation its confirmation and its good, its own power: it has in it a semblance of human existence. The class of the proletariat feels annihilated in its self-alienation; it sees in it its own powerlessness and the reality of an inhuman existence.[81]

It is important to realize that both the early and the mature Marx believe that alienation and the other limitations and distortions wrought by the capitalist economy and bourgeois-liberal society are not amenable to any political solution or fix. Rather, politics must be 'transcended' by "human emancipation." Marx gives a very abstract and theoretical account of such human emancipation at the close of the "Essay on the Jewish Question":

Only when the actual individual man absorbs the abstract citizen of the state into himself and has become in his empirical life, in his individual labour, in his individual relationships, a *species-being*, only when he has recognised and organised his 'own forces' as *social* forces and therefore no longer separates the social force from himself in the form of a *political* force; only then is human emancipation complete.[82]

Students of Hegel will certainly see his influence in this passage. But other readers are likely to be puzzled and dissatisfied: what would such a life actually be like? And how is it to be brought about?

Historical materialism and the coming of communism

Marx's particular brand of scientism allows him to answer or, perhaps to some degree, to avoid answering the preceding questions. Historical or dialectical materialism is a variety of determinism which, as understood by Marx, implies that social or political change is not really brought about by 'ideas', that is, by various schemes for social or political reform. To this sort of scheme for reform, to what one might term a 'moralizing' conception of reform, Marx applies the dismissive and contemptuous phrase "utopian socialism." If one adopts a 'compatibilist' conception of human agency (i.e., a conception of agency that is *compatible* with a principle of determinism according to which all events, including human actions, have antecedent determining causes), then Marx's historical determinism certainly leaves room for human agency. But, according to historical determinism, causality operates principally at the 'material' or economic level. It is the modes of production and distribution that determine social and political forms of organization, not vice versa. So there is a sense in which forms of social and political organization 'supervene' on their underlying economic basis. And, he usually maintains, other even 'higher-level' forms of culture – "forms of consciousness," systems of ideas, or "ideologies" – ultimately supervene on the material features of society in a similar way. Moreover, Marx maintains that the prevailing ideology of a society reflects the class interest of those who control the means of production and distribution within the society.

One conclusion that Marx draws is that, if one is to be an *effective* agent of social change, one will not moralize from the pulpit or harangue from the soap box. One's actions will be focused at the level where 'causation really operates', the socio-economic level. Social and political changes can only be brought about by economic changes to be wrought by members of the proletariat. This means the exploitation of class conflict and revolutionary struggle. Here the nineteenth-century optimism of Marx's scientism manifests itself. A proper understanding of the science of economics, in his view, not only guarantees the inevitability of "human emancipation" from capitalism and bourgeois-liberal society but also that this emancipation will be of the right sort: that it will yield a communist society where work will not be alienated and where political structures will have "withered away," or, more properly, will have been reabsorbed into the 'concrete' lives and social relations of persons.

Marx develops the details of how the seeds of their own inevitable destruction develop within capitalist societies in what he regarded as his 'scientific' work – especially *Capital* and in the material that became the posthumous *Theories of Surplus Value*. Of course, these details are now regarded by many economists as quite dubitable. I shall not attempt to describe them, instead referring the interested reader without antecedent, specialized knowledge in economics to the excellent introductory study by J. Wolff that I have previously cited.[83] One potential problem emphasized by Wolff is that, according to Marx, communism requires material abundance; but it is not obvious that an economy can generate abundance without possessing features (e.g., division of labor) that produce alienated labor. Some later thinkers within the Marxist tradition have argued that the right sort of advanced technology could solve this problem, but it is obvious that such issues tend to generate a good deal of empirical speculation (that is, speculation about matters of fact) on the basis of relatively little empirical evidence.

While Marx believes that the science of economics explains how capitalist, bourgeois-liberal society will inevitably be replaced by communism, he generally repudiates demands for an answer to the first question above, "What would non-alienated life in post capitalist, bourgeois-liberal society be like?" In the "Postface" to the second edition of the first volume of *Capital*, he contemptuously dismisses critics who expect him to write "recipes ... for the cook-shops of the future."[84] And in *The German Ideology*, Marx reiterates his fundamental scientistic, 'non-utopian' conception of communism:

> Communism is for us not a state of affairs which is to be established, an ideal to which reality will have to adjust itself. We call communism the real movement which abolishes the present state of things. The conditions of this movement result from the premises now in existence.[85]

Concluding thoughts: the cook-shops of the future made present

The political, social, and human effects of Marx's thought, in terms of actual political developments during the twentieth century, have been both immense and, in some sense, obvious. But at the beginning of the twenty-first century, Marx's effect on political *philosophy* is, I think, more subtle and less obvious. Aside from what is frequently regarded as a passing, Islam-centered challenge, bourgeois-liberal polity and capitalist or free-market economic organization now seem to be ascendant. Particularly in the universities of the United States and other English-speaking countries, a significant strand within contemporary political philosophy is devoted to the support and justification of some suitably perfected or idealized version of this combination of bourgeois-liberal polity and free-market economy.

One central aspect of Marx's thought that has found increasing acceptance is the assumption that there is some sort of necessary connection between bourgeois-liberal polity and capitalist economics. A frequent observation concerning Marx's critique of the duo of bourgeois-liberalism and capitalism is that the capitalist component bears the brunt of his criticisms, particularly the unfettered capitalism of the late nineteenth century. There have always been non-Marxist (and 'revisionist' Marxist) socialists who have entertained the ideal of the combination of a bourgeois-liberal state (characterized by its distinctive freedoms and rights) with a more-or-less strictly politically regulated economy (characterized by the public ownership of at least the major means of production and distribution). Whether practicable or not, such schemes certainly seem to contradict orthodox Marxist theory. But, with what seems to be the present, increasing acceptance of the so-called free-market economy as a natural or even necessary accouterment of liberal democratic government, Marx's idea of the necessary connection between the two appears to be winning the day. Of course, there is considerable irony here since those who now proclaim this indissoluble union typically regard it from a considerably more celebratory perspective than did Marx.[86]

At a more abstract theoretical level, contemporary liberal political philosophy has accepted as virtual orthodoxy Marx's diagnosis of the bifurcation of the person in the bourgeois-liberal state into *citoyen* and into *bourgeois/homme*, and the division of life in such a state into its public, political component and into its private, associational component (designated by Marx as "civil society"). This contemporary tradition – as we shall see in the next chapter – has really repudiated the classical political idea (revived, in a way, in the form of Marx's concept of the human species-being) of a common, objective function (*ergon*) or good, which it is the fundamental business of political organization to promote for its citizens. Rather, a person's good is a matter of his or her individual preferences (perhaps subject to rational reflection and prioritization), and it is the essential rôle of political organization to coordinate and balance the (often competing) preferences of its citizens. The reality of the person is assumed to reside in his or her *private* life, goals, preferences, associations, etc.; and it is the business of the state (and of the human person's rôle as a *citoyen*) to serve as a *means* for furthering these goals and preferences – that is, one's individual business – subject to some constraints of justice or equity.

In effect, the sort of contemporary political philosophy that we shall be subjecting to more detailed examination in the next chapter accepts 'without regret' what Marx regards as the defining antithesis of the bourgeois-liberal state: its division of human relationships into those of the political community and of civil society and the concomitant bifurcation of human persons within bourgeois-liberal society into the *personae* of *citoyens* (who are formally equal with one another and, in fact, formally indistinguishable from one another) and *bourgeois/hommes* (who typically are not at all equal and who are defined by their peculiar preferences, goals, and attachments). Theorists within this tradition, of course, do not at all follow Marx in regarding this division or 'diremption' of the human person as an unsatisfactory and 'contradictory' state of affairs that will (and should) eventually be transcended. Rather, they tend to regard it as a morally proper state of affairs and, at least in the case of some theorists, as the natural historical terminus of human political development.[87]

Marx is seldom given credit for this piece of conceptual apparatus, although it is quite central to contemporary liberal political thought. As we have seen, a version of the distinction is found earlier in Rousseau. I believe that it is fair to say that contemporary liberal political theory follows Rousseau in attempting to rationalize and balance the rôles of *citoyen* and *bourgeois/homme*, rather than following Marx in seeing this distinction as a human moral problem – that is, as a human "limitation" that history will inevitably overcome. In the next chapter we look at some of the details.

9

John Rawls: Liberalism Ascendant?

It may be thought that virtually any substantial claim concerning contemporary political theory will be controversial. However, with respect to contemporary 'real-world' *politics*, the claim that I made at the conclusion of the preceding chapter seems to me to be very close to uncontroversial: the combination of bourgeois-liberal polity and capitalist or 'free-market' economic organization is ascendant at the beginning of the twenty-first century. This state of affairs tends to be reflected in contemporary academic political philosophy, which for the most part is firmly grounded in assumptions that are derived from the bourgeois-liberal tradition.

Much of contemporary political philosophy *begins* with the liberal postulate that a fundamental function of the state is to guarantee to its citizens some favored set of liberties and rights (which, it is often assumed, should be equally distributed). This postulate is typically conjoined with a liberal-democratic or Rousseauian principle of political legitimacy: the legitimacy of the state (and the legitimacy of at least its most fundamental actions) depends on some form of agreement or consent of its citizens. A further fundamental assumption that is frequently made is that the state's business is to facilitate (in some just, equitable way) its citizens' getting what they *want*, rather than to make those citizens good or virtuous – according to some *formally or politically recognized* conception of human goodness or flourishing, that is, some conception of an objective human function or *ergon*. A final assumption common to the tradition but perhaps slightly more controversial is that enabling citizens to get what they want entails protecting their economic freedom. Doing so will include the guarantee of some form of private property, the right to choose (and to change) the way one makes one's living, the right to practice any legitimate form of business, trade, or profession, etc.

Of course, there continue to exist traditions critical of liberal political philosophy. Some – such as Marxism, other forms of socialism, and many varieties of so-called communitarianism – derive from the eighteenth- and nineteenth-century critiques of bourgeois-liberalism. Others, such as those based on a doctrine of natural law or the ideal of an Islamic state, derive from older Christian, Islamic, and 'pagan' classical traditions some of which we examined in the earlier chapters of this book. However, I think that it is fair to say that, despite the historical and contemporary criticisms of it, it is the bourgeois-liberal tradition that dominates in the contemporary academic political arena – at least within the universities of Western or so-called 'first-world' countries (perhaps particularly the English-speaking ones).

Consequently, much contemporary political philosophy is concerned with the nature and limits of various possible 'accommodations' with fundamental bourgeois-liberal principles. For example, what are the legitimate forms (by 'basically liberal' standards of legitimacy) of so-called paternalism, which would seem to amount to the attempt to give people what is good for them rather than what they may or may not want? In what form and to what degree is the political pursuit of economic and social equality legitimate (according to basically liberal standards of legitimacy)? In what ways and to what extent is it legitimate (according to basically liberal standards of legitimacy) for the contemporary state to accommodate the 'folkways' of those groups of its citizens who do not accept the social mores of the culturally and economically dominant groups (concerning, for example, the relations between the sexes or the nature of the family or the place of moral training in education)?

Questions such as the preceding ones clearly could be pursued in ways that would undermine the fundamental commitments of bourgeois-liberal political theory. The fact that they generally are *not* pursued in such a way among the practitioners of contemporary political theory perhaps indicates the continuing vigor of the liberal tradition of political theory. In this chapter, I use the recently deceased American political philosopher John Rawls as the primary representative of contemporary liberal political theory. This choice may perhaps, with some justice, be regarded as a bit provincial since Rawls' main influence has been strongest in academic circles within the United States. I find, however, that Rawls' writings set forth the contemporary liberal view not only in a form that is clear and cogent (to many persons, at least), but also in a form that readily manifests the conceptual tensions and problematic aspects of the tradition.

Egalitarian justice as the "first virtue of social institutions": basic assumptions

Political philosophy is nowadays commonly thought of as the canvassing of possible responses to concrete social and political issues – particularly *timely* ones. Thus, one's 'political philosophy' will comprehend one's response (a *reasoned* response, it may be hoped) to issues such as the legitimacy of politically mandated affirmative action programs, or of capital punishment, or of public subsidy and regulation of political campaign expenses. The list, of course, is open ended and depends on what, at a particular time and in a particular state, attracts the attention of the public (often through the mediation of the news and entertainment media). But, beyond considerations of narrow self interest, the response of the individual citizen will typically be grounded in one of two ways. It may depend upon the citizen's 'utilitarian' judgments (judgments concerning what provides the 'greatest good [happiness, welfare, satisfaction, etc.] for the greatest number'). Or it may depend upon the citizen's particular moral intuitions. But how, one might wonder, could some unified *public* response to some pressing political issue be forged out of the grab bag of differing, perhaps incompatible moral intuitions and judgments of utility?

With the publication in 1971 of the first edition of his principal work, *A Theory of Justice*,[1] John Rawls set out to address this issue by devising principles of justice that are capable both of adjudicating, in the public sphere, among competing moral intuitions and also of limiting, in the public sphere, claims based on the aim of furthering some conception of 'general' public utility or welfare. In Rawls' own words,

> laws and institutions no matter how efficient and well-arranged must be reformed or abolished if they are unjust. Each person possesses an inviolability founded on justice that even the welfare of society as a whole cannot override. For this reason justice denies that the loss of freedom for some is made right by a greater good shared by others. It does not allow that sacrifices imposed

on a few are outweighed by the larger sum of advantages enjoyed by many. Therefore, in a just society the liberties of equal citizenship are taken as settled; the rights secured by justice are not subject to political bargaining or to the calculus of social interests.[2]

As it turns out, Rawls' theory of justice rests on a set of assumptions that largely derive from the classical liberal tradition of the seventeenth and eighteenth centuries. But one important assumption echoes classical (specifically, Aristotelian) political theory and another important assumption is, I believe, distinctively contemporary. The Aristotelian assumption is that justice lies at the center of political theory: "Justice," Rawls says, "is the first virtue of social institutions, as truth is of systems of thought."[3] As we have seen, there was a tendency within the contractarian tradition of bourgeois-liberal political philosophy to privilege *commutative* justice, which can be identified with what parties would be willing to agree to, perhaps in idealized circumstances. But the sort of justice that Rawls has in mind as the "first virtue of social institutions" seems to be better conceived as *distributive* justice, which is a matter of how one 'fairly divides the pie' of the benefits and burdens of social cooperation among the citizens. Now, as we saw in the chapter on Aristotle, his assumption was that distributive justice is 'proportional' in the sense that this distribution should be 'in proportion' to the degree of possession of an appropriate sort of merit or worth on the part of the recipients of the distribution.

Rawls' distinctively *contemporary* assumption is that, with respect to the distributive justice that he takes to be of fundamental political importance, *equal* distribution is mandated. Indeed this egalitarian assumption is built into a general conception of justice that is affirmed by Rawls:

> All social values – liberty and opportunity, income and wealth, and social bases of self-respect – are to be distributed equally unless an unequal distribution of any, or all, of these values is to everyone's advantage.[4]

Although the last, qualifying clause of this principle may seem to offer the basis for mitigating its egalitarianism, we shall see that Rawls – at least in his *A Theory of Justice* – interprets the principle in such a way as to maintain his strong egalitarian commitments.

But what is the basis of those commitments? Perhaps the most straightforward and simple answer is that these commitments are taken as instantiating something Rawls (and many of his contemporaries) take to be morally fundamental or ultimate. With respect to the "liberties of equal citizenship," these are simply "taken as settled," as Rawls says in the passage quoted above.[5] And he certainly seems to be inclined to adopt an egalitarian stance, insofar as he can, with respect to other social values as well.

Although it may be unnecessary (or difficult or impossible) for a contemporary liberal theorist such as Rawls to justify such egalitarianism, I believe that something more can be said about its roots. To oversimplify a bit, what I have called the classical tradition of political philosophy assumes that the principal rôle of political organization is to further the common good, which is dependent on some conception of an objective human good, *telos* (end), or *ergon* (function). So the fundamental business of the state is to "make its citizens good (persons)," that is, to enable them to live up to the ideal of human potential embodied in the idea of a human function. Particularly if it is assumed that citizens have varying levels of potential for achieving the human function – or if we tend to find citizens at varying stages of progress toward full actualization of this function – distributive justice may mandate quite unequal treatment of citizens. The Christian conception of all humans as *equal* siblings within a divine family or as possessing *equally important* ultimate destinies has obvious egalitarian implications. But the import of such 'praeternatural egalitarianism' is not at all obvious. In particular, it is not clear that it entails equal citizenship in the sense that each citizen is entitled, in principle, to equal access to the political decision-making process.

It is perhaps some version of John Locke's Protestant conception of the human *ergon* as a private vocation or 'assignment from God' that best justifies the "*liberties* of equal citizenship": each citizen should have maximal liberty to work out and pursue his or her assignment from God, consistent with similar liberty for other citizens to work out and pursue their (equally important) divine assignments. And it is at least plausible to suggest that allowing all citizens equal access to political machinery is the best way to bring about and protect such maximal equal liberty. However, as such a theistic point of view became less widely accepted in Western constitutional democracies, it became less compelling as a 'public' foundation for the equal right to life, liberty, and the pursuit of happiness supposedly endorsed by those forms of polity. What remains to underwrite the egalitarianism of a secular liberal theorist such as Rawls in the late twentieth century? I suggest that an important foundation of contemporary egalitarianism is the idea of the 'moral arbitrariness' of various sorts of *inequality*.

Let me attempt to explain this idea. From a theistic perspective (such as a traditional Jewish, Christian, or Islamic one), various sorts of natural, and even social, contingencies can be thought of as having a larger purpose, even though that purpose may be quite obscure to human understanding. This may also be true of other views of the world (such as the classical Stoic one) that are teleological, in the literal sense of goal- or end-directed, but in which there is no intelligent creator God who is separate from the universe and directs its development. It is not difficult to understand how, from such a perspective, various forms of natural, or even social, inequality among persons might *not* be morally arbitrary. But a salient characteristic of many nineteenth- and twentieth-century forms of thought – particularly of many varieties of scientism that purport to take their point of departure from modern science – is the general repudiation of teleological premises. Within such a conceptual framework the causal influence on human beings and on their particular destinies by nature, that is, by our classical Greek *physis*, is momentous but non-teleological – that is, it operates without purpose. Perhaps somewhat surprisingly, such a non-teleological perspective is often extended to 'nurture', *nomos*, as well. So social-political developments are also often seen as occurring in seemingly random ways – or at least without any coherent, overarching purpose.

From such a perspective it is natural enough to see inequalities among human beings as the result of fortuitous natural or social causes – the result, in other words, of something like social and natural lotteries. It is then but a short conceptual jump to the idea that "natural and social contingencies" that result in human inequalities are somehow *unfair* or a violation of distributive justice. As Rawls argues,

> The existing distribution of income and wealth, say, is the cumulative effect of prior distributions of natural assets – that is, natural talents and abilities – as these have been developed or left unrealized, and their use favored or disfavored *by social circumstances and such chance contingencies as accident and good fortune.* Intuitively the most obvious injustice of a system of natural liberty [which does not attempt to compensate for such contingencies] is that it permits distributive shares to be improperly influenced by these factors so arbitrary from a moral point of view.[6]

Rawls notes that the concept of distributive justice that he develops is a "liberal interpretation," but one that seeks "to mitigate the influence of social contingencies and natural fortune on distributive shares."[7] The preceding line of thought best explains, I believe, Rawls' commitment to what he terms an "egalitarian form of liberalism,"[8] the features of which we shall soon consider in greater detail.

A final fundamental assumption underlying Rawls' principles of justice derives from both classical liberal sources and his more contemporary egalitarianism. This assumption has two components. (A) One is the supposition that the principles of justice are morally normative principles, the moral force of which should be universally compelling. (B) The other component is his supposition that these principles of justice need not presuppose what Rawls calls a "comprehensive doctrine" or "comprehensive conception of the good" – some richly normative religious, moral, or philosophical conception of human nature, purpose, and destiny. What explains Rawls' adherence to this rather extraordinary doctrine – which is somewhat like setting out to design a building but foregoing, as a matter or principle, the use of any blueprint in order to do so? I conjecture that the answer involves the concurrence of several related considerations.

One such consideration is Rawls' acceptance of the Rousseauian or liberal-democratic principle of political legitimacy: the legitimacy of at least basic political decisions requires the agreement or consent of each citizen. But Rawls assumes that a fundamental and ineliminable feature of contemporary constitutional democracies is a "diversity of opposing and irreconcilable religious, philosophical, and moral doctrines" (where "moral doctrines" has the sense of "moral conceptions of the good").[9] Such diversity suggests that, as a practical political matter, consensus or universal assent with respect to fundamental political issues will be difficult or impossible to achieve if it must be achieved on the basis of agreement that is dependent upon comprehensive conceptions of the good. But such diversity also, in Rawls' view, has an unfortunate *moral* implication for the Rousseauian principle of political legitimacy. Satisfaction of that principle becomes difficult or impossible *if* conceptions of the good (which are supposed to be diverse and irreconcilable) must be invoked in order to obtain the assent that confers political legitimacy. The resulting predicament is the following: a rational, moral basis of consent would seem to be required to preserve a fundamental liberal principle of political morality, viz., the Rousseauian principle of political legitimacy. However, it evidently cannot be found in a shared conception of the human good or *ergon* that derives from some (shared) religious, philosophical, or moral commitments of the citizens. The predicament makes quite attractive the idea of some rational basis of public, political morality that is *independent* of any comprehensive conception of the human good.

That there might exist such a basis of political morality is suggested by the moral philosophy of the eighteenth-century German philosopher Immanuel Kant, which certainly influenced Rawls' political philosophy. So Kant's thought is a second factor in Rawls' acceptance of the doctrine of a basis of political morality that is independent of any religious, moral, or philosophical conception of the human good. To simplify and shorten a much longer and more complex story, Kant holds that practical rationality can and should determine the foundation of morality without appeal to any 'ultimate premises' that are factual or empirical claims about human desires or happiness or about a distinctively human good, *ergon*, or *telos*. Kant famously finds the basis of morality in a principle of universalizability, the 'categorical imperative' which instructs us to act only on those 'maxims' or descriptions of our action that we could consistently will to be *universally* accepted and followed.[10] I shall not here attempt to discuss the details, or plausibility, of Kant's proposal. Rather, I merely point out that Kant supplies an eminent precedent for the attempt to divorce the foundations of morality from any conception of a human good or *ergon*. Moreover, as we shall see, the concept of universalizability figures as largely in Rawls' attempt to devise non-teleological principles of political morality (i.e., justice as fairness) as it does in Kant's attempt to specify a non-teleological basis of morality in general.

The final consideration involved in Rawls' assumption of the necessity of constructing a conception of distributive justice that does not appeal to any conception of the human good is perhaps most fundamental of all. It is a moral consideration, which is considered by Rawls to be a consequence of the egalitarianism that he (and many other contemporary liberal theorists) wish to affirm. Let us assume, with most liberal theorists, that it is the proper function of the state to give its citizens what they *want* according to some account of distributive justice (as opposed to what they *need* – in order to make them good persons, in terms of some objective standard of the human *ergon* or *telos*). Let us further assume, with many *contemporary* liberal theorists, that the correct account of distributive justice is an egalitarian one: citizens should be given what they want in as equal a way as possible (however we are to cash out "in as equal a way as possible," which is probably not such a simple or straightforward matter). Then we may ask if it is not an obvious violation of egalitarian distributive justice to make political decisions on the basis of some comprehensive conception of the good (that is, some religious, moral, or philosophical doctrines concerning the human *ergon* or *telos*) that is not universally shared by the citizens.

Rawls certainly thinks so:

> Citizens *as free and equal* have an *equal share* in the corporate political and coercive power of society. ... There is no reason, then, why any citizen, or association of citizens, should have the right to use the state's police power to decide constitutional essentials or basic questions of justice as that person's, or that association's, comprehensive doctrine directs.[11]

To interpret political egalitarianism as morally mandating a political stance of neutrality among different conceptions of the human good, *telos*, or *ergon* is an intellectual move that is by no means unique to Rawls. Another eminent contemporary liberal theorist who adopts essentially the same viewpoint is R.M. Dworkin:

> Political decisions must be, so far as is possible, independent of any particular conception of the good life, or what gives value to life. Since citizens in a society differ in their conceptions, the government *does not treat them as equals* if it prefers one conception to another, either because the officials believe that one is intrinsically superior, or because one is held by the more numerous or powerful group.[12]

The idea that egalitarian moral considerations require political neutrality among different conceptions of the human good might seem to create a real problem for Rawls' enterprise of devising principles of justice that are to capture the idea of justice as the "first virtue of social institutions." For distributive justice involves dividing up *something* (or some things) in an equitable way (which, for Rawls, is to divide it up as equally as possible). But decisions must be made about what things are *sufficiently important* that the principle of distributive justice in question must be applied to them. Quite typically, principles concerning the nature – simple or complex – of the human good have been explicitly invoked or implicitly assumed in making these decisions. But since Rawls, for the complex reasons we have been considering, has denied himself public political appeal to any such principles, to what is he to apply his principles of distributive justice? And on what basis? In order to answer these questions, we must first consider Rawls' principles of justice.[13]

Rawls' two principles of justice: what they apply to and why

Rawls' initial statement of his "two principles" of distributive justice in his *A Theory of Justice* reads as follows:

> First: each person is to have an equal right to the most extensive scheme of basic liberties compatible with a similar scheme of liberties for others.
>
> Second: social and economic inequalities are to be arranged so that they are both (a) reasonably expected to be to everyone's advantage, and (b) attached to positions and offices open to all.[14]

He further specifies that, in any situation in which these principles should come into conflict, the first is to take precedence: that is, "infringements of the basic liberties protected by the first principle cannot be justified, or compensated for, by greater social and economic advantages."[15]

With respect to the second principle, Rawls' strategy is to consider different interpretations of the two key ideas of (a) inequalities working "to everyone's advantage" and (b) of positions and offices being "open to all." Rawls proceeds to opt for the more egalitarian interpretation of both of these ideas. The interpretation of the idea (a) of inequalities working to everyone's advantage that Rawls rejects is that of "efficiency" or "Pareto optimality": according to this interpretation, inequalities built into the "basic structure" of society (particularly into its economic structure, which Rawls assumes will be "roughly a free market system, although the means of production may or may not be privately owned"[16]) will be to everyone's advantage "whenever it is impossible to change it so as to make some persons (at least one) better off without at the same time making other persons (at least one) worse off."[17] The most obvious problem with this interpretation, according to Rawls, is that it applies to "structures" that include distributions of wealth and income that are the "cumulative effect of prior distributions of natural assets – that is natural talents and abilities – as these have been developed or left unrealized, and their use favored or disfavored over time by social circumstances and such chance contingencies as accident and good fortune."[18] In other words, Rawls believes that such a principle would capture the concept of distributive justice "as fairness" only if it were fair (= distributively just) that those favored by the inequalities in a particular distribution of assets possess those advantages. So it would then be unjust to diminish their advantage for the sake of helping out other persons. But, Rawls claims, the good fortune of those that profit from inequalities is often the result of natural and social contingencies, which are "arbitrary from the moral point of view." He then seems to infer that, in view of his presumption of the fairness of as egalitarian a distribution as possible, such preexistent inequalities are *not* fair (= not distributively just) in at least the following sense: there is a *prima facie* moral obligation to adopt principles of justice that are designed to eliminate inequalities as much as possible and, where inequalities cannot reasonably be eliminated, to minimize their effects.

The interpretation of the notion of inequalities working to everyone's advantage (which is a matter of minimizing the effects of practically ineliminable inequalities) that Rawls favors he calls the "difference principle":

> Assuming the framework of institutions required by equal liberty and fair equality of opportunity, the higher expectations of those better situated are just if and only if they work as part of a scheme which improves the expectations of the least advantaged members of society. The intuitive idea is that the social order is not to establish and secure the more attractive prospects of those better off unless doing so is to the advantage of the less fortunate.[19]

Rawls notes the strongly egalitarian character of the difference principle. An inequality (of the relevant sort) is unjust unless its elimination would be detrimental to the persons occupying the lowest rung ("least advantaged representative position") in the political and socioeconomic structure.

With respect to the idea (b) of "positions and offices [being] open to all," Rawls also favors the more egalitarian interpretation. A weaker and less egalitarian interpretation would be the minimal requirement of an absence of legal or other formal kinds of discrimination that would bar some citizens or classes of citizens from some "positions or offices" in the political and socioeconomic structure. It is obvious, however, that the absence of such formal discrimination does not guarantee that all persons with similar motivation and relevant abilities and skills *actually* have similar chances of gaining desired positions. To consider just a few factors, class and racial membership, socioeconomic background, and personal or family connections can obviously make a difference. So Rawls opts for an interpretation of positions and offices being open to all that is guided by the idea of attempting to achieve actual "fair equality of opportunity" for attaining all positions and offices. Rawls is not so enamored of equality that he believes that equal access to any position or office should be sought even for those who are unequally qualified, in terms of abilities, skills, and knowledge that are relevant to the position or office in question. So his interpretation of "fair equality of opportunity" is typically cashed out in terms of some version of the principle that "those with similar abilities and skills should have similar life chances."[20]

This commonsensical limitation on the idea of equal access to positions and offices combines with another intuition of Rawls to motivate his adoption of the difference principle. That intuition, which certainly is not shared by all, is that "once we are troubled by the influence of either social contingencies or natural chance on the determination of distributive shares, we are bound, on reflection, to be troubled by the influence of the other."[21] According to this view, "natural chance" dictates what talents and abilities we either have or lack; it is even natural chance that determines whether we end up with the sort of personality (or as a member of the sort of family or class that inculcates that sort of personality) that is "highly motivated toward success" or vice versa. And so forth. But, as we saw, it is not reasonable for some inequalities that are deemed to be the consequence of natural chance to be entirely ignored in terms of determining the opportunity for occupying various positions and offices – because such inequalities may well affect the competence of the persons to perform actions essentially attaching to such positions and offices. On the assumption that disadvantages owing to natural chance tend to result in persons so disadvantaged gravitating to the least desirable socioeconomic and political positions, the difference principle represents a plausible mechanism of compensation.

It is not reasonable to expect to achieve equality with respect to all abilities, skills, motivation, mental and physical health, etc. Nor would it be morally or socially responsible always simply to ignore such inequalities. But those whose life chances are disadvantaged by them can be compensated by insuring that distributive inequalities are morally permissible only if they benefit those on the lowest rung of the political and socioeconomic ladder. Thus, Rawls' principles of distributive justice address what he takes to be the "morally arbitrary" character of inequalities due to the natural lottery, as well as morally arbitrary inequalities that are socially based.

Now, it is obvious that not *all* distinctions and differences among persons or among their political, socioeconomic, and cultural positions will constitute *inequalities* that Rawls' principles of justice should take into account – either by justifying them or by requiring that they be eliminated. We need not be much concerned, for example, with the supposed 'inequality' deriving from the fact that some persons are much more talented players of contract bridge than are other persons. The question, then, is how Rawls is to decide what the sorts of thing are to which his principles of distributive justice properly apply. The answer to this question that is given by 'classical' political philosophy will depend, at least in good part, upon one's particular conception of the human good, *telos*, or *ergon*. For it is the content of this conception of the human good or *ergon* that determines, in classical political philosophy, what is sufficiently important to demand that it be fairly or justly distributed. However, we have seen that Rawls explicitly denies the legitimacy of appeal to a particular "comprehensive conception" of the human good in order to undergird his principles of distributive justice. We thus return to the question of what *does* 'undergird' these principles in the sense of investing them with content: that is, what is it that determines what sorts of thing are sufficiently important that it is morally required that they be fairly distributed in terms of the principles of justice?

Rawls' answer to this question is "primary goods," which he defines as "things that every rational man is presumed to want."[22] One interpretation of this concept would make it a matter of empirical psychology: persons differ, of course, in their wants. But it *may* be the case that there is some degree of agreement or consilience of human wants. That is, whatever differences there may be among people in terms of their tastes and sentiments, their comprehensive conceptions of the human good, *telos*, or *ergon*, there is yet a core of things that all adult, minimally intelligent, and non-insane persons agree are desirable. So the Rawlsian principles of justice – which, you will recollect, must not depend on the particularities of individual citizens' comprehensive conceptions – are to be applied in order to effect a just distribution of just those things that all such persons agree in wanting.

While this interpretation of primary goods results in a straightforward and elegantly simple (but eminently disputable) principle of distributive justice, Rawls makes it quite clear in his introduction to the revised edition of *A Theory of Justice* that it is not the interpretation that he intends. Rather, he says that the proper conception of primary goods "depends on a moral conception of a person that embodies a certain ideal."[23] This "moral conception" of persons is, in brief, the conception of persons as possessing two moral powers, "their capacity of a sense of justice and their capacity of a conception of the good."[24] The result is that primary goods are now characterized as what persons need in their status as free and equal citizens, and as normal and cooperating members of society over a complete life. Interpersonal comparisons for purposes of political justice are to be made in terms of citizens' index of primary goods and these goods are seen as answering to their needs as citizens as opposed to their preferences and desires.[25]

This is about as clear a statement as possible of the doctrine that the purpose of political structures, through the mediation of the Rawlsian principles of distributive justice, is to allot – in a fair or just fashion – to citizens what they *need*, as opposed to what they may actually want or desire. In the jargon of contemporary political theory, it is a statement of a perfectionist doctrine – that is, it rests upon some conception of the human *ergon*, good, or 'perfection'. To that extent, it cuts against the grain of much contemporary liberal political philosophy, which assumes that the function of political structures is to give citizens, in some equitable way, what they want or to satisfy their preferences (whatever the basis of those preferences may be).[26]

But we then arrive back at a problem for Rawls and other contemporary liberal theorists. In order to specify what persons need, is it not necessary to appeal to a conception of the human good, *telos, ergon*? While there are features of Rawls' thought that may lead him to resist an affirmative answer to this question, I believe that he must ultimately answer 'yes'. The human good, *telos*, or *ergon*, according to Rawls' doctrine, is to develop one's *own* life plan, in conformity with one's *own* individual and concrete (rational and reasonable) conception of the human good within a social-political context that recognizes the moral equality of all citizens. Maximal autonomy in selecting one's own comprehensive doctrine or conception of the good, consistent with a similar autonomy for other citizens, really follows from Rawls' implicit conception of the *general* human good or *ergon* and is built into his principles of justice, which Rawls himself characterizes as "ideal-regarding" as opposed to "want-regarding" principles.[27]

Consequently, Rawls' primary goods are those things that are of value to all citizens in determining their particular, concrete conceptions of the human good and in developing and following life plans that they have formulated to advance those conceptions. The chief primary goods, according to Rawls, are "rights, liberties, and opportunities, and income and wealth."[28] To this list, Rawls adds self-respect or self-esteem on the grounds that "without it nothing may seem worth doing, or if some things have value for us, we lack the will to strive for them."[29] In other words, a sense of self-respect, of one's own worth, would seem to be necessary to achieve the human *ergon* or *telos* of formulating one's own, concrete, 'designer' conception of the good and devising a life plan to instantiate it. The Rawlsian conception of primary goods, then, is instrumental and teleological: primary goods are those things that citizens need in order to design a personal conception of the good and a life plan in conformity with that conception, *whatever the concrete content of that conception may be* – at least so long as it is a "rational and reasonable" conception and attendant plan.

This last qualification is important. Rawls would *like* to regard his principles of distributive justice as 'non-perfectionist' because they do not depend upon a *concrete* conception of the human good, *ergon,* or *telos* that is to be applied to all citizens – whether or not they individually subscribe to it. However, I submit that his political philosophy *is* perfectionist to the degree that it imposes on its citizens (whether they subscribe to the doctrine or not) the idea that citizens have a moral right to develop their own (rational and reasonable) conceptions of the good. To use a bit of Rawlsian jargon, his principles of justice require that persons, at least insofar as they are citizens, be regarded as "self-authenticating sources of valid claims."[30] At least a part of what this phrase seems to mean is that Rawls' principles of justice require that any rational and reasonable comprehensive conception of the good be accorded public, political respect and accommodation simply because it is "affirmed" by some citizen or citizens, irrespective of considerations of its truth or falsity, adequacy or inadequacy. One normative consequence of Rawlsian doctrine is that concrete comprehensive conceptions of the human good are to be accounted "rational and reasonable" (and, hence, as conceptions entitled to public, political accommodation) only if: (a) they can affirm – at least at the public level – the doctrine of the independence of the moral basis of society (the principles of justice) from any concrete, particular conception of the good; (b) they endorse the public priority of this moral basis to any such particular conception; and (c) they are willing to deny that any different ('more concrete', particular) conception of the human good, *ergon,* or *telos* should have public normative force. In other words, Rawls maintains that citizens have a moral obligation not to attempt to impose, politically, law or policy that is directly derived from a particular conception of any particular, concrete conception of the human good, *telos, or ergon* (other than the generic liberal one that I have just outlined).

I have suggested that Rawls' principles of justice and the political theory in which they are embedded *do*, in fact, presuppose elements of a conception of the human good or function. In particular, *from the point of view of the state*, a fundamental feature of the human good or function consists in each citizen's developing his or her particular, concrete (rational and reasonable) conception of the good and attendant life plan. This may be viewed as a sort of generic conception of the human good, *telos*, or *ergon*. Nonetheless, I believe that a conception of the human good or *ergon* is precisely what it is. In other words, it turns out that Rawls' liberalism cannot avoid presupposing what I have termed a normative anthropology. The Rawlsian normative anthropology is inconsistent with other normative anthropologies or conceptions of the human good. In particular, it is inconsistent with any philosophical, moral, or religious doctrine (and there are many) that maintains that any correct principle of distributive justice must depend on some concrete, 'fleshed-out' conception of the human good, *telos*, or *ergon*. And it is inconsistent with any political theory that asserts that fundamental legal and political decisions should be guided by the correct conception of this human good or *ergon*.

Consensus, public reason, and the distinction between *citoyen* and *bourgeois*

The suggestion of the preceding section was that the Rawlsian conception of which goods are primary goods and his principles of justice determining the equitable distribution of these primary goods are best understood as presupposing a certain normative anthropology or conception of the human good – although a rather generic conception in which the importance of individual autonomy in developing one's own, 'fleshed-out', *concrete* comprehensive conception of (one's own) human good is accorded great importance. However, this suggestion would be highly unwelcome to Rawls, and to many other contemporary adherents to what has come to be known as 'political liberalism'. According to the doctrine of political liberalism, it should be possible to find a public, political basis for egalitarian liberal principles (such as Rawls' principles of justice) without appeal to any deep or 'thick' normative anthropology. In writings subsequent to *A Theory of Justice*, particularly his book *Political Liberalism*, Rawls explores the possibility of grounding his principles of justice in an "overlapping consensus" of (rational and reasonable) comprehensive doctrines of the human good that are current in contemporary constitutional democracies.

One might be inclined to regard Rawls' idea of "overlapping consensus" in terms of the "idea of consensus used in everyday politics."[31] That is, it might be identified with whatever actual agreement can be achieved in a given society at a given time among divergent conceptions of the human good or *ergon*, employing actual political mechanisms of piecemeal negotiation and compromise. The overlapping consensus thus achieved would be the result of agreement, compromise, or acquiescence that might well prove to be qualified, conditional, and shifting. It would certainly be an empirical or factual notion of consensus – and, consequently, one relative to place and time:

> One [way to proceed] is to look at the various comprehensive doctrines actually found in society and specify an index of such [primary] goods so as to be near to those doctrines' center of gravity, so to speak; that is, so as to find a kind of average of what those who affirmed those views would need by way of institutional claims and protections and all-purpose means. Doing this might seem the best way to insure that the index provides the basic elements necessary to advance the conceptions of good associated with the existing doctrines and thus improve the likelihood of securing an overlapping consensus.[32]

Rawls insists, however, that this is *not* "how justice as fairness proceeds; to do so would be to make it political in the wrong way. Rather it elaborates a political conception as a freestanding view working from the fundamental idea of society as a fair system of cooperation and its companion ideas."[33] The reason why Rawls rejects the empirical idea of an overlapping consensus of doctrines as a foundation for his principles of justice is, I believe, his conviction that this would be no foundation at all. Persons agree to all sorts of things for all sorts of reasons. And such agreement can be highly context-dependent; it might prove to be quite selective or to evaporate in certain circumstances. The liberal egalitarianism of Rawls' principles of justice is for him a fundamental *moral* ideal. So, what is at stake for Rawls is the moral correctness of his political liberalism; and this, he evidently believes, must be grounded in principles and ideals, not in the empirical vagaries of concrete political compromise.

For Rawls it was imperative that he should find some foundation for his principles of justice, a *tertium quid* – that is a third or intermediate way – between a teleological, comprehensive (perfectionist) conception of the human good, on the one hand, and 'mere' actual political compromise, on the other. He seeks this alternative foundation in certain fundamental ideas seen as implicit in the public political culture of a democratic society. This public culture comprises the political institutions of a constitutional regime and the public traditions of their interpretation (including those of the judiciary), as well as historic texts and documents that are common knowledge. ... In a democratic society there is a tradition of democratic thought, the content of which is at least familiar and intelligible to the educated common sense of citizens generally. Society's main institutions, and their accepted forms of interpretation, are seen as a fund of implicitly shared ideas and principles.[34]

These "implicitly shared ideas and principles" must be interpreted and applied in terms of what Rawls terms "public reason," which (a) is the "reason of citizens as such" and (b) is concerned (only) with the "good of the public and matters of fundamental justice." And, as I just indicated, (c) public reason's "nature and content" is "given by the ideals and principles expressed by society's conception of public justice, and is conducted open to view on that basis."[35] One of the most important features of the application of this notion of public reason is to exclude appeal to any particular comprehensive conceptions of the human good or *ergon* when considering (in a public context) the public matters that are the objects of public reason. Peculiarly enough, Rawls does not seem to regard the "implicitly shared ideas and principles" with which public reason begins as constituting such a conception of the human good – even a generic, liberal one.

Public reason, then, is the reason prescribed for a person functioning as a *citoyen*. According to Rawls' moral doctrine, a person may indeed utilize practical reason as guided by his or her own 'designer' comprehensive conception of the human good or *ergon*. But he or she must do so 'privately' – as a *bourgeois* – within the realm of what Rawls himself calls "the 'background culture' of civil society":

This is the culture of the social, not the political. It is the culture of daily life, of its many associations: churches and universities, learned and scientific societies, and clubs and teams, to mention a few.[36]

One of the ironies of Rawls' later work, such as *Political Liberalism*, is its adoption as liberal orthodoxy of the basic conceptual framework of Marx's critique of the liberal state: the division of human relationships into those of the political community (which must be regulated by public reason, without reference to any comprehensive conception of the good) and those of civil society (which is characterized by 'voluntary associations' conceived as directed toward the satisfaction of the entirely private desires, preferences, and goals of individual persons). Of course, the concomitant distinction is the bifurcation of human persons into *citoyens* (who are formally indistinguishable from one another) and *bourgeois/hommes* (who are defined by their differences – their peculiar preferences, goals, and attachments).

As I remarked at the conclusion of the preceding chapter, while Marx regards these distinctions as limitations imposed upon human beings by the bourgeois-liberal, democratic forms of polity, contemporary liberal theorists such as Rawls accept them as natural and morally proper features of human relationships. For Rawls, and indeed much of the liberal tradition of political philosophy, there is an important sense in which the person's rôle as a *citoyen* must always simply serve as the political means for furthering the private ends of the entity that is taken to be the 'real' person, that is, the *bourgeois/homme*. But for Rawls, the person's rôle as *citoyen* really also has one peculiarly moral component: it is what Rawls terms "reasonableness," "the form of moral sensibility that underlies the desire to engage in fair cooperation *as such*, and to do so on terms that others *as equals* might reasonably [*sic*] be expected to endorse."[37] According to this conception, "reasonable persons ... are not moved by the general good as such but desire for its own sake a social world in which they, as free and equal, can cooperate with others on terms all accept. They insist that reciprocity should hold within that world so that each benefits along with others."[38] Rawls understands practical rationality, in contrast to reasonableness, to be a matter of efficiently advancing one's own private ends, whatever they may be. The result is that

> merely reasonable agents would have no ends of their own they
> wanted to advance by fair cooperation; merely rational agents
> lack a sense of justice and fail to recognize the independent valid-
> ity of the claims of others.[39]

Rawls' ideal of public reason, then, essentially involves the concept of reasonableness – and, in fact, may not amount to much more than that concept. Rawls here clearly exemplifies a claim about liberal political theory made by the contemporary political theorist R. Geuss: "What is characteristically liberal is the attempt always to see society *sub specie consensus.*"[40]

The reason for this emphasis on consensus and the moral-political primacy of Rawls' conception of reasonableness is not hard to detect. It is what I have termed the liberal-democratic or Rousseauian principle of political legitimacy: the legitimacy of the state (and the legitimacy of at least its most fundamental actions) depends on some form of agreement or consent of its citizens. Rawls himself refers to such a principle as the "liberal principle of legitimacy" and characterizes it as the doctrine that "our exercise of political power is proper and hence justifiable only when it is exercised in accordance with a constitution the essentials of which all citizens may reasonably be expected to endorse in the light of principles and ideals acceptable to them as reasonable and rational."[41] He further claims that this principle imposes a "moral, not a legal, duty – the duty of civility," which requires that citizens advocate public, political policies and principles only on the basis of the "political values of public reason."[42] We have seen that public reason may not appeal to any distinctive comprehensive doctrine of the human good.

The ultimate justification of Rawlsian liberalism?

What does 'propel' public reason, then? The most plausible answer is the desire to endorse the list of primary goods supplied by Rawls and to distribute them equitably – that is, to distribute them in terms of his two principles of justice. But why *that* particular list of primary goods and *those* particular principles of distributive justice? Again, the most plausible answer seems to be that *that* list of primary goods and *those* principles of justice and fairness best respect the combination of rational self-interest and moral reasonableness that Rawls attributes to human agents engaged in social (specifically, political) cooperation. The 'attribution' here is, of course, a *normative* moral ideal, particularly with respect to Rawls' privileging of his notion of reasonableness as *the* foundational social virtue.

One could go on to inquire into the reasons for Rawls' adopting his conception of practical rationality as properly directed by *private* conceptions of the human good, *telos*, or *ergon* as well as his reasons for morally privileging reasonableness as the virtue of social cooperation 'as such'. It would be possible, and perhaps even reasonable, for Rawls to reply that justification and explanation must eventually come to an end and that we have here reached fundamental moral intuitions which are not susceptible to further justification or explanation.

The reader with familiarity with Rawls' thought may wonder why I do not here refer to what is often taken to be the distinctive apparatus of the political philosophy of *A Theory of Justice* as a justification and explanation of Rawls' principles of justice. This feature is Rawls' contemporary, game-theoretic version of the social contract. Idealized "representatives" of persons are placed in a symmetrical bargaining situation. That is, none has any bargaining advantage over any other. They are curtained behind Rawls' famous "veil of ignorance," which denies them any information about the socio-economic particulars of the society of which they (or the persons they represent) are to be members, any information about the social or educational background or level of talent and ability of the persons they represent, and any information about the social or economic positions that are to be occupied by the persons they represent. They are also denied any information about the comprehensive conceptions of the good of the persons they represent.

On the basis of this information (or lack thereof), representatives are asked to select general principles of justice to be used to evaluate any political society. Rawls argues that they will select his principles of justice and his list of primary goods. More specifically, they will select an egalitarian distribution of "basic liberties." And with respect to "social and economic inequalities," they will adopt a 'maximin' strategy in an attempt to maximize the 'minimal' or worst level of position in any socio-economic setup (because, as far as each representative knows, the person he represents *might* end up occupying a position of that level). Thus, they will choose Rawls' difference-principle interpretation of the second principle of justice.

It is perhaps possible to interpret this contractarian device as an *argument* for (or a *proof* of) Rawls' two principles, from rationally incontrovertible premises. However, it is clear that this is not Rawls' own interpretation of his contractarian apparatus. Rather, he regards it as a "model" or "device of representation." But a model or device of representation of what? The answer seems to be a combination of (1) the liberal-democratic or Rousseauian principle of political legitimacy (in terms of the model's basic contractarian element of consent or agreement) and (2) the two moral powers that he attributes to persons: i.e., the capacity to exercise practical rationality and the capacity to form a sense of justice. The former power apparently is represented by the model's game-theoretic assumption of rational agents exclusively motivated by the attempt to maximize the interest of the persons they represent; the latter power seems to be represented by the constraints on the agent's behavior that are due to the symmetry of the bargaining situation and to the various features of the veil of ignorance. It is difficult to decide what sort (and how much) elucidation of Rawls' basic assumptions this contractarian, game-theoretic model really provides. My own view is that it may actually tend to obscure his specifically *moral* assumptions concerning fairness, reasonableness, etc.

I believe that, by way of further grounding of his principles of justice, Rawls would be more likely to return to his "shared ideas and principles implicit in the public political culture of a democratic society." With respect to the question of why these shared ideas and principles are to be accorded the fundamental, theoretical political significance that Rawls accords them, I believe he has really only two strategies as options.

One strategy is to locate those shared ideas and principles supposedly implicit in the political culture of a democratic society within a pragmatic argument. The ideas and principles in question represent a consensus, in the sense of compromise, acquiescence, or *modus vivendi*, in social contexts characterized by divergent, irreconcilable comprehensive conceptions of the human good, *telos*, or *ergon*. According to such an argument, a key feature of contemporary constitutional democracies – and, perhaps, a key feature of modern or postmodern polity in general – is the presence of such divergent views of human life. It might then be maintained that the 'price' of any sort of even minimally successful social cooperation in such a context would be adoption of liberal egalitarian principles of justice such as Rawls', the privileging of something like his conception of reasonableness, the eschewal of appeal to any comprehensive conception of the good in the political realm, etc. Although there is the occasional suggestion of this line of thought in Rawls' writings, it is clear that he is uneasy with the idea.

What, for example, would happen to Rawls' principles of justice, to his privileging of reasonableness, and so forth were social conditions to change in such a way that irreconcilable diversity concerning 'ultimacies' was no longer a social given? (In fact, orthodox Marxist social theory would seem to regard such changes, which allow the bourgeois-liberal state to be transcended, as historically inevitable.) Rawls' considered view seems to be that such an empirical, pragmatic account of the nature and theoretical function of the shared ideas and principles of the political culture of a contemporary constitutional democracy is to make those ideas and principles "political in the wrong way."[43] In other words, such an account would make the fundamentals of liberal political theory hostage to the historical contingencies, for good or ill, of rough-and-tumble social struggle, negotiation, and compromise.

The other strategy, which I think is generally favored by Rawls, is a *moral* interpretation of the supposed shared ideas and principles implicit in the public political culture of a democratic society. The purported fact that these ideas and principles *are* "widely shared" in contemporary constitutional democracies (or the outcome of the method of reflective equilibrium as applied to ideas, principles, and judgments that are widely shared) does not confer upon them their foundational status in Rawls' liberal political philosophy. What confers that status is the moral correctness of these ideas and principles. My conclusion, which I trust will not surprise the reader at this juncture, is that such moral ideals must be seen as part of a normative anthropology (also known in 'Rawlsese', as we have seen, as a "comprehensive conception of the good").

There is a (fairly generic) conception of the human good, *telos*, or *ergon* to be associated with the development and exercise of the two "moral powers" that Rawls holds to be of fundamental importance. Of primary moral value is the maximally autonomous development and exercise of the power of formulating and acting upon one's own private but concrete conception of the human good. That is, fundamental to the Rawlsian moral view of the human good is the requirement that political structures furnish each citizen with the (neutral) means for autonomously determining what is going to be of fundamental, directive value in his or her *own* life. Also fundamental to this view of the human good is the requirement that political structures develop a liberal sense of justice in their citizens. The liberal sense of justice demands that persons, when considered in terms of their political relations, that is, as *citoyens* or (to use Aristotle's phrase) political animals, privilege the value of social cooperation 'as such' *even at the expense* of the *public* pursuit of their 'private' comprehensive conceptions of the good.

While such a normative anthropology may seem quite broad and inclusive, it is inconsistent with other conceptions of the human good or *ergon* that do not endorse the idea of the 'public subservience' of comprehensive conceptions of the human good to the primacy of the virtue of social consensus built into Rawls' concept of reasonableness. Comprehensive conceptions that require a public presence for themselves, sometimes at the expense of consensus 'as such', must be deemed unreasonable and uncivil by Rawls. They involve a breach of the moral obligations imposed by his conception of public reason. However, he must represent the requirements of public reason as *not* simply grounded in one conception (among many) of the human good or *ergon*. His notion of public reason, in other words, is not supposed to be merely the expression of one normative anthropology that is conceptually 'on all fours' with other normative anthropologies, such as ones that we have considered in earlier chapters of this book.

To function as Rawls intends it to function public reason (as expressing the shared ideas and principles implicit in the public political culture of a democratic society) must be a neutral adjudicatory device. It must steer between the Scylla of being an expression of contingent, factual agreement or consensus among persons of a particular time in a particular area (which consensus might prove to be quite 'illiberal') and the Charybdis of being an expression of some teleological conception of what human life is all about (even in the form of a 'generic' normative anthropology). I have argued that there is no room for passage here, that there is no real third alternative or *tertium quid.* However, Rawls' theoretical mechanism forcefully expresses a profound desire for some firm, intelligible, and public foundation for political association and action. I consider the implications of that desire for the enterprise of political philosophy in the following and concluding brief chapter.

10

A Very Short Conclusion

Some pages ago, in Chapter 1 of this volume, I made the following claim:

> A ... common assumption is that the task of political philosophy is to establish some principled justification of political organization, a justification that will properly discriminate between better and worse forms of polity and that can be used to establish basic norms of political justice. But, according to the point of view I have just sketched, it evidently must accomplish this task without essential reference to a particular conception of a human function or purpose – an idea about which many of us moderns have become skeptical or agnostic. So political philosophy is charged with giving a rich account of the proper rôle of political organization without appeal to any conception (which would almost certainly be controversial) of what human beings are 'for' – that is, without any rich conception of human nature, function, or purpose.[1]

I proceeded to suggest that I thought it unlikely that any political philosophy worthy of the name could be formulated without explicit or implicit assumption of a normative anthropology – that is, without the assumption of *some* conception of a human nature, good, *telos*, or *ergon*. As we have seen, such a conception of the human good or *ergon* is not a simple and straightforwardly empirical matter.

In the last chapter we encountered some of the conceptual reasons why a significant movement in contemporary political philosophy has committed itself to the project of constructing a political philosophy that purports *not* to be anchored in any normative anthropology: the contractarian tradition's grounding of political legitimacy in the notion of agreement or consent has been transformed into the liberal-democratic or Rousseauian principle of political legitimacy. The legitimacy of the state and of at least its most fundamental or important actions depend on some form of agreement of its citizens. If one additionally accepts the doctrine that the principal function of the state is to facilitate, in some equitable way, the satisfaction of the citizens' (rational) *wants*, it is not clear that any political rôle should be accorded to a rational anthropology – which purports to make objectively true claims about what citizens *need* in order to become the best persons possible – *unless* such a rational anthropology reflects the (rational) wants of all the citizens.

A characteristically modern conceptual move has been to transform the old idea of a supposedly *objective* human good, *telos*, or *ergon* into a *subjective*, personal ideal or set of ultimate commitments. Such an ideal can then be operationalized, to use current managerial jargon, by a set of personal goals, which in turn will determine the rational wants of the person. This conceptual move has become a fundamental feature of much contemporary liberal political philosophy. Thus, for example, R.M. Dworkin asserts that the truth of the principle that "human beings must be treated as equals by their government"[2] is a matter of fundamental, objective morality while maintaining that "claims about the relative value of *personal goals* do not provide competent justifications for regulative political decisions."[3] In a similar vein, C.E. Larmore writes that

> in modern times we have come to recognize a multiplicity of ways in which a fulfilled life can be lived, without any perceptible hierarchy among them. And we have also been forced to acknowledge that even where we do believe that we have discerned the superiority of some ways of life to others, reasonable people may often not share our view. Pluralism and reasonable disagreement have become for modern thought ineliminable features of the idea of the good life.[4]

I attempted to show, in the preceding chapter, how this attitude combines with fundamental moral commitments to the Rousseauian principle of political legitimacy and to some form of egalitarianism to yield the consequence that a normative anthropology – that is, a conception of the human good, *telos*, or *ergon*, now rendered subjective and personal although not necessarily irrational – has no proper rôle in a 'public' political philosophy. According to such a view, it would simply be *unfair*, a matter of distributive injustice, to privilege in the public sphere such a 'non-neutral' ideal or set of commitments.

But why should a political philosophy be 'public' in the sense that would demand such neutrality? From at least the time of Plato in the fourth century B.C.E. political philosophers have tended to see themselves as doing something more than simply describing the development of political organizations and assessing their relative merits and deficiencies. Many such theorists have also undertaken the task of making political *prescriptions*, in conformity with reason and what they take to be the truth about the human good or *ergon*. The 'republic' of Plato's *Republic* is the sort of *polis* that would be established, in idealized circumstances, by a philosopher-king who has been tutored by Plato. The 'republic' of Rousseau's *Social Contract* is the sort of *polis* that would be established by a group of idealized Enlightenment *hommes*, who are motivated by rational *amour de soi-même*, not too corrupted by *amour-propre*, and instructed by Rousseau in the subtleties of the general will and the proper place of religion and the 'legislator' in the state. And so forth.

This prescriptive feature of political theory is certainly not absent from contemporary political philosophy, particularly the influential tradition of contemporary liberal political philosophy. But the Rousseauian, liberal-democratic principle of legitimacy and the concomitant conceptual apparatus that I have been discussing present the picture not of a philosopher-king but of philosopher-parliamentarians devising an ideal *polis* – or at least the ideal, fundamental principles of distributive justice and "constitutional essentials" instantiating such principles. For the reasons we have considered, such philosopher-parliamentarians will be obliged to prescind from their *differing* "comprehensive conceptions" of the human good, *telos*, or *ergon* – at least in their public, political rôles.

The prescriptive feature of much political philosophy naturally issues in the ideal of a systematic theoretical doctrine that will both legitimate and guide the political order. I have suggested that the additional ideal of the *publicity* of such a doctrine – the claim that the doctrine should be something that virtually all citizens should (in a moral sense of 'should') be able to endorse – derives from distinctively liberal presuppositions. But the quest for what, at the close of the preceding chapter, I termed a "firm, intelligible, and public foundation for political association and action" may also represent a profound desire for social cohesion and solidarity. My claim in the preceding chapter was that political liberalism's attempt to ground such a public political theory on something other than a normative anthropology, a conception of the human good or *ergon*, is a chase after a will-o'-the-wisp.

In an earlier book,[5] I argued that within contemporary constitutional democracies as we find them, the desire for a unifying, public political theory is a vain desire. More cultural, religious, and moral homogeneity than is typically found in such societies would be necessary in order for such a public political theory to be a real possibility. Modern attitudes that predominate in Western constitutional democracies seldom welcome the prospect of such increased homogeneity. In particular, it seems Pickwickian to retain the ideal of such a public political theory while encouraging and celebrating pluralism and diversity as positive social values.

Where does this leave political philosophy? Within contemporary constitutional democracies, it leaves political philosophy as an essentially partisan or sectarian affair. My use of these adjectives is not pejorative. I simply mean that political philosophy will inevitably be situated within the context of a more comprehensive moral, philosophical, or religious point of view that has as an element its own normative anthropology – its own conception of the human good, *telos*, or *ergon*. And, as convinced as the adherent to such a doctrine may be of its truth, he or she has no compelling reason to believe that it will win the acceptance of all of his or her rational, decent, and non-fanatical fellow citizens. Consequently, I would endorse a variant of A. MacIntyre's view: Political philosophy, "reflects the debates and disagreements of the culture so faithfully that its controversies turn out to be unsettlable in just the way that the political and moral debates themselves are."[6] Moreover, in MacIntyre's opinion,

> What this brings out is that modern politics cannot be a matter of genuine moral consensus. And it is not. Modern politics is civil war carried on by other means . . .[7]

The following claims are controversial but, in my view, likely to be true. At the beginning of the twenty-first century in the constitutional democracies of the West, the point of studying political theory and its history is not to play the rôle of the philosopher-king or of the philosopher-parliamentarian. Rather, it is to consider the political implications of various normative anthropologies – that is, the implications of various conceptions of what human existence is all about. Therefore, it is entirely appropriate and, indeed, necessary to situate political philosophy within a larger philosophical, moral, and religious context. I hope that the preceding chapters have given the reader some idea of the way in which some of the most profound thinkers from the history of political philosophy have approached this task. And I hope that some readers will be motivated to continue the task by further reading and reflection.

But what is the public value of political philosophy that is, from the perspective of contemporary constitutional democracies, partisan and sectarian in the sense that I have described? Echoing a hope expressed in my earlier book *Partisan or Neutral?*, I would like to think that

> thoughtful engagement with theory that is partisan or sectarian in this sense ... can help us better to understand what can and cannot be compromised and to what degree and in what way. Within such democratic contexts, a good part of prudence and of public civility is developing an informed sense of when one must "go to the mat" politically and when one should not.[8]

This may seem to be a rather modest aspiration for the public rôle of political philosophy. But it is, I trust, a reasonable one. It also seems to me that perhaps the *principal* value of engagement with political philosophy is not 'public' at all. In my view (that is, my view of the human good or *ergon*), it is always a worthwhile endeavor to become clearer about one's commitments and principles and their consequences, irrespective of whether those commitments and principles have achieved or are likely to achieve a position of political dominance in one's society.

And, yet, the study of political philosophy may not be *exclusively* of 'personal value'. In my case, this rather optimistic conjecture is paired with what some readers may regard as an overly cynical view of the political structure of the Western constitutional democracies that are sometimes referred to (usually by themselves) as constituting the 'first-world' nations. The cynical (or realistic) view, for which there seems to me to be considerable evidence, is that the governments of these societies are, by and large, economic or corporate oligarchies masquerading as liberal democracies. Such governments continue to maintain popular allegiance, in large part, by means of a modern version of the old Roman political strategy of supplying bread and circuses: the promotion of (or claim to promote) a relatively high level of material affluence, the securing of 'personal freedoms' (at least those that are deemed to be to the advantage, or at least are not to the disadvantage, of the interests of the economic oligarchy), and the provision of at least a minimal level of social welfare and 'safety net' programs for the disadvantaged.[9]

Within such structures, public political discourse is typically quite circumscribed. The media categories of 'right' and 'left', 'liberal' and 'conservative', 'tory' and 'labor' often designate little more than disagreement about the proper distribution of the bread and circuses among the categories that I just mentioned. Of course, it may well be to the advantage of the controlling oligarchic interests to maintain a circumscribed public political discourse. But conceptual political blinkers of this sort make it quite difficult for citizens of the West to understand, for example, the attraction that the ideal of an Islamic state exerts in the Middle East. Such a narrowed perspective can lend substance to the appearance of smug (and hypocritical) democratic triumphalism[10] of the sort, for example, that so much of the world sees in current American foreign and military policy. My optimistic but, I hope, not altogether fond hope is that the study of political philosophy, particularly in an historical context, provides the means to transcend these limitations – to provide oneself with the means, to use another bit of current American managerial jargon, 'to think outside the box'.

Notes

Chapter 1

1. F.W. Nietzsche, *On the Genealogy of Morals*, trans. Walter Kaufmann and R.J. Hollingdale; *Ecce Homo*, trans. Walter Kaufmann, ed., Walter Kaufmann (New York: Vintage Books, 1967). See also, Raymond Geuss, *History and Illusion in Politics* (Cambridge, Cambridge University Press, 2001), 'Introduction'.

2. To consider a very recent example, R. Geuss questions the common assumption that "five distinct elements" of our contemporary conception of democratic liberal polity ("liberalism, democracy, the state, the capitalist economy, the doctrine of human rights") "form a more or less natural, or at any rate minimally consistent and practically coherent, set" (*History and Illusion in Politics*, 3).

3. Political organization, according to this conception, exemplifies the *Gesellschaft* (association) paradigm of social organization, in the typology devised in the late nineteenth century by the German social philosopher Ferdinand Tönnies. *Gesellschaft* is an ideal type of social organization, at one end of a continuum, that has the following characteristics: (1) it is artificially created; people voluntarily join such an association; (2) it is organized on a formal basis – e.g., with a charter, constitution, and clearly defined positions within organization; (3) it has clearly circumscribed and limited aims and purposes; (4) the goals and purposes of its members typically are conceptually isolatable from their membership in such an association, the association being an 'external means' for satisfying the interests or desires of its members; and (5) it is a created, artificial entity without any existence

228

beyond that of its members. See Ferdinand Tönnies, *Community and Civil Society* [*Gemeinschaft und Gesellschaft*], ed. Jose Harris, trans. Jose Harris and Margaret Hollis (Cambridge: Cambridge University Press, 2001).

4. This conception of political organization exemplifies Tönnies' other, *Gemeinschaft* (community) paradigm of social organization. At the other end of the continuum from the *Gesellschaft* type, *Gemeinschaft* is an ideal type with the following characteristics: (1) it is natural; people are born into it; (2) its organizational structure is informal; (3) it does not have limited, clearly defined aims or purposes; (4) the goals and purposes of members typically are not conceptually isolatable from membership in such a community; and (5) it is conceived as having a 'life of its own' beyond that of its members.

5. Aristotle, *Politics* 3.9.1280b38–1281a4.

6. By 'state', I do not necessarily mean the modern nation-state. I use the term simply to signify the political organization, in whatever form it may exist, of a certain group of persons in a particular geographical location at a particular historical time. Of course, this characterization leaves quite unaddressed the question of which aspects of the social relations of such a group of persons should be considered to be distinctively political.

7. I do not mean to suggest that empirical matters are irrelevant to political philosophy. But the *sort* of empirical considerations relevant to political philosophy will often be quite different from those relevant, say, to concrete public policy. This is not to say that it is always easy to draw this distinction in a clear and convincing way. In particular, it is not always easy to say what empirical matters are relevant to a normative anthropology – or exactly how they are relevant.

8. This introduction to political philosophy is limited to what I term the 'Western' tradition, beginning with Greek (and Roman) antiquity, proceeding through the so-called Christian era to the classical modern and Enlightenment period of seventeenth and eighteenth century Europe, and concluding with American and European political thought of the nineteenth and twentieth centuries. This emphasis should not be interpreted as an implicit judgment that the political thought of, say, the orient or of the Islamic world is uninteresting or unimportant. The principal reason (or excuse) for this limitation is the limited competence of the author. However, I do think that it is fair to say that the political thought that has developed within the Western tradition, as I have just characterized it, is very much a part of the broader Western culture that gained global influence, for better or worse, in the nineteenth and twentieth centuries.

Chapter 2

1. Plato, *Protagoras*, trans. W.K.C. Guthrie, 318e–319a.

2. W.K.C. Guthrie, *The Sophists* (Cambridge: Cambridge University Press, 1971), 3.

3. Guthrie, *The Sophists*, 55.

4. The singular is '*aretê*'. The English noun 'virtue', which is traditionally used to translate this term, may have quaint, somewhat 'Victorian', or perhaps religious, connotations to the contemporary ear. Some prefer the translation 'excellence'. I shall often simply stick with a transliteration of the Greek.

5. Plato, *Protagoras* 320d.

6. *Protagoras* 322a.

7. *Protagoras* 322b.

8. *Protagoras* 322c–d.

9. *Protagoras*, trans. Guthrie [modified], 322d–323a.

10. *Protagoras* 326d.

11. *Protagoras* 327e–328a.

12. *Protagoras* 328a–b.

13. Thucydides, *The Landmark Thucydides: A Comprehensive Guide to the Peloponnesian War*, rev. ed. of the Richard Crawley translation, ed. Robert B. Strassler (New York: The Free Press, 1996), 6.38.5–39.2 (p. 384).

14. Aristotle, *Rhetoric*, trans. W. Rhys Roberts, 1.10.1368b8–9.

15. *Rhet.* 1.1373b6–9.

16. Plato, *Meno*, trans. W.K.C. Guthrie, 71e–72a.

17. In particular, the functionalistic model supplies a way of thinking about a *human* nature or essence.

18. Plato, *Laws* 890a.

19. Plato, *Republic* 359c.

20. Plato, *Republic*, trans. G.M.A. Grube, 358e–359b.

Chapter 3

1. We know surprisingly little about the life of Plato (427–347 B.C.E.). He came from a wealthy, aristocratic family, which had been politically prominent in the anti-democratic circles of Athenian society. Plato certainly had some position in the group surrounding Socrates; but it seems likely that some of his older male relations (e.g., his older brother Glaucon, who figures as an important character in the *Republic*, as we saw in the preceding chapter) were closer than Plato to Socrates. After the final defeat of Athens by Sparta in the Peloponnesian War and the subsequent defeat by the democratic faction of an oligarchic 'puppet government' (The Thirty) installed by the victorious Spartans, Plato's family lost its political influence. Probably sometime during the 380s Plato established his 'school', the Academy, at Athens. During his life, he seems to have paid three visits to Syracuse and maintained connections with the governors or 'tyrants' of Syracuse, Dionysius the Elder and his son Dionysius the Younger. There has been much speculation, partly based on letters attributed to Plato, about the influence of Plato's 'real-world' experience of politics in Syracuse

on the shape and development of his political philosophy. There has also been a rather astounding variety of interpretations of Plato's political thought. These interpretations range (to mention several of the more extreme examples) from the view, particularly associated with some of the followers of the twentieth-century political philosopher Leo Strauss, that Plato really was not much concerned with politics at all, to the view set forth by another twentieth-century philosopher, Karl Popper in his *The Open Society and its Enemies* (2 vols., 1945), according to which Plato becomes a paradigmatic spokesperson for repressive, intolerant, and anti-democratic ideas. So the reader should be aware that the interpretation that I develop in the text of Plato's political thought is certainly not the only one to have found favor in scholarly and philosophical reflection on Plato's thought.

2. The historical Socrates (470–399 B.C.E.) wrote nothing. He is a principal character in most of the dialogues of Plato. The most common, but not universal, scholarly view is that only the earliest dialogues of Plato give a sort of portrait of the historical Socrates at work. According to this view, Socrates is the character who expresses Plato's own views in most of the so-called middle and late dialogues.

3. Plato, *Republic*, trans. G.M.A. Grube, 369b–c.

4. *Rep.* 370a–b.

5. *Rep.* 372a.

6. The Latin phrase '*do ut des*' (which literally means "I give so that you will give") is sometimes used for this concept of prudential reciprocity. And this is also one interpretation of the Golden Rule: "Do unto others as you would have done unto yourself."

7. *Rep.* 372d.

8. *Rep.* 372d.

9. *Rep.*, trans. Grube, 373a.

10. *Rep.*, trans. Grube, 373d.

11. "I think that justice is the very thing, or some form of the thing which, when we were beginning to found our city, we said had to be established throughout. We stated, and often repeated, if you remember, that everyone must pursue one occupation of those in the city, that for which his nature best fitted him" (*Rep.*, trans. Grube, 433a). "In some way then possession of one's own and the performance of one's own task could be agreed to be justice" (*Rep.*, trans. Grube, 433e–434a).

12. *Rep.*, trans. Grube, 431c–d.

13. Plato, *Phaedo* 64a.

14. Of course, it might be claimed that some version of Plato's tripartite conception of the human *psychê* (as found in the *Republic*, *Phaedrus*, or *Timaeus*) constitutes such a conception of practical rationality, that is, reason directed toward action. This is not the place for a full response to such a claim. However, I would suggest that the tripartite conception of *psychê* does not really constitute the foundation of a theory of practical

rationality – reason in the service of practical ultimate ends. Instead, it gives a picture of ('blind', irrational) appetite or desire (Plato's faculty of *epithymia*) working *against* reason (Plato's faculty of *nous*) and, if the individual person is lucky, somehow being controlled and checked by *nous* through the rather mysterious mediation of *thymos* (the 'spirited' and honor-loving faculty of *psychê*).

15. Plato, *Republic*, trans. Grube, 516c–d.

16. *Rep.*, trans. Grube, 516e–517a.

17. *Rep.*, trans. Grube, 517a.

18. From a psychological perspective, perhaps Plato's most forceful argument why the most able should rule is found in the first book of the *Republic*: "Now the greatest punishment is to be ruled by a worse man than oneself if one is not willing to rule. I think that it is fear of this which makes men of good character rule whenever they do. They approach office not as something good or something to be enjoyed, but as something necessary because they cannot entrust it to men better than, or even equal to, themselves" (*Rep.*, trans. Grube, 347c–d). Note that this line of thought does not supply one with a reason (either prudential or moral) for ruling when there are others "better than, or even equal to," oneself available for the job.

19. *Rep.*, trans. Grube, 519d.

20. *Rep.* 519d.

21. *Rep.* 519d.

22. *Rep.*, trans Grube, 519e–520a.

23. *Rep.*, trans Grube, 520a–c.

Chapter 4

1. Unlike Socrates and Plato, who were Attic Greeks with well-established family connections in Athens, Aristotle (384–322 B.C.E.) was an Ionian Greek, who was born in the town of Stagira on the peninsula of Chalcidice in Thrace. His father had been the court physician to the Macedonian king Amyntas, father of Philip II and grandfather of Alexander the Great (whom Aristotle briefly tutored). At the age of seventeen (in 367) Aristotle went to Athens to study in Plato's school, the Academy, leaving twenty years later, in 347 after Plato's death. He remained away from Athens (traveling, doing research, and tutoring Alexander) until 335, when he returned and opened his own school, the Lyceum or Peripatetic school. In 323, after the death of Alexander, an anti-Macedonian reaction in Athens (and in other Greek *poleis*) caused Aristotle to depart for a family estate in Chalcis, where he died the following year.

2. Aristotle, *Nicomachean Ethics* (*EN*), trans. W.D. Ross, revised by J.O. Urmson, 1.2.1094a18–1094b1.

3. *EN* 1.2.1094b5–6.

4. What argument there is comes in *EN* 1.7, where Aristotle develops what I earlier term the 'functionalistic conception' of a human *aretê* (excellence or virtue) and of human goodness: a good person is a human being who is good at being a person, that is, one who fulfills the human function or lives up to the human nature well; and human virtues or excellences (*aretai*) are the qualities or capacities that allow a human agent to do that. As D. Bostock argues, Aristotle also seems to assume that the good person in this sense is to be identified with one who successfully "secures the good *for* man"; consequently, Aristotle also identifies the chief human good with the successful achievement or performance of whatever turns out to be the distinctive human function. See David Bostock, *Aristotle's Ethics* (Oxford and New York: Oxford University Press, 2000), 25–29.

5. I shall use the phrase 'contemplative life' for Aristotle's '*bios theôrêtikos*' because it is a translation that is traditionally used and, more importantly, because it supplies a handy English tag phrase for Aristotle's concept. However, contemplative (*theôrêtikos*, in the Greek) pertains simply to knowing or understanding the truth. It is not necessarily a form of intellection different in kind from that provided by what Aristotle calls the sciences (*epistêmai*); and it seems to me that Aristotle's use of the term certainly has none of the connotations that the English adjective, contemplative, has acquired from Eastern religious and philosophical traditions and from Christian mysticism.

6. Aristotle, *Metaphysics* 12.7.

7. Aristotle, *EN* 10.8.1178b18–19.

8. *EN* 10.7.1177b27–28.

9. *EN* 10.7.1177b33–34.

10. *EN*, trans. Ross/Urmson (revised), 10.8.1178a9–22.

11. Aristotle, *Politics* 1.2.1253a3.

12. *EN* 1.3.1094b14–16.

13. Sarah Broadie, *Ethics with Aristotle* (Oxford and New York: Oxford University Press, 1991), 198.

14. D. Bostock, *Aristotle's Ethics*, 211.

15. Bostock, *Aristotle's Ethics*, 210–211.

16. Aristotle, *Politics* 7.9.1329a1–2.

17. *Politics*, trans. Jowett (revised), 8.2.1337b8–14.

18. *Pol.* 3.5.1278a20–21.

19. Bostock, *Aristotle's Ethics*, 190.

20. Aristotle, *EN* 10.8.1179a4–5.

21. Broadie, *Ethics with Aristotle*, 210.

22. Broadie, *Ethics with Aristotle*, 211.

23. Aristotle, *Politics*, trans. Jowett (revised), 1.2.1252b27–1253a4.

24. *Pol.* 1.2.1253a2–3.

25. *Pol.* 1.2.1252b12–14.

26. *Pol.* 1.2.1252b15–16.

27. *Pol.* 1.2.1252b28, 1253a19.

28. *Pol.*, trans. Jowett (revised), 1.2.1253a25–29.

29. *Pol.*, trans. Jowett (revised), 3.9.1280a31–b12.

30. *Pol.* 4.1.1288b23–24.

31. *Pol.*, trans. Jowett, 4.1.1288b24–27.

32. *EN* 10.9.1180a25–32.

33. *EN*, trans. Ross/Urmson (revised), 10.9.1180b3–8.

34. John Finnis, *Natural Law and Natural Rights* (Oxford: Clarendon Press, 1980), 147–148.

35. Fred D. Miller, Jr., *Nature, Justice, and Rights in Aristotle's 'Politics'* (Oxford: Clarendon Press, 1995), 358.

36. *EN*, trans. Ross/Urmson, 10.9.1180a22–24.

37. *EN*, trans. Ross/Urmson (revised), 8.1.1155a22–28.

38. *Pol.*, 3.7.1279a25–26.

39. *Pol.*, trans. Jowett, 4.1.1289a15–18.

40. *Pol.*, trans. Jowett, 3.7.1179a27–31. A correct/true constitution in which rule is vested in one person is a kingship; one in which rule is vested in a few is an aristocracy; and one in which rule is vested in many, he (curiously) calls just a 'constitution' (*politeia*), "using the general term," as he himself points out. Aristotle associates the last form of constitution with the *poleis* where citizenship and/or participation of political decision-making is associated with citizen-soldier military status and thinks that such a form of constitution is not really capable of furthering "complete *aretê*" but only the martial virtues (*Pol.* 4.11.1295a25–40; 3.7.1279b1–3). The perversions of these sorts of constitution are, respectively, tyranny, oligarchy, and democracy; they are perversions because the political decision-makers pursue not the common interest but their own perceived (really, misperceived) class interest.

41. *Eudemian Ethics (EE)* 7.9.1241b13–14.

42. *Pol.* 3.12.1282b17–18; *EN* 8.9.1160a13–14.

43. *EN* 5.1.1130a10–13.

44. *EN* 5.2.1130b30–1131a9.

45. *EN*, trans. Ross/Urmson, 1.3.1131a25–29.

46. *Pol.*, trans. Jowett (revised), 3.18.1288a32–b2.

47. Broadie, *Ethics with Aristotle*, 369.

48. *Ethics with Aristotle*, 219.

49. *EN* 10.9.1181b12–15.

50. The meaning of Aristotle's phrase '*anthrôpeia philosophia*' is not altogether clear. I certainly do not mean to *equate* it with my idea of a normative anthropology, although I think it presupposes such a notion. I think something fairly broad, like the eighteenth-century idea of 'moral science' (which may include, *inter alia*, moral, political, aesthetic, and even psychological and epistemological elements), may be what Aristotle has in mind. I extend thanks to my colleague Thomas Blackson for discussion on this point.

Chapter 5

1. A notable exception, perhaps, is Plato's *Crito*. In that dialogue, Socrates, awaiting execution by the Athenian government, is urged by Crito and other supporters to escape. He considers what the reaction to this proposal by the personified 'Laws' of the *polis* would be. The doctrine that seems to emerge is that certain obligations of reciprocity oblige a citizen to obey the legitimate (legal?) commands of the *polis*, even if those commands are unjust or threaten one's physical welfare: "we (the Laws) maintain that anyone who disobeys is guilty of doing wrong on three separate counts: first because we are his parents, and secondly because we are his guardians, and thirdly because, after promising obedience, he is neither obeying us nor persuading us to change our decision if we are at fault in any way" (*Crito*, 51e [trans. H. Tredennick]). The *Crito* thus certainly suggests a "special sort of moral obligation owed to the state, which is not to be reduced to considerations of individual self-interest or [perhaps] even to the promotion of the common good." However, the doctrine does not seem to have been widely or enthusiastically adopted in Greek or Roman political *theory* (as opposed to practical exhortations to patriotism). And the doctrine seems to have had its limits even in the practice of Socrates, who evidently believed himself to be quite justified in ignoring a command, issued to him by the government of the 'Thirty Tyrants', after Athens' defeat in the Peloponnesian War. Obeying the command in question would have involved 'wronging' *another* citizen (Leon of Salamis), whom the rulers wished to execute (and who, in fact, was executed). In this case, it is clear that Socrates believed that his disobedience was justified because of the fact that he had been ordered to do something "wrong and wicked", although he may have questioned the legitimacy of the government as well (see Plato's *Apology*, 32c–d). Also in the *Apology*, Socrates informs his jury that, should they agree to acquit him on the condition that he cease philosophizing, he would disobey such an order because "I owe a greater obedience to god than to you" (*Apology* 25d).

2. For passages from the New Testament in this chapter, I use (sometimes in a slightly altered form) the text of *The Jerusalem Bible* (Garden City, New York: Doubleday and Company, Inc., 1966).

3. Ernest L. Fortin, "Introduction," *Augustine: Political Writings*, trans. Michael W. Tkacz and Douglas Kries, ed. Ernest L. Fortin and Douglas Kries, with Roland Gunn (Indianapolis and Cambridge: Hackett Publishing Company, Inc., 1994), vii–viii.

4. 'Gnosticism' refers to a collection of religious-philosophical systems particularly influential in the second and third centuries C.E. In general, these systems emphasized the duality between spirit and matter, tended to conceive the material world as intrinsically evil, and believed in salvation for a small group of elite souls, which is to be effected by means of ascetic practice and reliance on secret, specialized knowledge (*gnôsis*). In the 1940s

additional knowledge of gnostic beliefs was gained through the discovery of texts at the Egyptian site of Nag Hammadi. Manichaeanism, which may be regarded as a particular form of gnosticism, was founded by the Parthian religious figure Mani (216–276 C.E.). It elaborates gnostic dualism between the spiritual (good) and the material (evil) by means of an elaborate mythology, which includes the doctrine of a war between heavenly and demonic souls. As a result of this war, the former ('seeds of light' or 'suffering Jesuses') are entrapped in some biological organisms. Ultimately, there will be complete separation of the two kingdoms. Rigorous asceticism practiced by elect souls (aided by the ministrations of less exalted 'hearers') will help to effect this final separation.

5. Filmer's theory is the object of criticism in the seldom read *First Treatise of Government* by John Locke, whose competing political theory we shall consider in Chapter 7.

6. See *Romans* 3:30.

7. See, for example, Abraham J. Malherbe, *Paul and the Popular Philosophers* (Minneapolis: Fortress Press, 1989).

8. Troels Engberg-Pedersen, *Paul and the Stoics* (Louisville, Kentucky: Westminster John Knox Press, 2000), 53. As the etymology of the term '*oikeiôsis*' suggests, it bears the connotation of moving from seeing oneself as a separate entity, with idiosyncratic desires, aims, and motives, to an ever wider social identification of oneself with the surrounding *cosmos*, particularly with the directing, rational element of the *cosmos*. Because of the term's etymology and the associated connotations, J. Christiansen uses the term 'sociation' to translate it (Johnny Christiansen, "Equality of man and Stoic social thought," *Commentarium Humanarum Litterarum*, Vol. 75 [1984], 50).

9. Engberg-Pedersen, 59.

10. Engberg-Pedersen, 59.

11. Cicero, *De finibus bonorum et malorum*, trans. H. Rackham, second edition, The Loeb Classical Library (Cambridge, Mass. and London: Harvard University Press and Wm. Heinemann, Ltd., 1931), 3.21.

12. Engberg-Pedersen, 61.

13. Engberg-Pedersen, 61.

14. Engberg-Pedersen, 53. 'Passions' here signifies 'evil passions', of course. For orthodox Stoicism (as for the seventeenth-century philosopher Baruch Spinoza), a passion (which, in terms of its Latin etymology, is something we suffer or undergo – that is, something that is done *to* us) is a sort of irrational behavior response, a manifestation of ignorance or unclear ideas. From a contemporary perspective, one might refer to 'good passions' such as love. But it is pretty clear that for St. Paul (as for Spinoza) the love of God is not a passion in anything like this sense – despite the fact that there is a sense in which God permits and enables those who love him to do so.

15. Diogenes Laertius, *Lives and Opinions of the Eminent Philosophers*, 7.32.

16. Diogenes Laertius, 7.33.

17. Engberg-Pedersen, 75.

18. Engberg-Pedersen, 77.

19. Cicero, *De finibus bonorum et malorum*, trans. H. Rackham, 3.64.

20. Engberg-Pedersen, 77.

21. This term is taken from the essay of J. Christiansen cited earlier in this chapter: "Equality of man and Stoic social thought," 52. It nicely suggests the cooperative, communal character of the Stoic ideal – but a sort of cooperativeness that does not depend upon any formal 'political' structure of rule and subordination.

22. Arianism, named after the Christian priest Arius, was a doctrine according to which the Son, Jesus Christ, is a creature, superior to other creatures and created before time but distinct in essence from God the Father. It was condemned as heretical at the Council of Nicaea (325 C.E.). Although the division between Arianism and orthodox or Catholic Christianity may seem to depend on a rather abstruse theological issue, the division also came to coincide with other social, economic, and political differences.

23. Fortin, "Introduction," *Augustine: Political Writings*, xx.

24. Eusebius of Caesarea, *The Ecclesiastical History*, trans. Kirsopp Lake, The Loeb Classical Library (Cambridge, Mass. and London: Harvard University Press and Wm. Heinemann, Ltd., 1926), 1.2.23.

25. Eusebius, *Eccl. Hist.*, 10.4.60.

26. Eusebius, *Eccl. Hist.*, 10.4.63.

27. Eusebius, *Life of Constantine*, 4.13.

28. Eusebius, *Eccl. Hist.*, 10.9.6–8.

29. Hippo was a seaport in north Africa (in what is now Algeria). Augustine served as Catholic bishop there from 390 until 430 C.E., when he died while the city was being besieged by the Vandals.

30. Fortin, "Introduction," *Augustine: Political Writings*, xvii.

31. Paul Orosius, *Seven Books of History against the Pagans*, trans. Irving Woodsworth Raymond (New York: Columbia University Press, 1936), 7.35.

Chapter 6

1. This is the succinct characterization of the human function found in the *Baltimore Catechism* that was memorized by generations of American Roman Catholics. The same idea is expressed more fully in the new universal *Catechism of the Catholic Church* (Liguori, Missouri: Liguori Publications, 1994): God "calls man to seek him, to know him, and to love him with all his strength. He calls together all men, scattered and divided by

sin, into the unity of his family, the Church" (1, p. 7); and "of all visible creatures only man is 'able to know and love his creator.' He is 'the only creature on earth that God has willed for its own sake,' and he alone is called to share, by knowledge and love, in God's own life" (356, p. 91).

2. St. Thomas Aquinas, *Summa Theologiae* (*Summa Theologica*), I–II q. 92, a. 1 (my translation).

3. Ernest L. Fortin, "Introduction," *Augustine: Political Writings*, trans. Michael W. Tkacz and Douglas Kries, ed. Ernest L. Fortin and Douglas Kries, with Roland Gunn (Indianapolis and Cambridge: Hackett Publishing Company, Inc., 1994), vii.

4. Augustine, *Concerning the City of God against the Pagan*, trans. Henry Bettensen (Harmondsworth, England and New York: Penguin Books, Ltd.), bk. v, ch. 17 (hereafter cited in the form '*City of God*, 5.17').

5. Fortin, "Introduction," *Augustine: Political Writings*, xvi.

6. Fortin, "Introduction," *Augustine: Political Writings*, xvi–xvii.

7. Augustine, *City of God*, 1 (preface).

8. Augustine, *City of God*, 1 (preface).

9. Augustine, *City of God*, 1.1.

10. Augustine, *City of God*, 18.49.

11. Augustine, *On Christian Doctrine*, trans. J.F. Shaw (Chicago and London: Encylopaedia Britannica, Inc. [The Great Books], 1952), 1.3.

12. Augustine, *On Christian Doctrine*, 1.5.

13. Augustine, *Confessions*, 1.1.

14. Augustine, *On Christian Doctrine* 1.4.

15. Augustine, *City of God*, 14.1.

16. Augustine, *City of God*, 14.1.

17. Augustine, *City of God*, 14.1.

18. Augustine, *City of God*, 14.28.

19. Augustine, *City of God*, 15.2.

20. Augustine, *City of God*, 12.28.

21. Augustine, *City of God*, 5.19.

22. Augustine generally follows a tradition extending back at least to Socrates, according to which human persons do not desire an object *because* they perceive it as evil but because they believe (perhaps mistakenly) that it will yield them some good. Augustine's doctrine in this matter is subtle, however: he certainly admits the possibility of taking a perverse pleasure in sinful acts (as in the famous account, in *Confessions* 2.9–18, of his youthful theft of pears, pears which he did not want to consume). At one point, Augustine suggests that such acts are rooted in the love of a "maimed liberty," which can express itself in a desire to transgress the moral law; he also suggests that a love of companionship was involved in this famous act of 'pointless wrongdoing' – since he was not attracted toward solitary theft.

23. Augustine, *City of God*, 12.8.

24. Augustine, *City of God*, 14.4.

25. Augustine, *City of God,* 14.5.

26. See, for example, Augustine, *City of God,* 5.8–10.

27. Augustine, *City of God,* 29.26.

28. Augustine, *City of God,* 29.27.

29. Augustine, *City of God,* 29.28.

30. Augustine, *City of God,* 15.4.

31. Johannes van Oort, *Jerusalem and Babylon: A Study of Augustine's* City of God *and the Sources of His Doctrine of the Two Cities* (Leiden and New York: E.J. Brill, 1991), 151.

32. Augustine, *Letters, Volume III* (131–164), trans. Sister Wilfrid Parsons, S.N.D., The Fathers of the Church, Volume 20 (New York, Fathers of the Church, Inc. 1953), Letter 153 (p. 302).

33. See, for example, Edmund N. Santurri, "Rawlsian Liberalism, Moral Truth and Augustinian Politics," *Journal for Peace and Justice Studies* 8:2 (1997), 1–36.

34. Michael J. White, "Pluralism and Secularism in the Political Order: St. Augustine and Theoretical Liberalism," *The University of Dayton Review* 22:3 (1994), 147.

35. White, "Pluralism and Secularism in the Political Order," 146.

36. Augustine, *Letters* 131–164, Letter 138 (pp. 41–42).

37. Augustine, *Letters* 131–164, Letter 138 (p. 44).

38. Augustine, *Letters* 131–164, Letter 138 (p. 44).

39. Augustine, *Letters* 131–164, Letter 138 (p. 45).

40. Augustine, *Letters, Volume I* (1–82), trans. Sister Wilfrid Parsons, S.N.D., The Fathers of the Church, Volume 12 (Washington, D.C.: The Catholic University of America Press, 1951), Letter 47 (p. 230).

41. Augustine, *The Problem of Free Choice (De libero arbitrio),* trans. Dom Mark Pontifex (New York and Ramsey, New Jersey: Newman Press, 1955), 5.11 (p. 44).

42. Augustine, *Free Choice,* 5.12 (pp. 45–46).

43. Augustine, *Free Choice,* 5.12 (p. 46).

44. Augustine, *Free Choice,* 5.12 (p. 45).

45. Augustine, *Free Choice,* 5.13 (pp. 46–47).

46. Fortin, "Introduction," *Augustine: Political Writings,* xxvi.

47. Only some of the logical writings of Aristotle had survived the rigors of late antiquity as part of the intellectual heritage of the Latin-speaking and -reading Europe.

48. Josef Pieper, *Guide to Thomas Aquinas,* trans. Richard and Clara Winston (New York: Mentor-Omega Books, 1962), 34.

49. The term 'fundamentalist', in its contemporary sense, might well have been used in this context had that term then existed.

50. St. Thomas Aquinas, *Summa Theologica,* trans. Fathers of the English Dominican Province (New York: Benziger Bros., 1948), Part I–II, Question 1, Article 7 (hereafter cited in form 'I–II, q. 1, a. 7').

51. Aquinas, *Summa Theologica*, I–II, q. 55, a. 1.

52. Aquinas, *Summa Theologica*, I–II, q. 1, a. 7.

53. Sarah Broadie, *Ethics with Aristotle* (Oxford and New York: Oxford University Press, 1991), 369.

54. Aquinas, *Summa Theologica*, I–II, q. 91, a. 1.

55. Aquinas, *Summa Theologica*, I–II, q. 91, a. 2.

56. Aquinas, *Summa Theologica*, I–II, q. 91, a. 2.

57. Aquinas, *Summa Theologica*, I–II, q. 94, a. 2.

58. Aquinas, *Summa Theologica*, I–II, q. 5, a. 3.

59. Aquinas, *Summa Theologica*, I–II, q. 3, a. 6.

60. See Aquinas, *Summa Theologica*, I–II, q. 4, aa. 7 and 8.

61. Aquinas, *Summa Theologica* I–II, q. 3, a. 8.

62. Aquinas, *Summa Theologica*, I–II, q. 4, a. 1.

63. Aquinas, *Summa Theologica*, I–II, q. 63, a. 4.

64. Aquinas, *Summa Theologica*, I–II, q. 91, a. 4.

65. Aquinas, *Summa Theologica*, I–II, q. 91, a. 4.

66. Aquinas, *Summa Theologica*, I–II, q. 91, a. 4.

67. Aquinas, *Summa Theologica*, I–II, q. 91, a. 4.

68. Aquinas, *Summa Theologica*, I–II, q. 90, a. 1.

69. Aquinas, *Summa Theologica*, I–II, q. 90, a. 2.

70. Aquinas, *Summa Theologica*, I–II, q. 90, a. 3.

71. Aquinas, *Summa Theologica*, I–II, q. 90, a. 3.

72. Aquinas, *Summa Theologica*, I–II, q. 90, a. 4.

73. Aquinas, *Summa Theologica*, I–II, q. 96, a. 4.

74. Aquinas, *Summa Theologica*, I–II, q. 96, a. 4.

75. Aquinas, *Summa Theologica*, I–II, q. 95, a. 2.

76. Aquinas, *Summa Theologica*, I–II, q. 95, a. 2.

77. Aquinas, *Summa Theologica*, I–II, q. 95, a. 4.

78. Aquinas, *Summa Theologica*, I–II, q. 94, a. 6.

79. Aquinas, *Summa Theologica*, I–II, q. 95, a. 2.

80. Aquinas, *Summa Theologica*, I–II, q. 75, a. 3.

81. Aquinas, *Summa Theologica*, I–II, q. 96, a. 3.

82. Aquinas, *Summa Theologica*, I–II, q. 95, a. 1.

83. Aquinas, *Summa Theologica*, I–II, q. 92, a. 1.

84. Aquinas, *Summa Theologica*, I–II, q. 96, a. 3.

85. Bishop of Seville in Spain, whose approximate dates are 602–636 C.E., and who (along with Augustine) was one of the most important intellectual links between pagan antiquity and the Middle Ages.

86. Aquinas, *Summa Theologica*, I–II, q. 96, a. 2.

87. Aquinas, *Summa Theologica*, I–II, q. 96, a. 2.

88. Aquinas, *De Regno* (*On Kingship: To the King of Cyprus*), trans. Gerald B. Phelan, revised by I. Th. Eschmann, O.P. (Toronto: The Pontifical Institute of Mediaeval Studies, 1949), Book II, sec. 114 (hereafter cited in the form 'II, 114'). In the fourteenth century this work was conflated

with another work *De Regimine Principium* (*On the Governance of Rulers*) attributed to Tolomeo of Lucca. That Latin title continues sometimes to be used either for the conflated work or for what now is taken to be Aquinas' original work. The introduction to this edition contains a very full discussion of its history.

89. Aquinas, *De Regno*, II, 115.

90. Aquinas, *De Regno*, II, 118.

91. Aquinas, *De Regno*, II, 118.

92. Aquinas, *Summa Theologica*, II–II, q. 12, a. 2.

93. Aquinas, *De Regno*, I, 8.

94. Aquinas, *De Regno*, I, 9.

95. Aquinas, *De Regno*, I, 17.

96. Aquinas, *Summa Theologica*, I–II, q. 71, a. 2.

97. Aquinas, *Summa Theologica*, I–II, q. 97, a. 1.

98. See Dino Bigongiari, "Introduction," in *The Political Ideas of St. Thomas Aquinas* (New York: Hafner Press, 1953), xxv.

99. Aquinas, *De Regno*, I, 31.

100. Aquinas, *De Regno*, I, 32.

101. See Bigongiari, who cites Aquinas' commentary on Aristotle's *Politics* (iii. 8 *et passim*) in "Introduction," *The Political Ideas of St. Thomas Aquinas*, xxix.

102. Bigongiari, "Introduction," *The Political Ideas of St. Thomas Aquinas*, xxxiii.

103. Aquinas, *Summa Theologica*, II–II, q. 104, a. 3.

104. Aquinas, *Summa Theologica*, II–II, q. 104, a. 4.

105. Aquinas, *Summa Theologica*, II–II, q. 104, a. 4.

106. Aquinas, *Summa Theologica*, II–II, q. 10, a. 10.

107. Aquinas, *Summa Theologica*, II–II, q. 10, a. 10.

108. Aquinas, *Summa Theologica*, II–II, q. 10, a. 10.

109. Perhaps the most historically significant exercise of this right occurred in the excommunication of Elizabeth I of England by Pope Pius V in the bull *Regnans in excelsis* of 1570.

110. Aquinas, *Summa Theologica*, II–II, q. 12, a. 2.

111. Aquinas, *Summa Theologica*, I–II, q. 90, a. 3.

Chapter 7

1. Thomas Hobbes, "T. Hobbes Malmesburiensis Vita, Scripta Anno MDCLXXII," in *Thomae Hobbes Malmesburiensis Opera Philosophica quae Latine Scripsit*, ed. William Moleworth, Vol. 1 (London: John Bohn, 1839; second reprint at Darmstadt: Scientia Verlag Aalen, 1966), lxxxvi.

2. My story about Hobbes emphasizes his modernity, which was surely very central to his self-conception. However, Hobbes' education was a classical one, he came to mathematics (and natural science) relatively late,

and his interest in classical literature and culture never abated. Thus, he was by no means detached from preceding, Renaissance humanism. Quentin Skinner has usefully explored the connection between humanistic rhetoric and Hobbes' development of *scientia civilis*, arguing that while Hobbes repudiated the use of rhetoric in the human sciences in the 1640s, he later adopted a much more accommodating and positive attitude toward the rôle of rhetoric in this context. See, in particular, Skinner, *Reason and Rhetoric in the Philosophy of Hobbes* (Cambridge: Cambridge University Press, 1996).

3. Thomas Hobbes, *Leviathan, Parts I and II*, introduction by Herbert W. Schneider (Indianapolis and New York: The Liberal Arts Press, Inc., 1958), Part I, ch. 6 (I, 6). The *Leviathan*, one of Hobbes' two principal works of political philosophy, was written in English and published in 1651. The other work is the *De Cive* (*On the Citizen*), which was originally written in Latin and published in 1642, with notes and introduction added in 1647 and an English translation (perhaps by Hobbes himself) published in 1651.

4. Hobbes, *De Cive*, I, 2, in *Man and Citizen* (*De Homine* and *De Cive*) [*De Homine*, trans. C.T. Wood, T.S.K. Scott-Craig, and B. Gert; *De Cive*, trans. attributed to Thomas Hobbes], ed. and intro., Bernard Gert (Indianapolis and Cambridge: Hackett Publishing Company, 1991).

5. Hobbes, *De Cive*, I, 5.

6. Bernard Gert, 'Introduction' to Thomas Hobbes, *Man and Citizen*, 5.

7. It seems quite implausible to claim that the explicitly conscious goal of all my intentional actions is to achieve some pleasure or avoid some pain. However, one may perhaps admit this point and still consistently claim, as Hobbes does, that the ultimate *causal* origin of each of my actions is some-how correctly analyzed in terms of pursuit of pleasure or avoidance of pain.

8. My colleague Jeffrie G. Murphy has emphasized this point to me in his very helpful comments on a draft of this chapter.

9. Hobbes, *De Cive*, I, 2.

10. Hobbes, *De Cive*, I, 2.

11. Hobbes, *De Cive*, I, 12.

12. Hobbes, *Leviathan*, I, 13.

13. Hobbes, *De Cive*, I, 4.

14. Hobbes, *De Cive*, I, 5.

15. Hobbes, *Leviathan*, I, 14.

16. Hobbes, *Leviathan*, I, 14.

17. Hobbes, *Leviathan*, I, 14.

18. Hobbes, *Leviathan*, I, 14.

19. Hobbes, *De Cive*, II, 1 and I, 7.

20. Aquinas, *Summa Theologica*, I–II, q. 91, a. 2.

21. Aquinas, *Summa Theologica*, I–II, q. 94, a. 2.

22. René Descartes, *Principles of Philosophy*, Part II, Principle 37 in

The Philosophical Works of Descartes, trans. and ed. E.S. Haldane and G.R.T. Ross (New York: Dover Publications, Inc., 1955), Vol. I, 267.

23. Hobbes, *De Cive*, I, 7.

24. Berlin draws his distinction between positive and negative liberty in a lecture delivered in 1958, "Two Concepts of Liberty." This essay has most recently been reprinted in Isaiah Berlin, *Liberty: Incorporating Four Essays on Liberty*, ed. Henry Hardy (Oxford: Oxford University Press, 2002), 166–217.

25. Hobbes, *De Cive*, II, 1.

26. Hobbes, *De Cive*, I, 10.

27. Hobbes, *Leviathan*, I, 13.

28. Hobbes, *De Cive*, I, 7.

29. Hobbes, *De Cive*, II, 2; see *Leviathan*, I, 14.

30. Hobbes, *Leviathan*, I, 14.

31. In fact, Hobbes argues that there is a sense in which all of natural law amounts to the principle "*quod tibi fieri non vis, alteri ne feceris: do not that to others, you would not have done to yourself.*" The natural laws are easy for any person to discern because "when he doubts whether what he is now doing to another may be done by the law of nature or not, he [should] conceive himself to be in that other's stead" (Hobbes, *De Cive*, III, 26).

32. Hobbes, *Leviathan*, I, 15; *De Cive*, III, 1.

33. Hobbes, *De Cive*, III, 32.

34. Hobbes, *De Cive*, XIV, 1.

35. Hobbes, *De Cive*, XIV, 1.

36. Hobbes, *De Cive*, III, 33.

37. Hobbes, *De Cive*, III, 27.

38. Hobbes, *Leviathan*, I, 15.

39. Hobbes, *Leviathan*, I, 15.

40. Hobbes, *De Cive*, III, 27.

41. Hobbes, *De Cive*, I, 15.

42. Hobbes, *De Cive*, V, 2.

43. Hobbes, *De Cive*, I, 3; *Leviathan*, I, 13.

44. Again, it is easy to think of the social contract as an historical event, something along the lines of the outcome of a constitutional convention. But, like the state of nature, it is best understood as an analytical, conceptual device, which may or may not have (approximate) historical instantiations.

45. Hobbes, *Leviathan*, II, 17.

46. Hobbes, *Leviathan*, II, 17.

47. Hobbes, *Leviathan*, II, 17.

48. Hobbes, *De Cive*, XV, 7; in this same section Hobbes argues, on the basis of this analysis of natural obligation, that the obligation of yielding obedience to God derives "from fear or conscience of our own weakness in respect of the divine power."

49. Hobbes, *De Cive*, VIII, 3.
50. Hobbes, *De Cive*, IV, 2.
51. Hobbes, *De Cive*, IV, 2.
52. Hobbes, *Leviathan*, II, 20.
53. Hobbes, *Leviathan*, II, 20.
54. Hobbes, *Leviathan*, II, 20; *De Cive*, VIII.
55. Hobbes, *De Cive*, XIV, 2.
56. Hobbes, *De Cive*, III, 6.
57. Hobbes, *De Cive*, III, 4; *Leviathan*, II, 18 and 21.

58 The sense of 'positivistic', as I use the term here, derives from the idea of *positive* law. That is, positivistic conceptions of law, morality, and religion are conceptions that equate the sum and substance of law, morality, and religion with the specific 'enactments' or pronouncements of some person or group of persons – in this case, the sovereign.

59. Hobbes, *De Cive*, VI, 11.
60. Hobbes, *De Cive*, XII, 1.
61. Hobbes, *De Cive*, XII, 1.

62. The term 'Erastianism' derives from the name of Thomas Erastus (1524–1583), who was a Swiss physician, theologian, and professor (in Germany and Switzerland). He argued that the penalty of excommunication is unscriptural and that punishment of sin belongs to the secular authority alone, but was not an Erastian in the stronger sense of holding that religious matters should be exclusively the business of the secular government or of ecclesiastics completely subject to it.

63. Hobbes, *De Cive*, XII, 2.
64. Hobbes, *De Cive*, XVII, 21.
65. Hobbes, *Leviathan*, II, 31.
66. Hobbes, *De Cive*, XIII, 2.
67. Hobbes, *De Cive*, XIII, 2.
68. Hobbes, *De Cive*, XIII, 4.
69. Hobbes, *De Cive*, XIII, 4.
70. Hobbes, *De Cive*, XIII, 6.

71. The term 'Whig', as well as the term 'Tory' for the opposing political perspective, began as terms of abuse and were first used in their English political sense with respect to the issue of the succession of James II to the throne. Tory interests were generally those of the Anglican church and the old landed gentry or 'squirearchy', while Whig interests were those of one considerable segment of the aristocracy and the wealthy, mercantile elements of the middle class. Tories generally supported the Stuart monarchy (although many balked at the Catholic James II, who supported religious toleration that included Catholic toleration, which was opposed by most Tory Anglicans) and Whigs opposed it. From the time of the so-called Glorious Revolution of 1688, but particularly after the death of Queen Anne (another Protestant daughter of James II and sister of Queen Mary)

in 1714, Tory political fortunes declined at the national political level while the Whigs were ascendant for the remainder of the eighteenth century.

72. John Locke, *Second Treatise of Government*, ed. C.B. Macpherson (Indianapolis and Cambridge: Hackett Publishing Company, Inc., 1980), Preface.

73. C.B. Macpherson, "Editor's Introduction," to John Locke, *Second Treatise of Government*, ed. C.B. Macpherson (Indianapolis and Cambridge: Hackett Publishing Company, Inc., 1980), vii.

74. John Locke, *An Essay Concerning Human Understanding*, ed. Peter H. Nidditch (Oxford: Clarendon Press, 1975), Book IV, Ch. iii, Sec. 18 (IV, iii, 18).

75. Locke, *Essay*, IV, xii, 11.

76. Locke, *Essay*, IV, xii, 11.

77. Locke, *Second Treatise*, Ch. II, Sec. 10 (II, 10).

78. Locke, *Second Treatise*, II, 8.

79. Locke, *Second Treatise*, II, 6.

80. 'Theodicy' is sometimes used in a narrow sense of a doctrine pertaining to God's justice and the so-called 'problem of evil'. I use it here in the broader sense of a doctrine pertaining to the government of the universe by God, particularly as such government pertains to the destiny of souls.

81. Richard Hooker, *Book I, Laws of Ecclesiastical Polity*, quoted in Locke, *Second Treatise*, II, 5.

82. Locke, *Essay*, II, xxi, 61.

83. Locke, *Essay*, II, xxi, 55.

84. Locke, *Essay*, II, xxi, 55.

85. Locke, *Essay*, II, xxi, 60.

86. John Locke, *Epistola de Tolerantia, A Letter on Toleration*, ed. Raymond Klibansky (Oxford: Clarendon Press, 1968), 134.

87. Locke, *Second Treatise*, II, 4.

88. Locke, *Second Treatise*, VII, 90.

89. Macpherson, "Editor's Introduction," *Second Treatise of Government*, xiv.

90. Locke, *Second Treatise*, IX, 128.

91. Locke, *Second Treatise*, IX, 124.

92. Locke, *Second Treatise*, IX, 124.

93. Locke, *Second Treatise*, IX, 125.

94. Locke, *Second Treatise*, IX, 125.

95. Locke, *Second Treatise*, IX, 126.

96. Locke, *Second Treatise*, IX, 128.

97. Locke, *Second Treatise*, IX, 129.

98. Locke, *Second Treatise*, III, 19.

99. Locke, *Second Treatise*, III, 17.

100. Locke, *Second Treatise*, VII, 90–91.

101. Locke, *Second Treatise*, VIII, 99.
102. Locke, *Second Treatise*, VIII, 95.
103. Locke, *Second Treatise*, VIII, 96.
104. Locke, *Second Treatise*, XI, 131.
105. Locke, *Second Treatise*, XIII, 149.
106. Locke, *Second Treatise*, XI, 135.
107. Locke, *Second Treatise*, XIII, 149.
108. Locke, *Second Treatise*, XI, 136.
109. Locke, *Second Treatise*, XI, 138.
110. Locke, *Second Treatise*, XI, 141.
111. Locke, *Second Treatise*, VII, 94.
112. Locke, *Second Treatise*, XI, 134.
113. Locke, *Second Treatise*, IX, 123.
114. Locke, *Second Treatise*, V, 25.
115. Locke, *Second Treatise*, V, 26.
116. Locke, *Second Treatise*, V, 27.
117. Locke, *Second Treatise*, V, 31.
118. Locke, *Second Treatise*, V, 31.
119. Locke, *Second Treatise*, V, 50.
120. Locke, *Second Treatise*, V, 31.
121. Locke, *Second Treatise*, XII, 139.
122. Locke, *Second Treatise*, XII, 139.
123. Macpherson, "Editor's Introduction," *Second Treatise of Government*, xxi.
124. Macpherson, "Editor's Introduction," *Second Treatise of Government*, xxi.

Chapter 8

1. As a noun, the French 'bourgeois' originally meant the same thing as 'burgher', "a citizen or freeman of a city or burgh, as distinguished from a peasant on the one hand, and gentleman on the other; *now* often taken as the type of the mercantile or shopkeeping middle class of any country" (*Oxford English Dictionary* [Oxford: Oxford University Press, 2002]). The term eventually acquired pejorative connotations in some circles and was used to signify a person of conventional or vulgar moral, political, or aesthetic sensibility. In communist usage, it was used disparagingly of someone who advocated or defended the capitalist economic system or who was regarded as condoning the exploitation of the proletariat by such a system and its political underpinnings.

2. Rousseau later (in 1754, on a visit to Geneva) renounced his Catholicism and formally, if not actually, reverted to the Calvinist Protestantism of his youth.

3. Deism was a form of rationalistic theism particularly popular among

intellectuals in the eighteenth century. According to this doctrine, God exists as the creator of the universe. But he has constructed it so perfectly that he has very little if any continuing rôle to play in temporal matters. In particular, he takes no direct interest in human affairs. Deists were usually dismissive of the concepts of personal immortality and divine revelation (through supposedly inspired writings) as well as of the cultic practices (e.g., offering prayer, sacrifice) associated with revealed religions such as Christianity, Judaism, and Islam.

4. Peter Gay, "Introduction," *Jean-Jacques Rousseau: Basic Political Writings*, trans. and ed. Donald A. Cress, introduced by Peter Gay (Indianapolis and Cambridge: Hackett Publishing Company, 1987), xii.

5. In the *Social Contract*, Rousseau uses as synonyms the three terms '*Cité*', '*République*', and '*Corps politique*': *Du Contrat social ou Principes du Droit politique* (final version of 1762) I, 5 (book I, ch. 5), in *The Political Writings of Jean-Jacques Rousseau*, ed., introduction, and notes by C.E. Vaughan (New York: John Wiley and Sons, Inc., 1962), Vol. II, 33–34.

6. Rousseau, *Discourse on Inequality* (Second *Discourse*), Part II, in *Jean-Jacques Rousseau: Basic Political Writings*, 79.

7. Rousseau, Second *Discourse*, trans. Cress, Pt. I, 59.

8. Rousseau, Second *Discourse*, trans. Cress, Pt. I, 40.

9. Rousseau, Second *Discourse*, trans. Cress, "Notes to Part II," 106. For French terminology, see *Political Writings of Rousseau*, ed. Vaughan, "Notes du Discours," Vol. I, 217.

10. Rousseau, Second *Discourse*, trans. Cress, Pt. I, 53.

11. Rousseau, Second *Discourse*, trans. Cress, Pt. I, 53.

12. Rousseau, Second *Discourse*, trans. Cress, Pt. I, 52.

13. Rousseau, Second *Discourse*, trans. Cress, Pt. II, 60.

14. Rousseau, Second *Discourse*, trans. Cress, Pt. II, 64.

15. Rousseau, Second *Discourse*, trans. Cress, Pt. II, 64.

16. Rousseau, Second *Discourse*, trans. Cress, Pt. II, 64.

17. Rousseau, Second *Discourse*, trans. Cress, Pt. II, 65.

18. Rousseau, Second *Discourse*, trans. Cress, Pt. II, 67.

19. Rousseau, Second *Discourse*, trans. Cress, Pt. II, 67–68 (translation altered).

20. Rousseau, Second *Discourse*, trans. Cress, Pt. II, 69.

21. Rousseau, Second *Discourse*, trans. Cress, Pt. II, 69.

22. Rousseau, Second *Discourse*, trans. Cress, Pt. II, 70.

23. Rousseau, Second *Discourse*, trans. Cress, Pt. II, 70.

24. Rousseau, Second *Discourse*, trans. Cress, Pt. II, 79.

25. Rousseau, *On the Social Contract, or Principles of Right*, Book I, Preface, in *Jean-Jacques Rousseau: Basic Political Writings*, 141.

26. Rousseau, *Social Contract*, trans. Cress, I, 5 (Book I, Ch. v), 147.

27. Rousseau, *Social Contract*, trans. Cress, I, 3, 144.

28. Rousseau, *Social Contract*, trans. Cress, I, 5, 147.

29. Rousseau, *Social Contract*, trans. Cress, I, 6, 148.

30. Rousseau, *Social Contract*, trans. Cress, I, 6, 148.

31. Rousseau, *Social Contract*, trans. Cress, I, 6, 148.

32. Rousseau, *Social Contract*, trans. Cress, I, 7, 150.

33. Rousseau, *Social Contract*, trans. Cress, II, 1, 153.

34. Rousseau, *Social Contract*, trans. Cress, II, 1, 153.

35. Rousseau, *Social Contract*, trans. Cress, I, 7, 150.

36. Rousseau, *Social Contract*, trans. Cress, I, 7, 150.

37. Rousseau, *Social Contract*, trans. Cress, II, 4, 157.

38. Rousseau, *Social Contract*, trans. Cress, I, Preface, 141.

39. Rousseau, *Social Contract*, trans. Cress, II, 7, 164.

40. Rousseau, *Social Contract*, trans. Cress, II, 7, 164–165.

41. Rousseau, *Social Contract*, trans. Cress, II, 7, 163.

42. Rousseau believes that even what he regards as the best form of Christianity ("not that of today, but that of the Gospel") is "contrary to the social spirit," and that a "society of true Christians would no longer be a society of men" (*Social Contract*, trans. Cress, IV, 8, 224). In fact, he maintains that "these terms ['Christian' and 'republic'] are mutually exclusive. Christianity preaches only servitude and dependence. Its spirit is too favorable to tyranny for tyranny not to take advantage of it at all times. True Christians are meant to be slaves. They know it and are hardly moved by this" (*Social Contract*, trans. Cress, IV, 8, 225). From a political perspective, what is required is "a purely civil profession of faith, the articles of which it belongs to the sovereign to establish, not exactly as dogmas of religion, but as sentiments of sociability, without which it is impossible to be a good citizen or a faithful subject" (*Social Contract*, trans. Cress, IV, 8, 226).

43. Rousseau, *Émile or On Education*, introduction, translation, and notes by Allan Bloom (New York, Basic Books, Inc., Publishers, 1979), Book I, 40.

44. Rousseau, *Émile*, trans. Bloom, I, 38.

45. Rousseau, *Émile*, trans. Bloom, I, 39.

46. Rousseau, *Émile*, trans. Bloom, I, 41.

47. Gay, "Introduction," *Jean-Jacques Rousseau: Basic Political Writings*, xv.

48. Rousseau, *Émile*, trans. Bloom, I, 66.

49. Allan Bloom, "Introduction," Rousseau, *Émile*, 18.

50. Bloom, "Introduction," *Émile*, 18.

51. Bloom, "Introduction," *Émile*, 19.

52. Bloom, "Introduction," *Émile*, 28.

53. Jonathan Wolff, *Why Read Marx Today?* (Oxford: Oxford University Press, 2002), 7. Wolff's quite recent and quite short study is an excellent introduction to Marx's thought – conceptually sophisticated but wearing its scholarship lightly, and neither doctrinaire nor forbiddingly technical.

54. The reader is once again alerted to the fact that the interpretation of even the general shape and development of Marx's thought is controversial: It is by no means the case that all reputable Marx scholars would accept my story about Marx. To consider but one example, the French communist philosopher Louis Althusser sees a radical "'epistemological break' in the history of Marx's thought, a basic difference between the ideological 'problematic' of the Early Works and the scientific 'problematic' of *Capital*" (Louis Althusser, *For Marx*, trans. Ben Brewster [New York: Pantheon Books, A Division of Random House, 1969]).

55. Wolff, *Why Read Marx Today?*, 3–4.

56. The Young Hegelians were a group of philosophers that pursued 'radical' themes in social-political and religious thought under the inspiration of the German philosopher Georg W.F. Hegel (1770–1831) and that included (among others) Marx, Ludwig Feuerbach, David Strauss, and Bruno Bauer.

57. Marx, "On the Jewish Question," in *Marx: Early Political Writings*, ed. and trans. Joseph O'Malley with Richard A. Davis, Cambridge Texts in the History of Political Thought (Cambridge: Cambridge University Press, 1994), 31.

58. Marx, "On the Jewish Question," in *Marx: Early Political Writings*, 32.

59. Marx, "On the Jewish Question," in *Marx: Early Political Writings*, 32–33.

60. Marx, "On the Jewish Question," in *Marx: Early Political Writings*, 34–35.

61. Marx, "On the Jewish Question," in *Marx: Early Political Writings*, 35.

62. Marx, "On the Jewish Question," in *Marx: Early Political Writings*, 35.

63. Marx, "On the Jewish Question," in *Marx: Early Political Writings*, 35.

64. Marx, "On the Jewish Question," in *Marx: Early Political Writings*, 34.

65. Marx, "On the Jewish Question," in *Marx: Early Political Writings*, 36.

66. Marx, "On the Jewish Question," in *Marx: Early Political Writings*, 37.

67. Marx, "On the Jewish Question," in *Marx: Early Political Writings*, 36.

68. Marx, "On the Jewish Question," in *Marx: Early Political Writings*, 37.

69. Marx, "On the Jewish Question," in *Marx: Early Political Writings*, 43.

70. Marx, "On the Jewish Question," in *Marx: Early Political Writings*, 45.

71. Marx, "On the Jewish Question," in *Marx: Early Political Writings*, 45.

72. Marx, "On the Jewish Question," in *Marx: Early Political Writings*, 45.

73. Marx, "On the Jewish Question," in *Marx: Early Political Writings*, 45.

74. Marx, "On the Jewish Question," in *Marx: Early Political Writings*, 46.

75. It should be noted that in the early contractarian tradition, the phrase 'civil society' generally designates a state in which persons' relations are regulated by political relations. In other words, it is largely synonymous with 'political society'. However, for Marx, the phrase designates the *non-political* status and 'voluntary associations' of persons considered as *bourgeois* or egoistic *homines economici* within capitalistic, bourgeois-liberal states.

76. Marx, "On the Jewish Question," in *Marx: Early Political Writings*, 46.

77. Marx, "On the Jewish Question," in *Marx: Early Political Writings*, 46.

78. Marx, *Economic and Philosophical Manuscripts*, in *Karl Marx: Selected Writings*, ed. David McLellan, second ed. (Oxford: Oxford University Press, 2000), 88.

79. Marx, *Economic and Philosophical Manuscripts*, in *Karl Marx: Selected Writings*, 89.

80. Marx, *Economic and Philosophical Manuscripts*, in *Karl Marx: Selected Writings*, 91.

81. Marx, *The Holy Family*, in *Karl Marx: Selected Writings*, 148.

82. Marx, "On the Jewish Question," in *Marx: Early Political Writings*, 50.

83. Jonathan Wolff, *Why Read Marx Today?* especially ch. 2, "Class, History, and Capital."

84. Karl Marx, *Capital: A Critique of Political Economy*, Volume One, introduced by Ernest Mendel, trans. Ben Fowkes (New York: Vintage Books, 1977), 99.

85. Marx, *The German Ideology* in *Karl Marx: Selected Writings*, 187.

86. An influential but controversial expression of this point of view was a semi-popular book of the last decade of the twentieth century: Francis Fukuyama, *The End of History and the Last Man* (New York: The Free Press, 1992).

87. For expression of this attitude, see Fukuyama, *The End of History and the Last Man*.

Chapter 9

1. John Rawls, *A Theory of Justice* (Cambridge, Massachusetts: The Belknap Press of Harvard University Press, 1971). Rawls began to develop the ideas of this book in a series of scholarly essays dating from the late 1950s and 1960s. A revised English edition of *A Theory*, from which I shall quote unless specified otherwise, was published much later: *A Theory of Justice*, revised edition (Cambridge, Massachusetts: The Belknap Press of Harvard University Press, 1999).

2. Rawls, *A Theory*, 3–4.

3. Rawls, *A Theory*, 3.

4. Rawls, *A Theory*, 54.

5. Rawls, *A Theory*, 3.

6. Rawls, *A Theory*, 62–63 (emphasis added).

7. Rawls, *A Theory*, 63.

8. John Rawls, *Political Liberalism*, The John Dewey Essays in Philosophy, Number Four (New York: Columbia University Press, 1993), 6.

9. Rawls, *Political Liberalism*, 3–4.

10. See Immanuel Kant, *Critique of Practical Judgment*, trans. Lewis White Beck (Indianapolis and New York: The Bobbs-Merrill Company, Inc., 1956), especially Part I, Book I, Chapter I.

11. Rawls, *Political Liberalism*, 61–62 (emphasis added).

12. Ronald M. Dworkin, "Liberalism," in *A Matter of Principle* (Cambridge, Massachusetts: Harvard University Press, 1985), 191 (emphasis added).

13. An anonymous reader of the manuscript of this book quite correctly pointed out that I have underplayed the issue of development and change in Rawls' thought from *A Theory of Justice* (and the articles that gave rise to it) to *Political Liberalism* (and the subsequent, last works of Rawls). Although scholars of Rawls' thought disagree about the nature and extent of changes in his thought, I do believe that, in order to develop this part of my story about political philosophy, I have constructed a somewhat artificially 'seamless' Rawls. The most noticeable change in Rawls' thought, it seems to me, is what appears to be his diminished commitment to social and economic egalitarianism as mandated by his favored interpretation, in *A Theory of Justice*, of his second principle of justice. In *Political Liberalism* he seems willing to accommodate under the umbrella of 'public reason/reasonableness' varieties of liberalism that downplay or reject political commitment to promoting egalitarianism. It is not surprising that supporters and critics of Rawls on the 'left' (to use the term in its popular media sense) have tended to deprecate this perceived change, while those on the 'right' have tended to welcome it.

14. Rawls, *A Theory*, 53.

15. Rawls, *A Theory*, 53–54.

16. Rawls, *A Theory*, 57.

17. Rawls, *A Theory*, 58.

18. Rawls, *A Theory*, 63.

19. Rawls, *A Theory*, 65.

20. Rawls, *A Theory*, 63.

21. Rawls, *A Theory*, 64.

22. Rawls, *A Theory*, 54.

23. Rawls, *A Theory*, xiii.

24. Rawls, *A Theory*, xii.

25. Rawls, *A Theory*, xiii.

26. While Rawls may have been uncomfortable with the perfectionist elements of his political philosophy, there certainly are contemporary political theorists within the liberal tradition who advance perfectionist doctrines quite forthrightly. One such political philosopher is Joseph Raz (as in his *The Morality of Freedom* [Oxford: The Clarendon Press, 1986]); another who might be placed into this category is Will Kymlicka (as in his *Liberalism, Community, and Culture* [Oxford: Clarendon Press, 1989]). However, adherents to what has come to be called political liberalism have generally eschewed the 'perfectionist turn' – at least officially. In this chapter I suggest what I have argued for elsewhere at greater length: that there are reasons deriving from liberalism's own favored historiography (which can easily be transformed into conceptual reasons) for liberalism to be wary of the perfectionist turn. (See my *Partisan or Neutral? The Futility of Public Political Theory* [Lanham, Maryland: Rowman and Littlefield Publishers, Inc., 1997].)

27. Rawls, *A Theory*, 287.

28. Rawls, *A Theory*, 54.

29. Rawls, *A Theory*, 386.

30. Rawls, *Political Liberalism*, 32, 33.

31. Rawls, *Political Liberalism*, 39.

32. Rawls, *Political Liberalism*, 39.

33. Rawls, *Political Liberalism*, 39–40.

34. Rawls, *Political Liberalism*, 13–14.

35. Rawls, *Political Liberalism*, 213.

36. Rawls, *Political Liberalism*, 14.

37. Rawls, *Political Liberalism*, 51 (emphasis added).

38. Rawls, *Political Liberalism*, 50.

39. Rawls, *Political Liberalism*, 52.

40. Raymond Geuss, *History and Illusion in Politics* (Cambridge: Cambridge University Press, 2001), 4.

41. Rawls, *Political Liberalism*, 217.

42. Rawls, *Political Liberalism*, 217.

43. Rawls, *Political Liberalism*, 40

Chapter 10

1. Michael J. White, [this volume, p. 2].

2. Ronald M. Dworkin, "Liberalism," in *A Matter of Principle* (Cambridge, Mass.: Harvard University Press, 1985), 203.

3. Dworkin, *Law's Empire* (Cambridge, Mass.: Belknap Press, 1986), 441, note 19 (emphasis added).

4. Charles E. Larmore, *Patterns of Moral Complexity* (Cambridge: Cambridge University Press, 1987), 43.

5. Michael J. White, *Partisan or Neutral? The Futility of Public Political*

Theory (Lanham, Maryland: Rowman and Littlefield Publishers, Inc., 1997).

6. Alasdair MacIntyre, *After Virtue: A Study in Moral Theory* (Notre Dame, Indiana: University of Notre Dame Press, 1981), 235. MacIntyre is referring to "moral philosophy" here; but I would claim – and I believe that he would agree – that his claim is equally applicable to political philosophy.

7. MacIntyre, *After Virtue*, 236.

8. White, *Partisan or Neutral?*, 166–167.

9. It may also be important for such contemporary constitutional democracies to maintain the illusion of popular government. A recent book (which covers some of the same ground as Machiavelli's *History of Florence*) details a striking Renaissance anticipation of this phenomenon: the combination, in fifteenth-century Florence, of a radically democratic formal constitution and of the effective oligarchic manipulation and circumvention of this constitution, first by the Albizzi and then by the Medici families. See Lauro Martines, *April Blood: Florence and the Plot Against the Medici* (Oxford: Oxford University Press, 2002). In a review of this book, Tim Parks writes that, in the fifteenth century, "it had become important for the Florentines, as it is important for us today, to imagine that they shared as equals in a process of collective self-government" with the result that "a very special state of mind developed: a fizz of excited and idealistic political thought constantly frothing over the intransigent reality of protracted if veiled dictatorship" (Tim Parks, "Mad at the Medicis," *The New York Review of Books*, Vol. 50, no. 7 [May 1, 2003], 37).

10. I borrow this apt phrase from Mel Thompson, who has kindly served as one of my editors at Oneworld Publications.

Index